Buffalo Bill on Stage

Buffalo Bill on Stage

SANDRA K. SAGALA

UNIVERSITY OF NEW MEXICO PRESS ⊕ ALBUQUERQUE

LIBRARY OF CONGRESS CATALOGING-IN-PUBLICATION DATA

Sagala, Sandra K.
Buffalo Bill on stage / Sandra K. Sagala.
p. cm.
Includes bibliographical references and index.
ISBN 978-0-8263-4427-4 (CLOTH : ALK. PAPER)
1. Buffalo Bill, 1846–1917. 2. Pioneers—West (U.S.)—Biography.
3. Entertainers—United States—Biography.
4. Actors—United States—Biography.
5. Melodrama, American—History—19th century.
6. Wild west shows—History—19th century.
7. West (U.S.)—Biography.
I. Title.
F594.B94S23 2008
978'.02092—dc22

[B]

2007051642

❦

Book and jacket design and type composition by Kathleen Sparkes
This book was composed with Minion Pro OT 10.5/14 26P,
and with display type Voluta Pro and Brioso Pro.

for Mom and Dad

Contents

Acknowledgments

TELEVISION PRODUCER ROY HUGGINS LOVED HISTORY AND CREATED
Old West characters just a tad left of normal. One of his television pilots—
This Is the West That Was—tells the story of Wild Bill Hickok, Buffalo Bill
Cody, and Calamity Jane in Deadwood. In Huggins's version, Hickok is
a peaceable man who never fired his gun. Calamity Jane, however, brags
about his gunfighter's reputation until J. W. McCanles and the Wellman
brothers come to town seeking vengeance. Rumors say Hickok killed their
kin at Rock Creek station; instead, according to Huggins, Hickok was out
cold with a head wound during the shootout. Hoping to one day dance
with the Queen of England, Cody attempts to appropriate Hickok's inflated
reputation by challenging him to a gunfight "out by the snake dump."

The satirical drama aroused my curiosity about the real Hickok and
Cody. It seems ironic now that I first encountered the two men in a dramatic setting. I found Joseph G. Rosa to be Hickok's most reliable biographer and wrote to tell him so, setting off some of the many ripples God
caused when he dropped Wild Bill into the pond.[1] Since I live in an eastern
state Cody frequented with his theatrical troupe, Rosa wondered if I'd be
interested in researching the six months Hickok toured with Cody.

I agreed. Having a few dates and cities, it became a matter of going back-
ward and forward in time, guessing where the troupe played next and hoping
the library in those cities would have old newspapers to confirm my suspi-
cions. Many kudos to the Erie County Library's Interlibrary Loan Department
and to librarians across the country, especially the Western Genealogy staff

at Denver Public Library; Rosemary Cullen, Brown University; Joy Marlow Bevan, Columbus, OH; Lois Archuleta, Salt Lake City, UT; Tonya Boltz, Keokuk, IA; Kay Runge, Davenport, IA; Kay Weiss, Burlington, IA; Kathryn Pong, Fall River, MA; Jean Putch, Ilion, NY; and Amy Benckart. Soon news of Cody's whereabouts began pouring into my mailbox.

After *True West* published my article on the findings, Joe Rosa challenged me to unearth where Cody was every day during *his* theatrical career and continued to offer encouragement and guidance. With fourteen years more to cover, it seemed a daunting task, but discovery of the *New York Clipper* and *New York Dramatic Mirror* facilitated the research. The contemporary weekly theatrical newspapers published not only articles on actors and theatre goings-on but also listings of where various traveling companies were playing. A typical mention for Cody's troupe for a week in February 1878 might look like this: "BUFFALO BILL COMBINATION: Fort Wayne 16; Kokomo 17–18; Indianapolis 19–20; Terre Haute 22."

About this time I became acquainted with Paul Fees, who was curator of the Buffalo Bill Museum in Cody, Wyoming. As a result of his auspices, Garlow Fund trustees approved a grant for me to continue the research at the Buffalo Bill Historical Center's McCracken Library. To the trustees and library staff, especially Frances Clymer, I owe much appreciation for all their help and suggestions.

Back home, the postman continued to bring news of Cody from across the country. Critics had attended the performances, and reporters were eager to learn more about the popular new star, so with many of the ads came reviews of the production and personal interviews. Editors were keen to report his remarks about dealing with the Indian "problem," his political views, and personal details of his life. What I had supposed would be merely a list of Cody dates/cities was turning into a book, so I perused additional sources about theatre, melodrama, and border life. Steve Friesen, director of the Buffalo Bill Museum and Grave in Golden, Colorado, Timothy W. Fattig, Julie and Dennis Greene, Peter Alexis, Darlis Miller, and Joy Kasson graciously supplied information and photographs.

Why did some critics rave about the mediocre melodrama while others denigrated it? How was Cody's histrionic career influenced by changes in theatre itself in the latter half of the nineteenth century? When did Cody begin to envision himself as more than a mere actor in a frontier melodrama? What prompted him to initiate all the novelties? Over the course of several months, Paul Fees generously gave his time and expertise to help clarify and explain Cody's motivations. I owe him a tremendous debt of thanks. I am also grateful to Paul Hedren and Will Bagley for personally helping me describe events of 1857 and 1877.

At one point in the revisions, a letter Cody's biographer Don Russell had written came to light in which he responded to a man curious about Cody's troupe's itinerary. Russell thought plotting it "would probably take infinite time and patience." Friends and family certainly wouldn't credit me with either. That's why I relied on Lynn Houze, Ann Marie Donoghue, Clarence P. (Lefty) Blasco, Doreen Chaky, JoAnne Bagwell, John Marsh, Holly Labisky, Ellen Marler and many others to bring this project to fruition. Special thanks to my daughter Jennifer for her first edits and to my son Jeremy for keeping my computer up and running. Finally, to my husband Bill, many thanks for your willingness to share me, just for a while, with Mr. Cody.

Introduction

*It may be said that if Buffalo Bill had never existed
it would have been necessary to invent him.*

—Unknown Frenchman, quoted in brochure on display at the
Buffalo Bill Museum and Grave, Golden, Colorado

IN AN EARLY SCENE IN *THIS IS THE WEST THAT WAS*, BUFFALO BILL CODY and Wild Bill Hickok clamber onto a wagon driven by Calamity Jane. Cody has been out for months killing buffalo to supply the army with meat, but Hickok expresses surprise when Cody describes what he was doing as *hunting* buffalo. In reality, given the enormous herds roaming the plains, a man could stand in one spot and shoot them from dawn until dusk. Some called this sport, others butchery. As the wagon lumbers into town, Cody bristles at the insinuation he is a buffalo butcher. "Hey! Listen, friend, it takes a heap o' skill and craw to pick off them brutes."[1]

Cody did indeed possess "skill and craw." Into his seventy-one years on life's stage, William Frederick "Buffalo Bill" Cody crowded several lifetimes' worth of careers and adventures. Besides a buffalo hunter, he was a U.S. Army scout, Indian fighter, rancher, businessman, and world-renowned entertainer. A gentleman whose word was his bond, he used his wealth to help out friends, taking care of his sisters' families as well as his own and letting orphans into his shows for free. "He was totally unable to resist any claim for assistance . . . or refuse any mortal in distress. His philosophy was that of the plains, . . . more nearly Christian . . . than we are used to finding in the sharp business world."[2] In his later years, he became a conservationist, speaking out against the senseless slaughter of buffalo, as well as an advocate for American Indians and a supporter of women's suffrage.

His early plains years can be conjectured; they weren't much different from any other youngster's. Cody recalled he was "quite as bad, though no worse, than the ordinary every-day boy who goes barefoot, wears a brimless hat, one suspender and a mischievous smile."[3] Before he became a public figure and what one theatre manager called "the best drawing card on the American stage," he had already acquired a reputation as an exceptional frontiersman and hunter.[4] His years spent scouting for the army resulted in familiarity with officers whose accounts of Indian campaigns fill history books. Recognizing his charisma and gregarious nature, Lieutenant General Philip Sheridan asked Cody to lead Russia's Grand Duke Alexis on a lavish hunting expedition in January 1872. Under Cody's direction, the duke enjoyed a demonstration of how Indians hunt buffalo, a hellish ride in an open carriage, and a personal shooting lesson from Cody himself, leading his biographer to conclude that the occasion was, essentially, Cody's first Wild West show.[5] The widely publicized event brought him a degree of national fame.

Completion of the transcontinental railroad opened the West to immigrants, travelers, and sportsmen. After one hunt led by Cody, a "nobby and high-toned outfit" of eastern dignitaries including several generals and newspaper editors returned home raving about the skill and engaging personality of their guide.[6] All concurred Cody was a "mild, agreeable, well-mannered man, quiet and retiring in his disposition, though well informed and always ready to talk well and earnestly upon any subject of interest, and in all respects, the reverse of the person we had expected to meet."[7] Already demonstrating instincts for theatrics, Cody was eager and willing to be the center of attention. He impressed the men with his flair for costume, his forte for spreading tall tales, and his ability to organize and lead such a large contingent.

From 1883 when he started his Wild West show until his death in 1917, Cody personified the showman extraordinaire. People worldwide acclaimed his name as a star performer. He was known not only to common people from New York to San Francisco, who may have scrimped on groceries to afford seats in his arena, but also to European royalty who could command a personal performance.

But what of the period between his early plains years and the start of his Wild West show? From 1872 until 1886 Cody led a troupe of traveling actors, familiarly known as a "combination," around the country playing in frontier melodramas. The plays were mediocre at best, often causing theatre critics to shake their heads in wonder at the unreserved enthusiasm Cody incited in audiences.

Little has been known about these rather obscure years of Cody's life; however, they are important for fixing the course of his Wild West show career. He matured as an actor and impresario over the course of the Buffalo Bill Combination years, until he was finally ready to headline the nineteenth century's greatest outdoor program.

Don Russell neglected to give itineraries when he devoted thirty-five out of nearly five hundred pages of his Cody biography to the combination years. Most biographers gloss over them with quotations from the Chicago reviews of his debut and references to newsworthy forays he undertook before his exodus from the stage into the outdoor arena and the first performance of his Wild West show. This is understandable. Reviews of performances generally took the form of short news items on newspapers' theatre pages and are easily overlooked. Craig F. Nieuwenhuyse's dissertation, "Six-Guns on the Stage: Buffalo Bill Cody's First Celebration of the Conquest of the American Frontier," contains the most critical analysis of Cody's first season. His work, William S. E. Coleman's "Buffalo Bill on Stage," and James Monaghan's "The Stage Career of Buffalo Bill" contribute much to the initial years of Cody's theatrical career, but the information dwindles with each succeeding year.[8] Unlike his well-documented Wild West, few tour books, letters, or hotel registers survive to authenticate exactly where his dramatic troupe toured. Almost none of the plays is entirely extant, but programs revealing scene titles and character names hint at plots.[9] Reviewers, too, challenged to convey the wonder (or disaster) of it all, offer glimpses of story lines and suggestions of supporting casts, scenery, and special effects.

Only through newspaper media is a chronicle of Cody's adventures, mishaps, glories, and roastings available today. One must depend on contemporary drama critics who attended the plays and then spared no enthusiasm or scorn in their reviews. "Fine stage appearance," "admirable representation of border life," "good company, well drawn out"—these were phrases they used in attempting to explain the overwhelming adulation for Cody and his troupe of scouts and Indians.

Though he traveled with other, occasionally professional, actors, only two years into his thespian career, Cody could carry the program himself.

Emphasizing his dual careers as scout and actor, his very persona merged reality with theatre. Richard Slotkin wrote, "Under the aspect of mythology and historical distance, the acts and motives of [mythic heroes] have an air of simplicity and purity that makes them seem finely heroic expressions of an admirable quality of the human spirit."[10] After only a short time, the heroic Cody rarely did anything outside the theatre without an eye toward how it would play onstage. No matter how poor the melodrama, at least one reporter understood Cody's pure and simple effect: "He has captured the popular heart, knows how to keep it, and if that is not an actor's 'business' we know not what that business is."[11]

"I'm no d——d scout now; I'm a first-class star," Cody boasted to a reporter after only one season onstage. From the outset, it was obvious to anyone who was watching that Cody *was* a star and someone to be reckoned with.

Among those watching were some of his "pards" from the prairie. His first costar, Texas Jack Omohundro, found a wife and success with Cody's troupe. Wild Bill Hickok, swayed by the prospect of easy money but easily bored, amused himself onstage by harassing the actors in the Indian roles, much to their dismay. Jack Crawford and a mysterious scout named Kit Carson Jr. acted in Cody's troupe, but both left, arrogantly believing they could profit more on their own. During his stay at Fort Abraham Lincoln in Dakota Territory, George A. Custer proudly played the "Buffalo Bill" character in an amateur theatrical production of *Buffalo Bill and His Bride*.[12]

At one point during his dramatic career, Cody sat in the City Hotel office in Providence, Rhode Island, and confessed to a reporter, "I'm no actor. . . . I don't pretend to be anything of an actor, but you see the people seem to like it." During the winter, Cody admitted, he had "nothing else to do" and, during the summer, "I kin [*sic*] make more money this way than I can taking parties out on the plains or in hunting." He said he would settle down when he had got his "pile about where I want it."[13]

Each year his "pile" grew, and his success with border dramas led increasingly to displays and exhibits that would culminate in his Wild West show. Not content to rest on his laurels, he used his celebrity and wealth to invest in and develop the West he celebrated all his life, founding, for example, Cody, Wyoming, to lure tourists and sportsmen on their way to Yellowstone National Park. Throughout the nineteenth century, dime novels and stage plays popularized real-life heroes like Cody who blurred the line between fact and fiction and universalized the Western genre. But after forty-five years in show business, a new entertainment craze usurped his beloved Wild

West show and claimed America's entertainment dollars. Traditions of the West he depicted continued to be invoked in early films.

But before the movies and the Wild West show, there was the Buffalo Bill Combination. These pages chronicle his trail as he crisscrossed the country entertaining millions with his version of border life. They relay the excitement generated by a man who became larger than life and much more than Hickok's derided "buffalo butcher."

— CHAPTER ONE —

Setting the Stage

If exaggerated melodrama be the style, then Buffalo Bill is a success.
—*Daily Lexington Press*, September 30, 1873

IN 1893, FREDERICK JACKSON TURNER DELIVERED HIS NOW-FAMOUS paper, "The Significance of the Frontier in American History," at the American Historical Association in Chicago. He defined the frontier as "the meeting point between savagery and civilization." Imagine a scene in which, ironically, twenty years previously, Buffalo Bill's publicist John M. Burke pondered a snappy newspaper slogan to advertise Cody and his theatrical troupe. Until then, yellowback literature simply referred to him as "a frontiersman" or "a scout of the plains," but those descriptions just didn't do him justice. Burke stared off into space contemplating succinct phrasing to encapsulate Cody's character. Inspiration dawned, and Burke wrote, "ORIGINAL–LIVING HERO–LINK BETWEEN SAVAGERY AND CIVILIZATION."[1]

William Frederick Cody himself could hardly have conceived a more flattering or perceptive self-portrait. From 1872 to 1886, his dramatic persona bridged the Old West—the plains where buffalo roamed and soldiers and settlers fought Indians over land—and the newly civilized West through his retelling and dramatizing of the sometimes glorious, often bloody, and occasionally heroic Wild West story. He first strode onto the nation's stages at a most opportune time in America's theatrical history. Drama was then, as now, a vital form of entertainment and diversion from daily life. Almost overnight, his combination of traveling actors and frontier plays reached a pinnacle of popularity that other, often more professional, companies envied.

Cody's name conjures up the image a confident showman, star of the Wild West show, and not that of an inept amateur who often forgot his lines, because the apprenticeship he served as a traveling actor prepared him to undertake his outdoor show. He learned to handle complicated train schedules, fellow actors, and scenery and costume transportation; the management of these assumed greater proportions as the years progressed. Four actors were prominent members of his combination at his debut in December 1872. Fourteen years later, Cody was responsible for over twenty actors, including professional supporting theatre companies, and even a live animal or two. This was, however, mere training for the hundreds of persons and stock he would manage in his Wild West show. At the end of the first dramatic season, Cody counted only $6,000 in profit. Twenty years later, Wild West show revenue peaked near $1 million.

In typical Cody fashion, he couldn't have picked a better time for coming to the realization that his ever-enlarging dramatic program necessitated taking his show out of the theatre and into the arena. It seemed he possessed a knack for being in the right place at the right time. In the bleeding Kansas days, he dropped out of a jayhawking gang just before the Union army hunted down and killed its leader. When the railroad was building through Kansas, he was on hand to supply the workers with meat, earning his alliterative nickname. When the theatrical "star system" was born, Cody entered show business.

The first time Cody ever appeared onstage, J. B. Studley was starring in *Buffalo Bill, King of the Border Men*. The audience learned the real Buffalo Bill was in the theatre and insisted on his stepping up to say a few words. Studley scarcely recovered from being upstaged, even though Cody, frightened by the sea of eager faces, did little but stammer. By late 1872 when Cody finally allowed dime novelist Ned Buntline to talk him into trying acting as a profession, his entry into the dramatic venue coincided fortuitously with the emergence of "combinations."

A combination was a theatrical association of roving troupers who supported a star for the run of a single play. They traveled from city to city on the ever-expanding railroad system, often performing nightly. The advent of the star system spurred individuals to organize a group of actors and rent theatres on the circuit for a night or two. Depending on his talent, popularity, and chemistry with his supporting cast, the touring company could make or break the star's career. Though a season was usually devoted to one play, sometimes the company alternated between two to ensure the greatest attraction to potential audiences—hence the name "combination."

The actor first credited with the concept of road shows was Dion Boucicault. His idea, unique to the era, was not entirely new. From colonial days, professionals had taken their plays from town to town. With incredible rapidity, the new combinations undermined the old stock company system under which actors were organized on a permanent resident basis, headed by a theatre manager responsible for selecting entertainment that would gratify local audiences. On alternate days, they presented repertoire theatre—stock plays, farces, pantomimes, and musicals. The actors attached to any particular theatre were accomplished in playing standard dramatic roles, such as protagonist, leading lady, comedian, and villain. Management paid them according to the shares, or stock, they held in the company.[2]

By the 1870s, fewer theatres employed resident companies, and by decade's end, the *New York Times* could observe that

[a]t no time in the dramatic history of New York have so many of the theatres been occupied with what are called combination companies. . . . Not one of these theatres has any company of its own. The proprietors or managers are simply lessees, who make the best terms they can with the traveling troupe, at whose head is usually a star of some magnitude, for a given period, and when one troupe has gone another succeeds. This may seem to add to the variety of the entertainment, inasmuch as a new company as well as a new star is seen during each engagement.[3]

The *Times* article noted, on the other hand, however, that traveling companies "are prone to meet disaster, soon or late." How, critics wondered, could a roving troupe be as excellent as a trained, stable company? "The theater is sustained and elevated by permanent, unchanging companies. . . . The star system always has been and always will be injurious to the highest interests of the drama, sacrificing art to the immediate pecuniary gain; and going on the road brings histrionism down to the level of wandering shows."

Any program, after an initial run at a home theatre, could tour on the road. Although critics believed combinations did nothing to further dramatic art, advantages were, nevertheless, numerous: the cast was busy for the entire season; production costs were less if only one or two plays were performed; and the quality of the acting was superior because the actors were not locals of questionable talent. One-, two-, or three-night runs ensured maximum profits, and limitless audiences enjoyed a potpourri of entertainments—musicals, high drama, soloists, comedies, and border dramas—brought to their hometown.

Managers soon discovered the death of the stock system left them with empty houses, translating into financial losses until and unless they offered their theatres to combinations. This they did until, in most big cities, not a single stock theatre was left. New York, Philadelphia, and Boston, who once prided themselves on their professional dramatic companies, surrendered to the popularity of combinations. In 1886, almost three hundred combinations were touring; by 1900, that number had nearly doubled.[4]

Traveling troupers faced a grueling existence. Train schedules and curtain times outlined the days. Sleeping in cheap boardinghouses or strange hotel rooms, eating on the run, and waiting for trains or coaches became the daily routine. Oftentimes troupers played in six towns in as many nights. Because actors were not paid for missed performances, the show went on even if they were sick or weary. Hauling their own props and costumes required organization and cooperation. Train travel was dirty. Smoke and soot drifted in through open windows, demanding special attention to clothes and personal hygiene. Upon arrival, actors often found dressing rooms not much cleaner.[5]

At times troupers faced social prejudice, provisional pay, incompetent musicians, poor management, and drunken companions. "Sweatshop life," one actress called it, "the most sweatshop kind of work I ever heard of and the most exhausting for the brain and body." Actor Edwin Forrest complained about the "hateful, vagabond life."[6] Few visual reminders of all their hard work remain. Rare posed photographs of individuals or groups survive, but insipid theatrical lighting and early wet-plate cameras made it nearly impossible to shoot photographs during a performance.[7] Instead, for publicity purposes, stars were often photographed in studios surrounded by props.

Cody's combination allowed him to do onstage what he did best, exemplifying life on the western plains. Similar to Shakespearean dramas wherein heroes and scoundrels communicate directly with the audience, leaving no doubt about their motivations or intentions, Cody's especially winning quality, guaranteed to endear audiences, was his ability to step out of the role he was portraying and simply be himself. In St. Louis, during his second week of performing, he spotted his wife Louisa in the audience. Moving to the edge of the stage, he called out to her, "Oh, Mamma, I'm a bad actor!" Several years later, during a target shooting exhibition, he proudly confided to the audience that "[t]his Freund Bros.' improved Sharps is a perfect terror, isn't it?" as he pointed to his shots in the bull's-eye.[8]

Some of Cody's plays were dreadful, the acting worse, but his charisma and passion for authenticity delighted audiences. Already a hero in dime novels, having shot farther, saved more maidens, and killed more Indians than any other frontiersman, Cody's real presence on the stage actualized those feats. The fact that Cody *was* a brave Indian fighter, scout, and estimable man and that he could project that personality to the audience solidified his heroic status. Buffalo Bill of the dime novels and stage gelled with Buffalo Bill of the real West. Cody himself did little to dispel the fantasy that he had indeed committed all the gloriously heroic acts authors attributed to him. Dime novels jibed more or less with newspaper accounts of his true adventures. He spent the theatre's off-season actually doing the brave deeds, the shooting, and the scouting he was famous for, then returned to portray them onstage. After he overcame first-night jitters, whenever Cody strode out from the wings, he exuded self-confidence and authenticity.

The rough frontier melodramas he played early in his career were fine for a tyro. The sensational plays followed a common pattern of expressing exaggerated sentiments and yielding to happy endings. One distinguishing quality of melodrama incorporates large gestures and lavish facial expressions, necessary in Cody's plays so his young fans in the high balconies could understand the action. However, critics often congratulated him on his naturalness, noting his lack of "the stage business" evident in many professional actors.

Nineteenth-century melodramas embodied distinctly American elements, propagating popular myths about the nation's culture and character. Some presented new stereotypes, such as the Negro, Yankee, or Irish immigrant, though Negroes, Yankees, and Irish rarely portrayed themselves. White actors outfitted in wigs and greasepaint even filled Indian roles. Melodrama's basic premise offered an overly simplified view of life, particularly of morality. Black and white situations prevailed; shades of

Buffalo Bill Cody, c. 1872. Courtesy Buffalo Bill Historical Center (P.69.26), Cody, WY.

gray were rare. Characters, either completely good or completely bad, were seldom capable of change. When the villain hounds the lovely heroine, the brave hero comes to the rescue. At the finale, the hero must vanquish the villain, his deeds reflecting the contemporary moral code. Playwrights often used plot devices like disguise, abduction, concealed identity, and fortunate coincidence to keep the audience in suspense while friends of the hero provided comic relief.[9]

Credit goes to Buntline for spicing up melodramatic style by having a real person play himself. Cody, the "simon-pure character," a perceptive critic understood, is not an actor but plays himself, "and this fact constitutes the whole novelty of his performance."[10]

His fellow scout, Texas Jack, was Cody's first stage partner. Theirs was a unique partnership, a fine example of blue-gray alliance. After his Civil War service under Confederate Major General J. E. B. Stuart, Virginia-born John B. Omohundro headed to Texas, trailed a herd of longhorns to Nebraska, and remained in North Platte. Cody grew up in a strict abolitionist family and fought for the Union. Nevertheless, he befriended Jack and, as a result of Cody's success in overcoming military prejudice about hiring ex-Confederates, Jack joined him as scout.[11]

In the early dramas, the two frontiersmen bounded onstage armed with rifles and cried, "Death to the Indians!" further inflaming an already fevered audience. News of U.S. Army/Indian conflicts such as the Modoc war in northern California and the Ute war in Colorado had been telegraphed east. Cody's bold assertions, both onstage and off, that, if given the chance, he and Jack would head west and wipe out the redskins thrilled easterners.

In later years of the Buffalo Bill Combination, Cody subdued or removed such ravings and simulated Indian slaughters. His personal attitude toward Indians as their employer and friend superseded the audience's jubilant reaction to their misfortunes. In press interviews, he more compassionately emphasized how Indians had been much maligned and were not entirely to blame for problems whites encountered in settling the West. Personal experience led him to believe the government's Indian policy was wrong, and he adopted a reformer's viewpoint, observing,

> You can't compel a man who has lived by the chase, who has
> followed the bow and arrow, to take up the plough. The Indian
> is a man of feeling and intelligence and he knows right from
> wrong. . . . He has been driven from post to pillar and he doesn't

know what the white man wants him to do. . . . So the Poor Indians are kept at sixes and sevens all the time. But they are gradually becoming civilized. The process is necessarily slow, but it is sure, and they will certainly fall in line with our great civilization some day.[12]

His introductions of live action on horseback and marksmanship exhibitions also marked an evolution in his dramatic style. His legacy, however, would not be merely his portrayal of the Old West. He depicted a dynamic period in America's history and strove to keep the image current by producing increasingly timely dramas.

Four years after he ventured onstage for his first sham Indian battle, in a high point in his career, Cody effectively incorporated drama into reality. During the summer of 1876 following Custer's defeat at the Little Bighorn, scout Cody, who wore his stage costume during a skirmish with Cheyenne Indians at Warbonnet Creek, Nebraska, killed a young warrior. As victor, he claimed the Indian's topknot and braid as the first scalp in revenge for Custer. Fully appreciating the topicality and popularity of the event, he replayed the victory in that season's melodrama.

The year after, he performed in a theatrical version of the Mountain Meadows Massacre. The 1857 slaughter of innocent Arkansas emigrants traveling through Utah was news again because of the twenty-year-delayed execution of John D. Lee, one of the Mormon leaders involved. In another novel move, following negotiations with the U.S. Indian Bureau, for the first time Cody hired Sioux from the Red Cloud agency to portray Indians in the drama. Instead of bloodthirsty savages, they played the good guys, and Cody lived up, in prime fashion, to his publicity as link between savagery and civilization.

When he auditioned Wild West show performers, Cody hired American Indians as a matter of course. Despite objections from Indian Affairs commissioners who believed Indians should remain at home as "educated, peaceful and productive proponents of the Protestant ethic," Cody argued that his employment provided them money as well as travel experiences and exposure to white culture.[13] Without them, his plan to show true western events would fail because he would be lacking an essential half of the white/Indian conflict. This would not do—realism was a primary consideration. His reasoning convinced most objectors.

By 1883, when Cody planned to perform in theatres during the winter months and in the Wild West during the summers, Major Frank North, leader of a Pawnee Indian battalion and one of his ranching partners, called him on his realism penchant. During the first rehearsal of the Wild West show, Indians were to chase a stagecoach with the town's mayor inside. Their whoops stampeded the mules hauling the hapless politician around the arena. After a melee of "din and confusion," Cody and North rounded up both the Indians and the mules. We don't know if North's response was tinged with amusement or disgust when he suggested to Cody that he might want to reorganize in order to create "a show of illusion not realism."[14] But Cody would have none of it. He said, "I can put a pair of boots, a big hat, and a red shirt on any man, call him a cowboy; but I cannot dress anyone up and call him an Indian."[15]

As the frontiersman aged, he became aware of his own role in the narrative of the West. He began his autobiography by remarking in theatrical terms how his "*debut* upon the world's stage" took place the day he was born.[16] After daylong hunts, sportsmen sat on logs around a roaring campfire while their guide Cody, honing his entertainment skills, spun yarns of western adventures. Neither was he shy about showing off his hunting prowess, pointing out where plentiful game grazed. Four days before his first performance, he didn't know not to recite the cues in dialogue, but when the curtain dropped, he "congratulated Jack and [himself] on having made such a brilliant and successful *debut*."[17] Within months, he exuberantly announced he and Jack would go through the states playing Shakespeare and put actors like Edwin Booth to shame.[18]

Throughout his touring career, critics in nearly every town had something to say about the man or the production. Even while he crammed scrapbooks full of their reviews, for the most part, Cody ignored critics who scorned his dramas (and his acting), much as he would ignore Frank North's criticism, preferring instead to rely on audience reaction. Cody seemed to delight in how those same critics "went crazy in trying to follow the plot" of one of his plays.[19]

As always, and rightfully so, "the mob that paid the piper called the tune."[20] In eastern states, where the combination toured nearly exclusively for the first five years, wealth-producing industrial development raised the standard of living for millions of Americans, creating a new middle class with discretionary money to spend.[21] Proletarian theatres such as New York's Bowery catered to workingmen who read the *Police Gazette*, a sensational tabloid featuring lurid coverage of murders, prostitution, and outlaws. Inevitably, theatres modified their offerings to accommodate the tastes of a growing population nostalgic for the simplicity of country life and those who sought escapist entertainment after working long hours at boring factory jobs. Sharing little in the trappings of the so-called Gilded Age, the new social stratum was more likely to be amused by a sensational frontier melodrama or a colorful spectacle than serious dramatic presentation. It was enough that the dramas furnished relaxation and escape from familiar reality.

Various social classes attended the same theatres to see the same attractions, though they sat in very different areas. In the pit, or orchestra, sat the "middling classes," which some contemporaries referred to as "the honest folks" or the "sterling part of the audience." The boxes were reserved for "the dandies, and people of the first respectability and fashion." Finally the high balcony or gallery held seats or standing room for children, servants, and poor workers who could not afford any better seats.[22]

During performances, the audience often and loudly demonstrated their approval or displeasure by stamping their feet or hissing and jeering. Their reputation as unruly and uncouth was well deserved. Highbrow critics disdained audiences who favored such lowbrow fare as border dramas, calling them the "great unwashed" that "the slums had been drained to supply."[23] Women, joining the workforce in increasing numbers, also began attending popular amusements alongside men. The ever-increasing excitement of all classes over Cody's dramas convinced many critics that "[t]he audience seemed delighted and after all we suppose success is the truest test with a play."[24]

Historical events provided the basis for some of his melodramas, but for the rest, it didn't matter if Cody had participated in the affair or not—he could act the West because he knew it, and he exploited his real life to full advantage. "The story of the westering experience has drawn packed houses for a long time," wrote historian Robert Athearn. "[I]t has been an enormous stage, with its characters set in place, ready to create the illusion that the audience has expected. The audience has paid its admission fee expecting to be enchanted, and the fact that it understood that this was all an illusion does not mean it was not satisfied. Nor does it mean that the characters were not telling the truth in their own way."[25]

Cody wanted to show those packed houses frontier reality, not illusion. But his name remains familiar nearly a century after his death not because of his stage performances. The process of his becoming a genuine American hero began with authentic experiences publicized in myriad dime novels and border dramas. His legacy as a Wild West entertainer earned him the reputation as an original, a link between savagery and civilization.

CHAPTER TWO

Treading the Boards

❧

Everything was so wonderfully bad that it was almost good.
—*New York Herald*, April 1, 1873

DURING THE TIME CODY SCOUTED FOR THE FIFTH CAVALRY, CHEYENNE chief Tall Bull and his mixed band of incensed Cheyenne, Sioux, and Arapaho terrorized emigrants along the route from Leavenworth to Denver. Graves of those the Indians had murdered mottled the trail. One outrage occurred in summer 1869 when Tall Bull abducted two women from Solomon, Kansas. Lieutenant General Philip H. Sheridan called on the Fifth Cavalry to stop him. Cody guided troops to Summit Springs, Colorado, where Major Eugene A. Carr attacked the camp, killing some fifty Cheyenne. One of the hostages was wounded; the other woman was killed, as was the Indian chief. Controversy has continued ever since over who actually killed Tall Bull, Cody or Frank North, but Cody was generally credited with the killing and never denied it. In his version, he said he noticed the Indian close by a ravine. "When he was not more than thirty yards distant I fired, and the next moment he tumbled from his saddle."[1] Contradicting her husband's account, Louisa wrote in her memoirs, "Many times afterward he laughed at the historical account of the killing—one out of the many heroic things with which he is credited that he did not accomplish."[2]

Shortly after the Summit Springs battle, Ned Buntline arrived at Fort McPherson, the home of the Fifth, from a temperance tour in California. Buntline was the pen name of Edward Zane Carroll Judson, an overweight, baggy-eyed New Yorker who wrote for eastern publications. Besides advocating various causes, he made his living giving temperance lectures (some while drunk), all the while on the lookout for new dime-novel material. A prolific author, Buntline churned out a number of books, some with social reform themes, a topic that kept him hopping, so he said, from the villains he exposed.[3]

There are a number of conflicting accounts about the first meeting between Cody and Buntline. Some suggest he came looking for Wild Bill Hickok whose adventures in *Harper's New Monthly Magazine* highlighted his recent fracas at Rock Creek station. Others claim Buntline hoped to make a fictional hero out of Frank North, the rumored champion of Summit Springs. North refused to have anything to do with such romance and instead pointed out Cody as a likely hero.[4] Cody's charisma captivated Buntline and, a few months after he went back to New York, his story *Buffalo Bill, King of the Border Men* appeared in print. Serialized in the *New York Weekly*, it reinforced Cody's name in the nation's attention.

The eastern sportsmen whom Cody had impressed as a hunting guide invited him to visit New York City, where they showed him off as being what a real scout and Indian fighter looked like. The *New York Herald* believed he came "from the land of the buffalo and red men to see for himself the difference between an Indian powwow and a genuine masquerade."[5] At the time, February 1872, actor and playwright Frederick G. Maeder had just dramatized the *King of the Border Men* story. Buntline thought it a fine idea for Cody to attend the play.

Forty years previously, *The Lion of the West*, James Kirke Spaulding's comedy about a rough, ill-mannered frontiersman named Nimrod Wildfire, had played in Washington. Spaulding modeled Wildfire after Tennessee congressman Davy Crockett. At one performance, when buckskinned actor James Hackett realized Crockett himself was in the audience, he bowed to him in acknowledgement. Crockett rose and bowed back. Perhaps Buntline fancied the scenario enough to harbor hopes of a repeat.

Cody, oblivious to Buntline's ruse, admitted to being "curious to see how I would look when represented by someone else."[6] For the play—actually a reworking of Hickok's Civil War adventures—Buntline had supplied a good description of Cody, so actor J. B. Studley made himself up to resemble him.

We don't know what Cody thought of this fiction, but the audience discovered his presence and insisted he step onstage. Years later in his autobiography, he confessed that, "I felt very much embarrassed—never more so in my life—and I knew not what to say. I made a desperate effort, and a few words escaped me, but what they were I could not tell, nor could any one else in the house."[7] Despite Cody's total lack of stage presence, the manager offered him $500 a week to play himself. Cody scoffed, thinking a government mule would make a better actor. However, Buntline knew a good idea when he heard one.

All summer, Buntline sent letters urging Cody to consider acting as a profession. Reflecting on his initial unease, Cody vacillated between rejecting the idea because he feared failure and accepting it because he was reassured by Buntline's pointing out that he could always return to his old life if he didn't like show business. "That I, an old scout who had never seen more than twenty or thirty theatrical performances in my life, should think of going upon the stage, was ridiculous in the extreme."[8] Not everyone agreed. His scouting partner, Texas Jack, intimated he would come along, and Cody acquiesced, thinking Jack "would make as good a 'star' as myself."[9] Perhaps his city-bred, sophisticated wife Louisa tried to discourage them, knowing "[n]either of them ever had seen more than a dozen stage plays in their lives. They had no idea of how to make an entrance or an exit, they did not know a cue from a footlight, and they believed that plays just happened."[10] In the end, her misgivings fell on deaf ears. Buntline's promise of big money convinced them they ought to at least try it, so Cody and Omohundro agreed to meet him in Chicago, a good place to begin their first theatrical venture. Flames from the great fire of October 1871 had spared the theatre district, and the city proclaimed itself second only to New York in dramatic arts.

A distraught Buntline greeted Cody and Texas Jack at the train station on December 12, 1872. While travelers hustled around them, he upbraided the scouts for not bringing the Sioux and Pawnee chiefs he had prematurely advertised in the *Chicago Evening Journal*. They probably knew nothing of his plans, nor could they have brought them anyway.[11] The previous year American Indians were made national wards, and Sheridan issued orders forbidding western Indians to leave their reservations without the permission of civilian agents.

That same day Buntline introduced the scouts to Mr. Nixon, the

Amphitheatre's manager. There they learned what the two men had already planned: "Buntline, it seems, was to furnish the company, the drama, and the pictorial printing . . . while Nixon was to furnish the theater, the *attachés*, the orchestra, and the local printing," for which he would receive forty percent of the receipts.[12] Nixon, however, was perturbed to discover on Thursday that Buntline had not yet written the play, which was to open the following Monday, and threatened to cancel their contract. Buntline declared a solution imminent and paid half down on the $600 rent for the week.

He then sat down and dashed off words to the play, blatantly borrowing from his novel *Buffalo Bill, King of the Border Men*. Having the title helped his artistic juices to flow. He said, "I never lay out plots in advance. . . . First I invent a title, when I hit a good one I consider the story about half finished. . . . After I begin I push ahead as fast as I can write, never blotting out anything I have once written and never making a correction or modification."[13]

Four hours later, he set hotel clerks to copying the scribbled pages. When he handed the script to the scouts, Cody recalled, "I looked at my part and then at Jack; and Jack looked at his part and then at me. Then we looked at each other, and then at Buntline. We did not know what to make of the man." They calculated it would take about six months to memorize their dialogue.[14]

As they settled down to memorization, Buntline hastened out to round up actors for the secondary roles. He hired and costumed forty or fifty "supernumeraries" in tan-colored frocks and flannel scalps to resemble Indians.[15] Costumes for Cody and Jack were no problem; they simply wore the "habiliments and trappings to which they . . . [had] been long accustomed, B. B. having only added a hem-stitched pocket handkerchief to his outfit."[16] Chicago's *Daily Tribune* critic noticed the discrepancy between the promised redskins and those onstage and, echoing one common eastern assumption, observed that Indians did nothing all day but get into mischief. He supposed genuine Indians "stood ready to accept a histrionic engagement. . . . The Pawnees, however, failed to keep their engagement, probably on account of prevailing duties with reference to a projected horse-stealing expedition, and in their places there have been substituted a collection of talented supers."[17] Ironically, professional actors would play frontier characters while the real frontiersmen played at acting.[18] For his heroine, Buntline engaged the already popular Italian actress Mlle. Giuseppina Morlacchi to play the Indian maiden and love interest. Born in Milan in 1846, she debuted at age ten and danced at La Scala. She appeared in several European cities before introducing America to her trademark, the cancan.[19]

On his return to the hotel, Buntline requested the two frontiersmen run through the script. Unwittingly, Cody had not only memorized his lines but the cues as well. He recited them perfectly, noting he was to "exit stage right" or "step to the footlights." When Buntline informed him that cues were not part of the dialogue, Cody slammed his script down. "Cue! What mischief do you mean by the cue? I never saw any cue except in a billiard room."[20]

After long hours of rehearsal, the scouts believed they were ready. The evening before opening night, the *Chicago Times* enticed the public with a blurb noting the drama was of the "red-hot type" written by "the prince of sensation-mongers." Buntline included himself as one of the "supposititious eaters of gunpowder." No one attempted to dissuade readers from the conviction that the play Indians were anything but "genuine savages from the plains, greased and painted with veritable scalps dangling at their belts."[21] Only four days after their arrival in the Windy City, two nervous scouts peeked out from behind the curtain to watch people filling the hall. Then the lights were dimmed, the curtain rose, and *Scouts of the Prairie, and Red Deviltry As It Is*, Cody's first experience as an actor, began.

Though no copy of the original drama exists, we can glean some idea of the plot from a New York program and various newspaper accounts. The curtain opened on a western scene where trapper "Cale Durg," played by Buntline, meanders onstage. In bad humor because Indians have stolen his traps, he vows revenge. "Cale has evidently been in the mountains, but never before on the stage[.] . . . [H]e speaks his first speech not trippingly on the tongue and he uses his arms like a pump handle." Shielding his eyes from a make-believe sun, he wonders where his comrades are tarrying.[22]

If they didn't recognize their cue, the stage manager would have pushed the scouts out onto the stage. Numb with fright, Cody could do naught but stare at an audience that included General Sheridan and other Chicago socialites as well as dime-novel aficionados from all classes. Now that the time had come to perform, it was painfully obvious how unprepared he and Jack were. They seemed "to labor under a distressing uncertainty as to what they ought to do with their hands, fidgeting uneasily when silent and when in the dialogue poking out the right and then the left at regular intervals, with an evident determination to show no favor between the two."[23]

In the midst of the fidgeting, according to Cody's undisputed version, he spotted a Mr. Milligan in the audience, with whom he had hunted several months previously. When Buntline cued him with "Where have you been, Bill? What has kept you so long?" Cody, having forgotten his lines, improvised a story about his hunt with the Chicagoan. Because the hunt had been well publicized, the audience cheered, eager for firsthand details. "I 'chipped in' anything I thought of," he said later.[24]

In the next scene, Dove Eye, the Indian girl, arrives to warn the scouts of danger because Wolf Slayer is on their trail. Mormon Ben, the villain, has fifty wives and believes one more would allow him to die a happy man. He confides this to his companions, Dutchman Carl Pretzel, Sly Mike, and Phelim O'Laugherty, the Irish stereotype constantly in need of a drink. Mormon Ben sends Wolf Slayer to capture Durg's orphaned ward, Hazel Eye, who, at that moment, is off poetically reciting a tribute to the generous man who adopted her. To the *Chicago Times*, this seemed incongruous:

> a beautiful maiden, armed with a rifle and a dagger, [is] roaming these deserts with evil intents on Indians. Possibly to the select and cultivated audience it would have seemed strange indeed to see this lovely damsel . . . suddenly pause in a passionate speech, and marching clear up to the footlights, troll off, in an artistic fashion, a select air from Offenbach. But to the dime novel audience all this was in perfect keeping.[25]

At that point, Buntline hissed to the stage manager that he should dispatch the war-painted Indians. "The Indians!" Louisa Cody recounted, "who had never seen the land beyond the border of Illinois, Indians painted and devilish and ready to be killed." The Indians surprise Hazel Eye, "which is not surprising under the circumstances, and after a hard fight on her part, and the orchestra has a severe tussle with their instruments, Hazel Eye is overpowered and bound over."[26] Cale Durg rushes in intent on rescue but is no match for the Indians. They tie the girl and Durg to a stake then demonstrate a war dance, tomahawk handling, and savage glares. The brave trapper shows no fear of death, heckling the Indians to burn him quickly to which the Indians retaliate with their own taunts. Dove Eye dances in and severs the bonds of the victims. Before the Indians can retie them to the stake, Cody and Jack appear and, remembering the dialogue in which they promise to "[w]ipe the red skins out," "roar and bang away at the hapless Illinois tribe." When all are "dead," they also vaguely recall

there was a heroine scattered somewhere around the stage, that
they must save her. Whereupon they leaped forward, hurdled the
bodies of the slain savages, grabbed the heroine around the waist
and dragged her off stage, while the curtain came down and the
house roared its approval at the bloodthirstiest Indian fight in
which either Will Cody or Texas Jack ever participated,[27]

all because "Buntline don't [*sic*] think any more of killing forty or fifty
Indians when he works up a story than he does of eating his breakfast."[28]

A powwow of the white villains and Indians begins act 2. While the
scoundrels plot their next move, Buffalo Bill and Texas Jack declare their
love for the women. Before any lovemaking can develop, however, the plotting is over, and the Indians secure both women and the rescuing trapper.
When Wolf Slayer confesses his disdain for firewater, calling it "the curse of
the Red Man as well as the White," Durg, still tied to a tree, pontificates on
the virtue of temperance, Buntline's pet theme. Not called a "great rascal"
by his biographer for nothing, Buntline enjoyed the respect of temperance
supporters while confounding them with his drunkenness.[29] Not expecting
to be preached to in such a venue, the press called the address "ludicrous
beyond the power of description."[30] Another reviewer sympathized with
the "terrible picture of the fall of the drunkard," which Buntline, "an earnest apostle of temperance," delivered.[31] When he trails off, once more the
heroes dash in in the nick of time to effect a rescue because, as Buffalo Bill
declares, "That's the kind of man I am."[32] Texas Jack lassoes the red men,
who refuse to die by bullet, but, unfortunately, not before Wolf Slayer gets
in a shot, killing Durg.

The third act reprises the action of the first two. In vengeance for their
friend's death, the scouts vow not to leave a redskin alive. "Being a little
short of Injuns, they had to be killed several times over." One critic "counted
sixteen times that one poor 'supe' was killed during the play."[33] When Wolf
Slayer and the renegades plan a sneak attack, the scouts must fight or die.
Cody's instructions to "Give it to 'em, boys" result in an earnest contest.[34] To
outwit the scouts, the renegades start a prairie fire, but the heroes prevail.
Cody picks up a dead Indian by his belt and carries him off, while Dove
Eye shoots Wolf Slayer.[35] With the desperadoes retreating, the scouts and
women find a moment for romance. The curtain falls on the final tableau
of triumph and love, a scene "wild and weird in the extreme and worth the
price of admission."[36]

Of their premiere, a dazed Cody remembered little beyond the spec-
tacular Indian fights, but instinctively he knew "[t]here was no backing out
after that."[37] The next day the press exploded with reviews. The *Chicago
Times* guessed "that each act would end with a grand tableau terminating
a general scrimmage in which the dead and wounded would appear by
scores, and in which the Indians invariably get the worst of it; that it would
abound in hairbreadth escapes, and that the scout would always turn up
just in the nick of time; the whole ending with a happy denouement.... All
this it does and more."[38]

In depicting the warfare among scouts, Indians, and renegades, the
drama showcased the entire cast. The scouts ably demonstrated their storytelling and Indian-fighting talents. One of the renegades "managed to keep
drunk for several days without a drop of anything." The Indians, appearing
to "have a strong desire to capture somebody and, consequently, jump about
and yell," fulfilled easterners' expectations of "western savages." Buntline
"delivered some opinions on the use of liquor which he said was injurious
and had done a great deal of harm." Last, but not least, was "the beautiful
Indian maiden with an Italian accent and a weakness for scouts."[39]

As the week progressed, critics wondered what Buntline had been
doing for the four hours it took him to write the play.[40] They called Texas
Jack and Cody the

> real attractions, not only as the heroes of the play, but as
> celebrities whose fame long ante-dates their appearance before
> the footlights. So when Buffalo Bill attempts a recitation, and
> accomplishes it . . . the audience felt bound to applaud and did it
> with a vim. On the whole, it is not probable that Chicago will ever
> look upon the like again. Such a combination of incongruous
> drama, execrable acting, renowned performers, mixed audience,
> intolerable stanch, scalping, blood and thunder, is not likely
> to be vouchsafed to a city a second time, even Chicago.[41]

Discerning theatre critics' backgrounds, particularly those big-city
newspaper editors sent to cover the dramas, is nearly impossible. They may
have been of the upper class and typically have reviewed Shakespearean
plays performed by the likes of Junius Booth. They may have been mere cub
reporters, as young and excitable as the audience, or have been dime-novel
readers or maligners of the yellow literature. Reviews in nineteenth-century

Buffalo Bill Cody, Ned Buntline, and Texas Jack Omohundro.
Courtesy Buffalo Bill Museum and Grave, Golden, CO.

newspapers rarely offered a writer's byline. However, professional critics often considered themselves "guardians of the cultural mantle" and as such disparaged those plays and actors who did not aim for a higher class of theatre, fearing lowbrow works would undermine the cultural norm.[42] As a result, they often qualified their reviews. The journalist might admit the performer was very good, but it was a shame the venue was so bad. Conversely, the play might be the best "of its kind," intimating there were other, better kinds.[43]

Despite the roastings, with first night receipts of $2,800, Cody's company exceeded expectations. Manager Nixon was happy because the production saved his theatre financially. Once "a long-neglected place of amusement," his amphitheatre "suddenly loomed up as the most patronized of any in the city."[44]

When news of Cody's initial success reached Omaha, the *Weekly Tribune & Republican* described Mlle. Morlacchi as "a mulatto dancer of Chicago."[45] Cody immediately sprang to her defense and chided the editor for his "allusion to an estimable lady, of irreproachable public and private character, whose skin is as white, and blood as pure as your own—if not purer—[as] simply *contemptible*."[46] The editor defended his opinion and reproached Cody for his acting presumptions. "To talk of comparing the part he plays in this 'sensational drama' to the artistic operations of Booth and Foorest [*sic*] . . . is simply asinine."[47]

Following the first prosperous week, the troupe moved on to St. Louis where Cody spotted his wife in the audience at DeBar's Opera House. He leaned over the footlights to ask, "Honest, Mamma, does this look as awful out there as it feels up here?" At that, the crowd urged Louisa to join the actors on stage. As she quivered with fright, Cody whispered, "Now you can understand how hard your poor old husband has to work to make a living." (He was twenty-six.) Embarrassed, thereafter Louisa sat in the darkest corner of the house.[48]

After six days in St. Louis, the troupers took the road to Cincinnati's Pike's Opera House. Admission to the evening performance cost seventy-five cents for a stall and twenty-five cents for the gallery. Boys who had saved their pennies joined the dense crowd collected near the ticket office that stretched out in both directions down the sidewalk. Though Cody was suffering from a severe cold, "he put vigor into his playing as well as gallantry." In one tableau, he raised his hat to acknowledge audience applause as the curtain fell.

The press advertised no Indians, yet a young Apache named Carlos Montezuma was in the party. He had been hired out to Cody's troupe by Italian photographer Carlo Gentile who "ransomed—or bought" him from a band of southwestern Pimas. His role, along with the other "Indian" supers, was to shoot arrows at the scouts.[49] In addition, it became apparent that another professional actress was needed. Cuban-native Eloe Carfano joined the troupe, but reviews are confusing, and it's not clear whether she and Morlacchi alternated the roles of Dove Eye and Hazel Eye or whether the critics were just unable to differentiate between the actresses and their characters.

One review came out sounding like a recipe for "the queerest compound imaginable":

> Take two scouts, one trapper, one Irishman, one Dutchman, one Mormon with his family, a dozen renegades, half-a-dozen Indian chiefs, a dozen or two of Indians, a lovely squaw, an equally charming trapper's daughter, 500 rifles, 500 revolvers, 500 knives, and 500 tomahawks. Mix so thoroughly together that the identity of each ingredient will be completely lost, and then roast, slowly, around a stake. Season abundantly with gunpowder, war-whoops, and war-dances, and serve steaming hot with blood sauce, cold chills and calcium light.[50]

After the troupe left for Indianapolis, the *Cincinnati Enquirer* contended that Cody was sad. The reason could not be because of "thin houses" for he will "go hence on the war-path with well-replenished wallet." Nor was it for lack of firewater; he was seen "raising foaming beakers of most villainous stuff to his facial orifice with an evident satisfaction." The reporter thought perhaps Cody had tired of city life, but that wasn't it. Instead, he had grown fond of one of the actresses. "He loved her with a devotion that was only equaled by his love for red-eye" and, drunk, he attempted to woo her. When he put his arm around her waist, she "picked up a war club used on the stage and laid it with such gentle force and precision over the bison hunter's occiput that he rolled to the floor." Then she sat on him "with a heftiness that left him little breath for war-whoops."[51]

Despite the inclement weather in Titusville, Pennsylvania, on January 23, no one who ventured out to attend the program left "without the feeling that he had received more than his money[']s worth of enjoyment." It was neither

Ned Buntline, Buffalo Bill Cody, Giuseppina Morlacchi, and Texas Jack Omohundro. Courtesy Julie and Dennis Greene.

the first time nor the last that a critic would compare the play to a dime novel. This particular critic associated audiences who flocked to border dramas with "book-worms" who read quickly just to get the story. The plot of Cody's drama, he rhapsodized, "is filled with the most romantic, but most natural love, with thrilling escapes from foolishly perilous situations, with plenty of fine sentiments in the mouths of the 'Lo's' and with all the glittering paraphernalia which is necessary to please the popular mind."[52]

Delighted audiences crowded opera houses across Pennsylvania and New York showing their appreciation with hearty applause. For many of them, the play was of secondary importance. They had come to see the fine specimens of manhood the handsome scouts represented. To entice more women and families to the show, management passed out photographs of the four main stars.

Buntline instituted a Friday matinee as well as an introductory sketch. His short drama, a "terpsichorean comedietta" titled *Love's Battle; or, Fairy Transformation*, introduced Morlacchi's dances.[53] Her fame as "the very poetry of motion" deserved to be highlighted, as did the ease with which she adapted to speaking lines foreign to her. Her voice and gestures were forceful, but at times she obviously had trouble with idiomatic expressions.[54] Notwithstanding the impressive entertainment she provided, unreserved praise was unusual. Consequently, she must have impressed the "two thousand bad breaths and smelly feet" enough for them to show their appreciation.[55] She also awed one reviewer with her "ability to fire a rifle with precision and accuracy, fetching her Indian down on the spot." The *Scouts of the Prairie*, though, remained the pièce d'résistance. Already critics were noticing how easily the plainsmen had settled into histrionic careers.[56]

Nearly five months into the season, newspapers began acknowledging Charles Melville, the combination's advance agent, whose job was to arrange show dates. For theatre owners and managers of the myriad troupes engaged in one-night stands, booking was serious business. If the company manager found a more desirable engagement, he would not hesitate to cancel a scheduled one. Such practice led theatre managers to book two acts for the same night, often resulting in both companies arriving to perform on the same stage. The solution was the theatrical circuit, a tour of theatres in adjacent cities on a logical transportation route. Combinations found it advantageous, considerably cheaper, and convenient to book a circuit than to reserve each theatre separately.[57]

Buntline filled the position of general manager for the troupe until then and scheduled dates, signed theatre contracts, and arranged transportation. One of his main concerns was seeing to it that potential audiences were aware the troupe was coming to town. In advertising "The Greatest Dramatic Event of the Age," Buntline gave himself top billing. In many newspaper announcements, his name appears prominently in large bold-faced letters; Cody's and Texas Jack's names were in much smaller type on the cast list. Even the "Ten Indian Warriors" and Morlacchi rated larger and bolder print.[58]

At times the local press, in extolling Cody's popularity, merely inserted his name into a formulaic story line. While in Hartford, the troupers were guests of Samuel Colt's armory where Cody allegedly favored citizens with a marksmanship exhibit. After exaggerated preparations, he pasted paper on a barn door, fired and, as the story goes, knocked a picket off a fence

ACADEMY OF MUSIC.

ONE NIGHT ONLY!

Monday Evening, Feb. 17th.

Greatest Dramatic Event of the Age!

The advent of the favorite author, Sailor,
Soldier and Actor,

NED BUNTLINE!

in his great realistic drama of the

SCOUTS OF THE PRAIRIE!

WITH THE

GENUINE WESTERN HEROES IN PERSON.

BUFFALO BILL,
(Hon. W. F. Cody.)

TEXAS JACK,
(J. B. Omohundro.)

TEN INDIAN WARRIORS!

The Italian Danseuse

MLLE MORLACCHI!

AND A

Full Dramatic Company of 30 Artists!

in a most accurate representation of

SCENES IN BORDER LIFE!

INDIAN WAR DANCES,

WAR-WHOOPS,

POW-WOWS,

SCALP DANCES,

THRILLING TABLEAU,

AND A VIVID

Scene of a Prairie on Fire!

Admission 50 and 75 Cents.

No extra charge for reserved seats. For
sale at Holland's, Post Office Building.

Pittsfield, MA, ad for the February 17, 1873, performance.

ten feet to the left. He hit the rifle barrel over a stone to straighten it, then shot again, "this time barking the shin of an old pie-woman on his right flank." On his final attempt, he "hit the barn fair in the center, and the shout that arose from the assemblage attested the joy of the spectators at his success."[59]

By early March, Boston's *Evening Transcript* invited its readers to see "The Genuine Western Heroes in Person!" presumably all three now being of equal importance, judging from the same bold font in which their names were listed. The enticement worked, as Boston Theatre manager J. B. Booth seldom experienced such a succession of overflowing audiences as he did for performances of *Scouts of the Prairie*. One critic felt the drama, written in the author's "highly spiced style," appealed not only to the least expensive, often children-filled, galleries but also to those in the parquet and in the high-priced seats. Spectators in the orchestra boxes divided their attention between the "quaint expressions" of the youngsters and the action onstage where Buffalo Bill and Texas Jack lent "an intensity to the piece that ha[d] never been witnessed as representations of the semi savage drama here before."[60]

The departure of the troupe led one columnist to rhapsodize with tongue in cheek.

> With our own eyes we have seen the simon pure Buffalo Bill,
> the renowned Texas Jack is no longer to us a myth, and when
> time and age have tinged our locks with silver, can we not relate
> to future generations our personal impressions of the veritable
> Ned Buntline? . . . Have we not seen the real heroes? Have we not
> witnessed the exploits of the real remorseless avengers with real
> guns and powder, real pistols and bowie knives? And can there
> be a doubt as to the reality of the Indians? Perish the thought.

The critic confessed he didn't remember much of the plot if there was one, but the scouts and even Buntline, "who looked as though he might be a tough Indian fighter, even at his advanced years," impressed him. The Indians' job—be they "real or sham . . . it didn't make much difference"—was to "stand round, crawl round a little, and serve as targets for the intrepid scouts until the stage became burdened with dead bodies, and the curtain was dropped to clear away and begin over again."[61] Newspaper ads varied in the language describing the Indians. In one, they were "ten Indian warriors;" in another, they became specifically "ten Pawnees." Buntline and Cody likely passed off the supers as authentic. It worked. The *New York Herald* believed them to be "the genuine article," who "imparted a realistic individuality that it would be hard to attain by professional supers."[62]

An extant program printed in Boston's *The Ray* listed several actors playing those parts. W. J. Fleming, Joseph P. Winter, and George B. Beach were obviously white men impersonating the noble red. However, "Grassy Chief," "Prairie Dog," "Water Chief," "Big Elk," "Great River," and "Seven Stars" also comprise the Indian chiefs, playing far less Anglicized characters such as Ar-Fi-A-Ka and As-Sin-An-Wa.[63] They may have been nonprofessionals simply listed as such for the program, or they may have been genuine Indians pulled from those touring the eastern circuit. The Portsmouth, New Hampshire, *Daily Evening Times* critic decided the Indians he watched "seem to be half-breeds—not much Indian." Though the advertising claimed the men were "fiery" and "untamed," they turned out to be "the most peaceable, docile, awkward squad one ever saw, with seemingly no idea of what was required of them." Obvious white men, "smoked for the occasion," were the only ones who seemed to have any concept of the Indian character; or, perhaps, the eastern idea of the Indian character.[64] As disenchanted with the program as the Portsmouth critic was, a rival newspaperman, uncertain if the Pawnees were genuine or not, nevertheless thought they "looked homely enough, made hideous noises enough; and some of them spoke bad English enough."[65]

The liveliness of the show overwhelmed one Maine audience reluctant to see it end, and some showed an unwillingness to accept the closing tableau as the grand finale. "[A]n urchin, remembering that one character, at least, in the play yet survived, exclaimed, 'Hold on; wait till the show's through—*Dutchy ain't dead yet!*'"[66] Buntline was fortunate to have made the performance at all, nearly being detained in Portland the day before after successfully bringing charges against one man in the troupe for stealing. In a turnabout, the alleged thief sued Buntline for nonpayment of his wages and for false imprisonment, demanding $20,000. Buntline counteroffered with $700, and they compromised.[67]

While "Dutchy" managed to survive night after night, the lurid battle scenes were not without incident, and an occasional war wound was inevitable. Both Cody and Omohundro, unaccustomed to the confines of the stage, became overexuberant in their attacks at times. According to the *New York Herald*, W. J. Halpin, who played Wolf Slayer, was stabbed during an

Indian fight onstage in Cincinnati and died soon afterward.[68] The unfortunate accident appears to have been accepted as an inevitable hazard and served to titillate the audience, bringing the production nearer to the realities of actual Indian fighting. However, with no other verification from Cincinnati, it may have been a perverse publicity ploy on Buntline's part.

Both scouts weathered the strain of touring and performing from December through March and were prepared for their debut on the New York City stage. Buntline wrote a new introductory farce called *The Broken Bank; or, A Rough Corner in New York*, which critics promptly slammed as "the worst ever written, and certainly the worst acted atrocity ever seen on any stage."[69] Such curtain raisers featured supporting actors in song and dance and were rarely well received. New York ladies and gentlemen, whom Cody the Plainsman had impressed only a year previously, anticipated seeing Cody the Actor. Critics from major New York newspapers attended the production, while editors awaited their remarks. The dailies gave ample space to alternately praising and lambasting the troupe.

James G. Bennett, a newspaper magnate whom Cody had once guided on a hunting trip, made sure his *New York Herald* reviewer cheered Cody and the play, daunting though the assignment was. Bennett, even more so than Buntline, can be credited with Cody's success, proving "how factors completely unrelated to the quality of the drama influenced critics."[70] According to the *Herald* critic,

> *The Scouts of the Prairie* . . . is about everything in general and nothing in particular. . . . Mr. Judson (otherwise Buntline) represents the part as badly as is possible for any human being to represent it and the part is as bad as it was possible to make it. . . . "Buffalo Bill" . . . is a good-looking fellow, tall and straight as an arrow, but ridiculous as an actor. Texas Jack . . . is not quite so good-looking, not so tall, not so straight, and not so ridiculous. . . . To describe the play and its reception is alike impossible. . . . Everything was so wonderfully bad that it was almost good.[71]

The critic for the *World* likewise pulled no punches:

> It scarcely coheres sufficiently to interest one in the story. . . . [The Indians] make bombastic speeches about the dew, the

> morning cloud, and the baseness of the white man. They . . .
> fall upon a trapper called Cale Durg. . . . At that moment Buffalo
> Bill and Texas Jack jump into the assemblage, kill pretty nearly
> everybody and form a tableau. . . . As a drama it is very poor stuff.

Cody, a "remarkably handsome fellow" with his "round uncultured voice and utter absence of anything like stage art," charmed the audience "disposed to laugh at all that was intended to be pathetic and serious." The critic understood the object of the play was to give the scouts the opportunity to show how they fight Indians. "None of them are actors. Least of all is Ned Buntline. His histrionism is even worse than his literature. But he has succeeded in getting a crammed house, which he and the management do not hesitate to say is better than doing a good thing."[72]

The *New York Times* weighed in with grudging admiration for Cody, even though the play left much to be desired. "Of [the drama], few will know much, even after repeated hearings. . . . The *Scouts of the Prairie* is, then, made up largely of wars and the rumors of wars. The characters are always either fighting or getting ready to fight. Most of them seem to be shot down in the course of the action, and come miraculously to life again in the sequel."[73]

Finally, the *Tribune* reluctantly admitted the spectacle might be "mildly and feebly characterized as extraordinary . . . but the play . . . is idiotic." Cody, though, was sublime "when surrounded with defunct Indians and standing stalwart in a cloud of smoke and dust, through which the yelps of the supers sounded in hideous discord." Buntline, the critic hoped, realized "his pretensions as a play-writer are ridiculous." Very little criticism usually came Morlacchi's way, but the *Tribune* reviewer condemned her acting as "very absurd. . . . [She] was laughed at, as she deserved to be." Indeed, he belittled the whole troupe for its "misuse of a beautiful stage" and seemed pleased to see it "dismissed in universal laughter."[74]

In Brooklyn, the impressive Rocky Mountain scenery remarkably resembled the backdrop for *Rip Van Winkle*, produced at the opera house a few weeks before. When Texas Jack and Buffalo Bill first appear, they "look at the leader of the orchestra and make that good soul shake in his boots as they swear to take his scalp at the first favorable opportunity." As Nieuwenhuyse noted, no information about the type of orchestra or the music played is mentioned in contemporary reports. While "orchestra" implies a cadre of musicians, often it was only a piano player and a violinist, occasionally accompanied by a cornet player. After threatening to shoot the pianist, the scouts "look to their arms and seeing evidently for the first time that they are new, proceed to puff the makers who presented them." The subsequent Indian fight, "in which several tribes are exterminated and about a ton of gunpowder is blown to blue blazes, . . . terminates only because every fighting man lies stiff in death upon the sanguinary sword."[75]

Censure ran rampant. Even Cody, who for four months could do little wrong, "has in his general aspect a great many features suggestive of the braggarts in all frontier towns, who are always talking fight, but, like the colored troops, fight nobody." With Texas Jack and Buntline, "the three together form as pretty a combination of frauds as the country has ever paid to see."[76]

The show business tabloid, the *New York Clipper*, chimed in with its opinion that the play "has no story or plot. . . . Brevity is, perhaps, its greatest merit." The stringer thought the only fun in the play was the Dutchman's question to the savages following the trail: "'Ingines, vat you lose?'"[77]

One journalist stood back to observe the humorous wrangling of the highbrow critics who couldn't decide what to write about the unique troupe.

> Being the dramatic sensation of the day, the critics had, of course, to give it respectful treatment. . . . It is a hard trial for them to admit that after all their fine writing Buffalo Bill and the Black Crook fill the largest theater in New York night after night for weeks in succession, while Edwin Booth and Fechter play the classic drama to empty seats but such is the fact. On the whole, it is a fair question whether the dramatic taste of New York is so far above that of the provinces after all.[78]

When the combination reached Philadelphia on April 28, reporter J. Noel de Snooks spotted the scouts walking down the street, costumed in moccasins and buckskin. Requesting an interview, Snooks sent his card to the scouts' hotel room. Cody wrote back to "Pass bearer to Buffalo Bill's room," and then, quoting a line in the play, he added, because "[t]hat's the kind of a man I am."

Snooks found Cody "put on more style than a cheap dry goods clerk" and observed that "if there are any comforts or luxuries in the market that these Indian-slayers do not enjoy, it is because the sellers do not advertise and the two latter do not see them." Despite the extravagant room, Snooks found the two scouts sitting cross-legged on the floor smoking cigars and pipes. After introductions, Cody boasted his share was $1,000 a night "for slaughtering the King's English." In another life, he had made that amount in one year hunting buffalo.[79]

At this time, the Modoc Indian War was making news. When whites tried to resettle them onto a reservation, Modoc leader Captain Jack led his people to northern California's lava caves where they maintained their position. After much bloodshed, Captain Jack agreed to a peace treaty. He did not trust the U.S. Army, however, and in a sudden outburst during negotiations, he shot and killed Brigadier General E. R. S. Canby, then escaped with his supporters back into the caves.

Snooks asked Cody what he thought of the situation and reported his response in what he supposed was western dialect.

"Well[,] Cap . . . I hear a heap of talk around the country since Capt. Jack lifted the hair of the commissioners and Gen. Canby. I'm surprised, I am, that the government don't clean 'em out forthwithly." The reporter countered that the Modocs were well hidden in natural caves.

Buffalo Bill declared, "Give me old 'Nancy Ann,' my breech-loader there, and let Jack have a lasso and scalping-knife, and I'll bet every cent I own we can clean out every bloody red son-of-a-corkscrew of 'em inside of thirty days, and do our own scouting and cooking. . . . I have shot and stabbed [Indians], cut their bowels out with my knife, harpooned 'em, clubbed 'em to death, in fact killed 'em in every way you can think of, except talking 'em to death." Cody asserted his intention to head west to take care of the Indian problem, but first, he said, he was going to "show the play-goers what real acting is. I propose to run Booth and Fechter into New Jersey by playing Shakespeare right through from beginning to end."

When Snooks suggested Cody take the contract to exterminate the Indians, he responded that, when the season was over, he and Jack would head to the lava beds "and see if we can't get enough hair to stuff a rocking-chair for the old woman." Once they got a look around the area, "if 'clean 'em out' is the orders, we won't leave a pappoose [sic] a week old."[80] It was, he said, "harder work to kill and drag off twenty Indians on the stage every night than to perform the same job in real earnest." If Cody indeed said all this, no evidence suggests he was doing more than indulging in flagrant exaggeration. Tall tales, teasing, and leg-pulling were frequent by-products of the boredom of frontier life. In his many tales, Mark Twain often indulged in "whoppers." On the other hand, editors encouraged over-the-top writing if it was done skillfully, so Cody's remarks may not have been what he actually said but rather what Snooks's editor thought would make good reading.[81]

The Philadelphia newspaper ran the scathing comment that "the play, considered as a literary work, was beneath contempt." The heroes playing themselves were the attraction, despite their lack of talent. "Imagine Julius Caesar playing his own part in the tragedy named after him. . . . It would be very interesting." Yet, the critic continued, if Caesar acted as badly as Cody and Jack, "we should rejoice that death had made such a terrible mischance impossible." Cody's lines were straightforward, requiring no great measure of intellect to convey their meaning to the audience, but "the wild and ineffectual struggles of the actor with them would make a contrary impression upon the uninformed." Texas Jack's awkwardness was such that it seemed as if he were "perpetrating a somewhat clumsy gag. The most effective members of the company are two or three Indians, who . . . stand grim and silent, looking as gloomy and sad amid all the hurley-burley and noise, as if their squaws and papooses had just been ushered to the happy hunting grounds at the very moment when those last fragments of baked dog disagreed with the bereaved relatives."[82]

Despite the ineptness the critic saw, Cody's increasing self-confidence became apparent when, after the first act of the performance in Baltimore, he extemporaneously addressed the audience and alluded to the fact that only a few months ago, he had been performing on the western plains the very same deeds of Indian warfare he was re-creating that evening. During their weeklong stay, the stage Indians roamed the streets clad in native costumes. Their appearance caused fear in "nervous old ladies, timid elderly gentlemen, young maidens with palpitating hearts in their bosoms, and small boys who had scared themselves at night reading dime novels by the light of surreptitious candles." Buntline inflated the Indian numbers, saying he "originally left the plains with forty, but half of them caught their deaths of cold when they were introduced to civilization and a bath tub."[83]

The discrepancy between the production and the actual Modoc war struck one reviewer as incongruous:

In these days when the Indians of the West are dancing war dances and scalp dances and uniting in a war against the pale faces, it seems very strange to have the genuine red man going through the pantomime of war upon the stage. . . . The noble savage, with his feathers and his war paint is on the boards of the Holliday Street Theatre and is doing the jumping, tearing, howling savage, with an abandon, and an enjoyment that inspires the pit with a desire to empty their six shooters in that direction.

He surmised that

the rate at which Buffalo Bill and Texas Jack dispose of the red skins . . . would be very satisfactory if practiced in earnest at the lava beds, but from some mistake in the arrangements out there it is the Modocs who do the shooting and our men who do the dying. If the Indians got up a drama for an Indian audience, they would probably present the war of external action in a light more in accordance with Captain Jack's ideas.[84]

By the time the combination reached Washington, D.C., Bessie Sudlow had replaced Mlle. Morlacchi. A new introductory comedietta titled *Jenny Lind at Last* highlighted Sudlow's singing and dancing and the "comicalities" of G. C. Davenport, the play's Irishman. Washingtonians at first appeared to have no interest in western men for, when the play began, the house was nearly half empty. But when people heard the volleys of shots and war whoops, they flocked into Wall's Opera House to learn what was going on. The final curtain dropped on one of the season's fullest houses.

Two weeks later, the crowd that filled Fulton Hall in Lancaster, Pennsylvania, was disappointed when Cody failed to appear because his wife was ill. The reviewer did not name the actor who took his part, nor is any mention made of Texas Jack. Perhaps because the original scouts were not in attendance, the understudies felt free to improvise, and "remarks that were decidedly *vulgar* were freely used by the principal characters." Through the whole play, "the genuine Indians gave a novelty to the performance— a *decided* novelty, we may say, for each and every one of them was killed no less than five times by actual count."[85] Between engagements in eastern Pennsylvania, Cody stopped in to visit Colonel Henry R. Guss of West Chester, a relative on his mother's side. Cody subsequently moved his family to that city, which was closer to the eastern theatrical circuit, and rented a home on Washington Street.[86]

Many historians contend that the combination's first season came to an end at Port Jervis, New York, on June 16, 1873, citing Cody's autobiography

Buffalo Bill Cody, c. 1873, by Rockwood, New York. Courtesy
Buffalo Bill Historical Center (P.69.1792), Mary Jester Allen
Collection, Cody, WY.

as the source of this information. However, Cody's memory was faulty; the season did not end until June 28 in Albany. On June 16, the troupe appeared in Lockport, New York, and in Auburn on June 18. Cody reported to the press that, when his tour ended, he expected to "return to the war path after Captain Jack" as chief scout under General Sheridan.[87]

Throughout the first season, they had made no claim to dramatic ability, and one *New York Clipper* journalist realized that to criticize them as actors would be "unjust as well as absurd."[88] The performance needed improvement, but Cody had certainly grown in stage presence; he started out in December a bumbling, naive frontiersman but by season's end, he had become a confident player. More importantly for his future career, he had learned some valuable lessons: a marksmanship exhibit was of interest, people enjoyed seeing the costumed actors wander about the street, and it paid to hire competent managers to plan routes and rent theatres.

Cody and Texas Jack had become accustomed to luxuries their newfound wealth could provide. No wonder, then, at the end of that first arduous season, Cody's paltry income of only $6,000 disappointed him. Audience acclaim should have translated into bigger profits.[89]

Convinced of their own ability to manage the show and their future fortunes, Cody and Texas Jack decided to exclude Buntline from the next season's plans. We don't know how Buntline took the discharge, but chagrined or stoic, he carried on, advertising a new dramatic company only two months later. True to his temperance inclination, he announced, "Every person in this organization is free from intemperate habits which so often mar entertainments and shock sensibilities."[90]

Though similar to *Scouts*, Buntline's new production failed to gain appreciative audiences. Cody was the draw and, lacking his presence, no rival drama could endure. In December 1875, Buntline resurrected *Scouts of the Prairie* and toured New England but with little success.[91] He is reported to have said, "I might have paved for myself a far different career in letters but my early lot was cast among rough men on the border; they became my comrades, and when I made my name as a teller of stories about Indians, pirates and scouts, it seemed too late to begin over again."[92] He continued writing stories until his death in July 1886. Cody never again partnered with the architect of his life as a showman.

Once he made the decision to carry on, Cody spent two weeks with his family, and then he and Texas Jack headed west to escort a hunting party. Arriving in Omaha on July 16, Cody, sporting a wealth of jewelry, "'loomed it up' for the boys right lively." He had a bridle "made of Indian scalps adorned with $400 worth of siver [*sic*]."[93] The blatant display of financial success was accepted custom in the nineteenth century; his boastful exuberance expected of someone who had prospered in his recent endeavors.

In the *Omaha Daily Bee*, Cody announced his new dramatic production for the 1873–74 season and an anticipated tour of Europe.[94] "This [is] more remunerative than the honor of being a Nebraska legislator," he told the reporter, "while Texas Jack is of the opinion that financially it eclipses buffalo hunting and scouting."[95] Cody boasted: "I'm no d——d scout now; I'm a first-class star."[96]

Around August 4, following the hunt, Cody returned to West Chester. During a visit by Texas Jack, the men engaged "in a game of tenpins which exercise and pastime they now refer to as 'horse billiards.'"[97] There was little time for leisure, however; the new season loomed closer, and a great deal remained to be done. They would be introducing a new character, one who would have a great impact on the combination.

CHAPTER THREE

Wild Times with Wild Bill

By heavens, you are safe with Wild Bill,
who is ever ready to risk his life and die, if need be.
—John Burke, *The Noblest Whiteskin*

FOLLOWING THE FIRST SEASON'S TRIUMPHS, NEWFOUND FAME, AND break from Buntline, Cody and Texas Jack planned their next season. Cody returned to New York City to a warm welcome from William B. Freligh, manager of the Bowery Theatre. Commencing August 28, he would play the lead in *Buffalo Bill, King of the Border Men*, the play he attended only eighteen months previously when he had stood tongue-tied on the same stage with no thought of ever becoming an actor. Now, he was once again about to meld his real self with his theatrical persona.

The drama, reconstructed and embellished with "Novel effects, Startling Tableaux, Thrilling Realistic Situations and a powerful cast," opens at the Cody family cabin, where villain Jake McKanlass murdered Buffalo Bill's father.[1] Twenty years later, Buffalo Bill has grown up and is seeking vengeance. In act 1, Cody wounds Jake, who next kidnaps Bill's sister Lettie. During a pursuit, Buffalo Bill tires and crawls into a hollow log to sleep. Unfortunately, during a powwow, Indians throw the log into their campfire. By tossing some gunpowder around, Buffalo Bill escapes and watches the explosion scatter the Indians. "A lot of music and a minimal plot encumber the last act," which concludes with a knife fight between the protagonists and results in Lettie's rescue.[2] "As Mr. Cody acted his own character, criticism is out of the question," jotted the New York Clipper, "yet it may be said that, as he becomes more familiar with stage business, his performances are more enjoyable." Had Cody accepted Freligh's first offer, his stage presence may have eventually improved, but his initial reluctance to embark on a histrionic career enabled him to return with confidence on his own terms.

Texas Jack and Mlle. Morlacchi married in Rochester, New York, on August 31, 1873.[3] While the newlyweds honeymooned, Joseph P. Winter replaced Jack in the drama. Frederick G. Maeder, who originally adapted the play from Buntline's novel, took the role of the Old Vet. Critics considered Maeder a good eccentric comedian, but he was best known as a prolific playwright.[4] His wife, Rena, played Kitty Muldoon, and Richard W. Marston was Snakeroot Sam.[5] Harry Irving joined the troupe and many years later enjoyed telling stories about the old days. Buntline, he had heard, "decided to quit the company for the lecture platform, for he was as fluent a talker as he was a writer." When he learned Cody was in New York, Buntline invited him and his troupers to the lecture hall, suggesting Buntline's dismissal was somewhat amicable.

A talented speaker, Ned had the audience in tears, then in gales of laughter. Throughout it all, he held a large pitcher from which he would occasionally drink. Everyone assumed it held water until, as he went along, "he was getting unusually oratorical. His face got redder . . . telling us of the awful things that would happen to any man who took a drink." Finally Cody leaned over to Irving and asked, "'What do you suppose he's got in that pitcher? I believe it's whiskey.' He was right. . . . [P]retty soon Buntline got all tangled up in his words and had to be carried out of the theatre by the arms and legs."[6]

A week after his marriage, Texas Jack rejoined Cody. John M. Burke, who had served as Morlacchi's manager during the first season, accompanied him. Born in Washington, D.C., Burke had been an actor, manager, drama critic, and city editor. Over the course of the next thirty-four years, he would become one of Cody's most constant and devoted companions. Buntline's discourses could convert a drunk away from the bottle, and he entertained more than a generation with his stories. But Burke, for all

Cody poses with a .42-caliber Remington rifle and a revolver in his belt, c. 1875. Courtesy Buffalo Bill Historical Center (P.69.131), Cody, WY.

his experience in publicity, "seldom constructed an intelligible sentence, although he so entangled flowers and figures of speech that the lack of a mere verb was unnoticeable." Critics of Buntline's so-called plot in *Scouts of the Prairie* found Burke's florid prose even more perplexing. As public relations manager, "he was a master of the adjective to the exclusion of other parts of speech."[7] One critic was Nate Salsbury, Cody's partner in his Wild West show. He wrote, "I do not believe there is another man in the world who could have covered as much space in the newspapers of the day as John Burke has done and I do not believe there is another man in the world in his position that would have had the gall to exploit himself at the expense of the show as much as John Burke!"[8]

In his baroque style, Burke recalled his first meeting with Cody:

Physically superb, trained to the limit, in the zenith of his manhood, features cast in nature's most perfect mold, on a prancing charger that was foaming and chafing at the bit, and in his most picturesque beaded buckskin garb, he was indeed a picture. When he dismounted I was introduced to the finest specimen of God's handiwork I had ever seen, and felt that for once there was that nearest approach to an ideal human, a visual interpretation given to the assertion that man was indeed a replica of His Maker. . . . I thought then that he was the handsomest, straightest, finest man that I had ever seen in my life. I still think so.[9]

Cody hired Burke with all his expertise to replace Buntline as manager. However, he still needed another actor and, after much consideration, decided on his old friend, James Butler "Wild Bill" Hickok. Discreet inquiries revealed he was living in Missouri, eking out a living as a gambler.

Cody recalled: "Thinking that Wild Bill would be quite an acquisition to the troupe, we wrote to him at Springfield, Missouri, offering him a large salary if he would play with us that winter. He was doing nothing at the time, and we thought that he would like to take a trip through the States, as he had never been East."[10] Contrary to Cody's belief, Hickok had been east. Having been involved in a "Grand Buffalo Hunt" fiasco, the legendary gunman was wary of all things theatrical.

The previous summer, Colonel Sidney Barnett of Niagara Falls decided to publicize his museum with a staged buffalo hunt and persuaded Hickok to take charge. When three buffaloes, instead of the expected herd, were released into the arena, cowboys and Indians costumed in full war regalia shot at them with blunt arrows. Though Barnett tried to make the event amusing, the three thousand onlookers went home disappointed. The *New York Times*, learning of the immense efforts to get the Indians and buffalo to the falls and of the deaths of several buffalo during transport, hoped that "the present experience may have the effect of inducing those who crave the excitement of hunting the animals, to seek it, in future, upon the plains."[11] For his part, a frustrated Hickok returned to the West. At first, he was dubious of Cody's invitation. Buntline had enticed Cody with the promise of money. Similarly, "[Wild] Bill did not think well of our enterprise on account of our unfamiliarity with the stage, but a large salary forced him to forego his diffidence before the public."[12]

Learning of this, the West Chester editor indicated that Hickok, "full of daring spirit, and act[ing] more from impulse than deliberation, . . . is considered a 'terror' by the 'red skins.'" Though many might regard Hickok, or any of the scouts, as rough and uncouth in manners, the newsman hastened to assure his readers that would be a mistake. "It is true they have necessarily inherited from their long wild Western associations some eccentricities of character, but these are to be admired rather than deprecated."[13] With Hickok set to come aboard, on August 9, 1873, the *New York Clipper* advertised a new drama with Cody, Omohundro, and Hickok, emphasizing "that the celebrated Wild Bill has pleased to avail himself of the opportunity to accompany his old comrade. His duties on the plains will only permit him to travel during one season," a caveat Hickok may have insisted on. On Thursday, September 4, before Cody finished the run of *Buffalo Bill*, Wild Bill appeared onstage with him; Texas Jack showed up the next night to give an exhibition of lasso throwing; and on Saturday evening, the trio treated audiences to the sights of Indians Jack brought from the plains. Jack's rope tricks, Wild Bill's rapid pistol-shooting and fancy shots, and the Indians' war dances "were most enthusiastically received."[14]

Cody took his new combination on the road, still playing in *Buffalo Bill, King of the Border Men*. Professional actors such as the Maeders, Lizzie Safford as Lillie Fielding, and Walter Fletcher as Snakeroot Sam accompanied the three actor/heroes. On September 8, the show was scheduled for eight p.m. at Greer's Hall, in New Brunswick, New Jersey. An hour before, people who were struggling to get beyond the closed doors packed the stairs and hallway. Twenty minutes later, they occupied every seat, and large numbers were standing. In anticipation, gallery patrons whistled and called, "'O Jack! O, Bill!' 'Hoera!' 'Bully for you!' 'Set 'em up again!'" When the scouts emerged onstage, the shouts grew louder. "The braves and border men who again and again sunk under the ruthless tomahawk and by the blank cartridge unerringly aimed, and who pluckily wouldn't die, made hit upon hit." Young boys especially enjoyed the performance, and the reviewer feared half of them would run off to become cowboys, leaving a paucity of butchers, bakers, and candlestick makers. "[W]hen the curtain falls on a stage full of slain red men, with Buffalo Bill in proud triumph standing over his victims, no boy who loves to be thrilled with wild Western scenes could refuse to yell."[15]

In one of the early scenes, the scouts sit around a fake campfire passing a whiskey jug and ad-libbing tall tales. The first time Cody passed the jug to Hickok, he took a good swig. A look of horror crossed his face before he turned and spat out the liquid. "Cold tea don't count—either I get real whisky or I ain't tellin' no story!" he thundered. Cody was outraged at the disruption, but Hickok's outburst so amused the audience that Cody not only kept him in whisky but probably made his tantrum part of the performance.[16] Becoming astute at judging what audiences wanted, he gave it to them.

Many years after his affiliation with the combination, former manager Hiram Robbins was entertaining a crowd with stories. One listener, a reporter for the *Arkansaw Traveler*, recorded his comments.

Wild Bill was really the character. . . . He was always under the influence of liquor, for it seemed that he could not do without a stimulant. Yet, he was far from being drunk, and was always modest and respectful until something occurred to claim his warlike attention. . . .

After I wrote a drama, full of gore and scalp, I found that it was necessary to assign Wild Bill, the actual hero, to a minor part, on account of his effeminate voice, . . . altogether too weak for the part which he would naturally take.[17]

Robbins's observation lacks credibility considering that many a man cowered at the prospect of facing Wild Bill. A gunfighter speaking with a soft, sissified inflection could hardly claim a reputation built on fear. In contrast, Cody maintained in his autobiography that Wild Bill "possessed a good strong voice, yet when he went upon the stage before an audience, it was almost impossible for him to utter a word."[18] Until Hickok became used to performing, perhaps all he was able to manage was a squeak, and it is to this that Robbins likely refers. Wild Bill's reluctance to speak up was also due to the banality of his lines, such as "Fear not, fair maid! By heavens, you are safe with Wild Bill, who is ever ready to risk his life and die, if need be, in defense of weak and defenseless womanhood!"[19]

In recognition of the two "scouting" parties traveling the theatre circuit (Cody's and Buntline's), the *New York Clipper* reminded its readers that

these sons of the forest are harmless and without guile; that the palefaced maiden is in no danger from their presence and that the white man may follow their path without let or hindrance. We can further guarantee that some of these Indians are not Indians, but merely imitators of the noble red man, and that their mission is not death to their natural foes, as the dime novels would lead us to believe but peace and goodwill to men who patronize them.

In honor of the bordermen, the *Clipper* proposed a poem:

They are all decent fellows and not marauding scamps . . .
"Wild Bill" and "Dashing Charlie" with long and tawny hair
Too often are their targets the beautiful and fair.
Without a "Jack" from Texas the pack is not complete,
Whene'er he throws his lasso he takes us off our feet. . . .
Fred Maeder and Ned Buntline will guard the flowing tills—
We hope they'll find the money when they *present their Bills.*[20]

Audiences continued to crowd theatres where Cody's combination played, while critics posted reviews alternately praising and denouncing the drama. Lexington's *Kentucky Gazette* predicted that "if some one would write a play suited to the actors, we have no doubt the company would create quite a sensation." Instead, the critic saw there was no plot, "[only] a succession of raids by the Indians, in which the young ladies are carried off and afterwards rescued in an impossible manner by their lovers. . . . However, the very absurdity of the scenes lends an interest which would probably be lacking if they approached nearer a true representation of border life."[21]

According to the *Louisville Courier-Journal*, the scouts moved in and slew "everybody laying around, loose, and nicely they finished the job, the last man grieving that there is no one left to 'to chaw up' having serious intensions [*sic*] to commit suicide for that reason, when the curtain falls." The next day, the same columnist thought the boys had been "lively as crickets, killing everything right and left. The galleries enjoy the wholesale slaughter, and only seemed to regret that they couldn't take a hand in the tustle [*sic*]. If the company would just elect a coroner, we think it would make the combination complete."[22]

Melodrama reflected contemporary life, so it was not unrealistic for even the border dramas to include, besides the shootings, scalpings, and free use of the bowie knife, some amount of lovemaking between the scouts and female characters of the cast. But Cody never forgot the audience had come to see genuine scouts acting as heroes. In one scene, the action represents a meeting between the plainsmen and a band of Indians on the warpath. They "are seeking an advantage which the keen eye of Buffalo Bill detects almost in the outset, and a terrific hand to hand encounter transpires, and the pipe of peace is incontinently snuffed out." Logic dictates that some in the audience attended border plays hoping to learn what the frontier was all about before making the trip themselves. One Indiana reporter supposed "[t]hose who witness the performance of this play will not care to take Greeley's advice to go West."[23]

The ad in the *Terre Haute Daily Express* offered a concrete indication of the program preceding the main event. Mlle. Morlacchi showed off her singing and dancing in Howard Paul's comedy *Thrice Married*. She assumed four different characters: Carlotta; Victoria La Page singing a French song; Senora Norona Marana in a Spanish Dance; and Gustavus Wellington De Vere with Hornpipe. The paper also reported Cody's practice of using himself, Texas Jack, and Wild Bill as the best form of promotion. "[W]ith their long, ambrosial locks streaming in the wind," the scouts attracted attention as they walked the streets. The frontiersmen, the paper went on, "have served their country nobly in years past; and not having been over-paid, (and those who serve their country best never are,) and wishing to travel through 'the States' profitably, financially, and otherwise, they take this way of accomplishing their purpose."[24]

Sometimes theatrical life became dangerous, particularly given the physicality of border dramas. During an engagement in Philadelphia, Cody "acted a rough and tumble night so well," he broke a rib. "[B]ut the actions of

'Buffalo Bill' certainly call for a full complement of these important bones," so theatregoers would have to be patient until "the illustrious bull-whacker" could return to the stage.[25]

When the combination reached Indiana months later, the *Indianapolis Journal* reminded its readers that Cody's troupers appeared there once before, but since then, "they have made a study of their new chosen profession, and everywhere the press and public are loud in praise of their marked improvement." The critic congratulated the scouts on surmounting the "numberless difficulties" of the actor's art. Considering that only a few months previously they had "trod the mimic stage" for the first time, their achievement was all the greater.[26]

The *Journal* pinpointed the crux of the troupe's popularity: Texas Jack's "quick agile movements, earnestness of manner and rapid gesture" earned him equal billing with Cody. Audiences flocked to see Hickok after reading about his legendary exploits in *Harper's New Monthly Magazine*.[27] Watching the legendary gunfighter, who reportedly had killed ten heavily armed members of the McCanles gang, they were amazed that "he had only a few weeks ago been on the plains and probably had scarcely ever visited a theatre and knew nothing of its workings. That he should get through a part, full of busy action, shows a wonderful adaptability." But Cody was the top attraction. "[T]he dash, grace, and rollicking bravery of the king of the border men were ably personified—the more life-like and natural from the remarkable fact, almost unprecedented in the annals of the drama, of the hero of a play being personated by the hero himself."[28]

When the plainsmen walked the streets, "large crowds of gaping men and open-eyed, awe-stricken youths" gathered around. If the three scouts were not genuine, the reporter guessed "their appearance and make-up is so nearly like the picture of them in the Beadle Dime Novels that they passed all the same with the crowd, and as such were honored and respected." Dime-novel enthusiasts who read and "more than half believe" blood-and-thunder stories composed the majority of the Lafayette, Indiana, audience in mid-October. Because the troupe did not claim to present a drama of great merit, once again editors concluded "criticism would be entirely out of place."[29]

Most critics realized that, although *Buffalo Bill, King of the Border Men* "is composed of a score of impossible situations, and the dialogue is disjointed and bad," the author's purpose afforded the scouts ample opportunity to display "the mode of warfare in vogue in savage life." Despite this,

Toledo, Ohio, opinion had it that Cody's combination was in many respects inferior to others.[30] The *Sandusky Daily Register* agreed that the drama was barely mediocre but insisted that, even if they had no interest in the scenes of strife and warfare, everyone ought to attend just to see the real heroes in person. "It is said of Wild Bill himself, that he alone has in his life probably killed one hundred men while the others are not far behind him in their sanguinary record. In short they are the most noted scouts in the world."[31]

Despite the acclaim accorded him, Hickok began to conclude playacting was not for him. He insisted to Cody they were making laughingstocks of themselves, and, out of boredom or devilment, he began to torment the "Indian" supers (the paid extras) by shooting at their legs instead of over their heads during the battles. Although the scouts' pistols were underloaded with black gunpowder, the shot could sting or cause minor burns. "This would make them dance and jump, so that it was difficult to make them fall and die—although they were paid twenty-five cents each for performing the 'dying business.'" They complained to Cody and threatened not to go onstage, so Cody remonstrated with Hickok, at which he would laugh and promise not to do it anymore. "But it would not be long before he was at his old tricks again."[32]

In Titusville, Pennsylvania, where the troupe was to appear at the Parshall Opera House in early November, some local toughs intended to cause trouble. Fearing the worst, the hotel's landlord asked the scouts to use the side door. Cody agreed and informed the others of the arrangement. Hickok immediately offered to "fight the whole mob," but Cody advised against it. Heedless of the warning, Hickok, intending to see just who it was that had it in for them, entered the room where the bullies waited. Instantly there was a hand on his shoulder. "Hello, Buffalo Bill! We have been looking for you all day."

When Hickok denied being Buffalo Bill, the bruiser called him a liar. To him, one long-haired scout looked the same as any other. Suffering no name-calling, Hickok immediately knocked him down and drove the rest away. He then exited the room "whistling a lively tune" and announced to Cody, "I have been interviewing that party who wanted to clean us out. . . . I got lost among the cañons and then I ran in among the hostiles, . . . but it is all right now. They won't bother us any more."[33]

Throughout the previous three months, advertisements for the combination publicized Cody, Hickok, and Omohundro as "scouts of the plains." During their travels, Hiram Robbins was busy writing a new play expressly

Wild Bill Hickok, Texas Jack Omohundro, Buffalo Bill Cody.
Courtesy Buffalo Bill Museum and Grave, Golden, CO.

for them. With little originality, he called it *Scouts of the Plains*, much to the confusion of later historians, owing to the similarity between this title and that of Buntline's play, *Scouts of the Prairie*. The new drama premiered in Buffalo, New York, on November 13, 1873. Newsmen expected that "[s]tirring scenes in which the Scouts have figured in actual life will be presented, and there will be, incidentally, many startling situations and much music and fun." Such anticipation did not go unfilled.[34]

The story begins when Buffalo Bill learns that Jim Daws, "a first class renegade and horse thief," kidnaps the daughter of Uncle Henry Carter, an old trapper friend. Predictably, Cody swears revenge and promises he will "take his life's blood, or die in the attempt." Daws, played by Robbins, vows revenge in return. He becomes leader of the Comanches, kills off Carter and his wife, and carries off their other two daughters. Time and again throughout the four acts, either the girls or the scouts are in imminent peril and, in several scenes, someone is dangerously close to being burned at the stake. At the perfect time, at least one scout happens along and handles either a rifle or pistol with such celerity as could only be attained by a great deal of practice. All through the play a Quaker peace commissioner drops in most inopportunely. He gets scalped—"as he deserves"—before the close. The scouts finally mete out justice to Daws and his cowardly sidekick Tom Doggett.[35]

Reactions to the troupe and the new drama were prompt and generally favorable. The *Jamestown Daily Journal* suggested "those in need of a jolly laugh had better attend." The *Erie Morning Dispatch* thought the drama, produced in the city's brand new opera house, had "scarce the shadow of a plot and is like an animated dime novel with the Indian-killing multiplied by ten, but . . . the bloodier the tragedy the broader was the comedy." None failed to notice "a slight incongruity in the piece and that is, the frequency with which the same tribe of Indians are wiped out, but the oftener they were shot down, the better the audience liked it." As for the heroes, they were "among the finest looking men on the Continent, each being above six feet in height and splendidly proportioned." The "'Modocs,' as the Indians attached to Buffalo Bill's party are generally called, attracted a good deal of attention by their quaint costumes, while promenading about the streets yesterday." The drama illustrated how the scouts conducted matters on the plains, "where it is a word and a revolver, the revolver first," observed the *Williamsport Gazette & Bulletin*. The production, with twelve hundred people in attendance, "was an unparalleled success."[36]

The *Easton Daily Express* of December 15 invited theatre patrons with a poem:

> Hark; Hark; the dogs do bark,
> The Indians are in town—
> Buffalo Bill and Texas Jack,
> William the Wild, the peerless Morlac
> Chi, as the maiden brown.

The next day the newspaper devoted a column to the border drama, describing it as historical as well as "instructive and agreeable." Easterners had the wonderful opportunity "to see men whose lives have been fraught with such perilous adventures and extraordinary dangers; who have encountered death a thousand times, and who have rendered so much service to our army and to the settlers on the plains."[37]

Hiram Robbins remembered Philadelphia was where Hickok again caused trouble. The troupe rented a calcium light—also known as a lime-light because of the brilliant illumination created when lime was heated to incandescence—and paid the owner a fee every time he turned it on. One night Hickok decided Cody and Texas Jack were receiving more light than he, and it "makes them look pretty." Keen to have his fair share of the blaze, Hickok climbed the ladder to the light "manipulator" and demanded he direct more light on him. When the man told him he could only turn it on at specific times, Hickok pulled out his revolver and threatened to "kill you nine out of ten [times] from below, . . . and [i]f you don't throw the light on me when I appear, I'll try you one just for luck." Fearful for his life, the man shone the full effect on Hickok during his scene. The intensity blinded his eyes, already weakened from a disease. Squinting, he yelled up at the operator to "'Turn the blamed thing off.' The entire act was spoiled."[38]

Following New Year 1874 celebrations, the three scouts set out for Bridgeport, Connecticut. The local press, anticipating their arrival, lauded them as "men who held their lives 'but at a pin's fee,' [who] endured hardships and danger to protect the borders from renegades and savages and now travel to contrast city life with prairie existence."[39] Besides hiring professional actor Frank Mordaunt as director, Cody added another expert to the combination team. The *New York Clipper* reported Harry Miner, manager of Miner's Bowery Theatre, joined the troupe in capacity of agent.[40]

At the end of the month, in a Portland, Maine, hotel, Hickok was unable to sleep because of loud noises coming from a neighboring room. His investigation revealed a group of men playing poker. When they invited him to join them, Hickok feigned ignorance of the game. Four hours later, after cleaning them out, he returned to his room but not before issuing the injunction, "Better think twice after this before waking a man up and inviting him to play poker."[41]

Irving related yet another incident in Maine involving Hickok that, no doubt, caused Cody to wonder by now if he had been wise to hire his old friend. The troupe arrived on a cold day and registered in one of the hotels. Hickok requested that a fire be lit in his room. In the middle of the night, loud cries of "Fire!" awakened the hotel guests. The hotel clerk and several others ran into the street and looked up to the top floor where Hickok, in his nightshirt with his head out of the window, was yelling "Fire!" "'Where is the fire?' the clerk shouted at the old Indian fighter. 'That's what I want to know!' Wild Bill yelled back. 'I ordered one four hours ago and it hasn't been built yet!'"[42]

After the last show in Worcester, Massachusetts, in mid-February, former Fifth Cavalry officer Edward Stevens gave a dinner at the Waverly House to renew his acquaintance with Cody. Omohundro was unable to attend because his wife was ill, and Hickok was "unavoidably absent," but John Burke and comedian Walter Fletcher attended. After dinner the men adjourned to the parlor where they spent hours smoking cigars and telling stories. A *Gazette* reporter gleaned tales of Cody's early years and a peek into his partners' characters. Cody admitted his participation in jayhawking activities during the "bleeding Kansas" days when he and other fellows "made it too hot" for Missourians as they settled old scores. Courting the displeasure of the government, they elected to serve as scouts and guides in lieu of being tried and punished for their "partially outlawed position[s]." Hickok's "daring character" led him into service as a spy where he showed "some of the coolest bravery of the whole secret service." Texas Jack was adept at trailing in his position as government scout and hunting guide.[43]

Burke told a story about one of the show Indians. This particular fellow was "a natural grumbler, and his propensities were always increased by his potations of 'fire water.'" He approached Burke with complaints about the play, saying, "John—no good—Indian killed all time. Indian no kill—no good—why not me kill Buffalo Bill?' The 'noble red man' had discovered that his position in the piece was emphatically that of 'Lo, the poor Indian,' and it was far from suiting him."

The actors joked about their attempts at playacting. Hickok's line "Boys, I'm with you heart and hand" and Cody's "I'll save my friend Texas Jack or die in the attempt" worked because they lacked common stage rhetoric. Hickok, they said, had told the others he wished the play rewritten so he could give the rascal Doggett a chance for his life instead of shooting him as he carried off the girl. The company's levity demonstrated a healthy mentality toward the theatrical profession, but it was serious business. Profits were important. If the dramas did not please, door receipts would suffer, their livelihood would be at stake, and the acclaim they had come to enjoy would be lost. Laughing about what they were doing kept it in perspective.

Rumors spread that Major General George A. Custer had requested Cody to guide his troops who were under orders to investigate a Sioux uprising. Cody planned on leaving the combination for the scene of the current Indian troubles at the end of February 1874. Shortly afterward, though, he changed his mind, deciding the Indians wouldn't move far "until the grass grows." He told a reporter he expected to head west at that time.[44]

The day after the scouts appeared at Troy, New York, the *Times* guessed every newsboy and bootblack had been in the gallery. Their enjoyment translated into feet stampings, whistles, and catcalls. With "open mouths," the "dirty faced" youngsters studied every action. During the two-and-a-half hours the scouts were onstage, "three hundred Indians must have bit the dust. Some of these days the material will give out, and there will be no Indians left to exterminate." The newspaper reported that there was not a week in which "the 'living heroes' have not each received $500 as his share of the profits, and some weeks the dividend has been $800. At the lowest sum this would give each $25,000 a year. Perhaps the agent has exaggerated a little."[45] With his most recent share, Texas Jack bought a thoroughbred colt.

Then it was on to Albany where the *Evening News* compared last season's drama with the current one, thinking it "a much higher grade than the trash which Ned Buntline inflicted upon the public." The next day, the reviewer focused on Morlacchi's part and praised her dancing in the opening farce. Associating with Cody's company didn't hurt her career; instead she had "developed into a sparkling *commedienne* [sic], singing, acting, and talking English with a pleasing accent, which captivates alike the parquette and the gallery." Nevertheless, *Scouts* remained the great attraction. "Abounding in incongruities, gun powder and Indians, . . . it is not more improbable than half the stuff that holds the stage at the present time."[46]

When the company appeared in Schenectady, Cody introduced himself at the livery stables of John H. Bame, who trotted out one of his best rigs and took the plainsmen for a drive. Upon their return, Cody purchased a horse whip from the harness emporium. At the jeweler's, he had a personal inscription engraved on it and presented it to the liveryman.[47] Then, out of courtesy or curiosity, the scouts followed their last performance in Utica, New York, with a visit to the state lunatic asylum. Cody met a man who claimed to be "Buffalo Bill No. 2," while a female inmate laughed at their long hair. The patients were pleased with the visit, and the "kind hearts of the border men were touched by the condition of many of the unfortunate patients."[48]

Despite such interesting diversions, Hickok's tolerance for the stage was exhausted after almost seven months. He repeatedly criticized his partners for their foolishness and talked about leaving. Hiram Robbins tried to persuade him to stay, pointing out how much money they were making, but Hickok said he was "merely sustaining Jack and Cody."[49]

By March 1874, Cody had moved his family to a house on Exchange Street in Rochester, New York. The *Democrat & Chronicle* reported that the city welcomed its newest resident by crowding into the opera house, filling seats, boxes, gallery, stools, aisles, stairs, and railings. Management opened doors on the side of the dress circle, and more people stood in the halls.[50]

Cody, hoping to impress his new neighbors, warned Hickok ahead of time "not to cut up any of his capers," so the performance would run smoothly. Hickok agreed to behave and kept the promise until the Indian fight in the second act, when he couldn't resist his old trick of singeing the supers' legs. Offstage, Cody remonstrated with him until Hickok stormed off to the dressing room, changed his buckskin costume for street wear, and elbowed his way out of the theatre. When Cody finished the next scene, the stage carpenter approached him and said, "That long-haired gentleman, who passed out a few minutes ago, requested me to tell you that you could go to thunder with your old show."[51]

Hickok had joined Cody on a lark. Perhaps he hoped traveling with his former companions would recapture the camaraderie of old times. Certainly the promise of wealth tempted him, but his boredom as well as his dread that they were a sham overcame any other motivation. Cody, Hickok realized, did not see acting merely as a pastime. Instead, Cody appreciated the impact he was creating. Being profusely welcomed in every town on the theatrical circuit was a heady experience. The members of the dramatic company, as well as Cody's astute managers, were professionals in their outlook and performance. The attitude impressed Cody. As his proficiency as an actor grew, he needed such supporting players who took the craft seriously. The play itself may have overindulged in sham heroics, but the talent and discipline were real. Cody respected Hickok but needed to let him go.

After the final curtain, the men met at the Osborn House.

> By this time he had recovered from his mad fit and was in as good humor as ever. He had made up his mind to leave for the West the next day. I endeavored to persuade him to remain with me till spring, and then we would go together; but it was of no use. I then paid him the money due him, and Jack and myself made him a present of $1,000 besides.[52]

The next day, a reporter glimpsed Hickok walking down Rochester's State Street and, knowing the troupe had departed for Lockport, sounded him out. As they talked, an "impudent youngster [approached], crying . . . 'Oh! stag his nibs wid the long hair.'" But Hickok was accustomed to remarks about his appearance. Suggesting they move along, they left behind the "few staring, mouth-opened children," including one who ran off when Hickok stopped and looked at him. Hickok informed the reporter he had been called to the frontier. After all, "his services are highly valued and eagerly sought when there is danger of war with the red man. . . . It is this, together with a longing desire to return to the free, wild life he loves so well that has called our hero away." His fellow scouts, Hickok said, "did not like to have him leave, but when he said he must go, the noble hearted fellows . . . each gave him a splendid revolver, bidding him to make good use of it among the 'Reds.'"[53]

Hiram Robbins remembered he had been trying to convince Hickok to stay, when John A. Stevens, the manager of a traveling Daniel Boone company, offered him $50 a week to join the Boone Combination and play himself, promising to make him a hero. Hickok acquiesced, admitting he was in no hurry to return to the West, but merely wanted to be out from under Cody's shadow. The first night he strode onstage only to stand about as though he had never been in front of an audience before. Robbins convinced him he was no better off with the Boone troupe, so Hickok decided to leave them as well. Since Stevens had already advertised his presence, he hired a tall actor, supplied him with a blond wig, and proffered him to the unsuspecting audience as Wild Bill. Hearing about the charade, Hickok entered the theatre in disguise and, when the faker walked out from the wings, Wild Bill "with a bound sprang upon the stage, and with a blow of his ponderous fist, knocked the fellow down." Following the commotion, the police jailed Hickok until Robbins paid his fine.[54]

Afterward, Hickok became a familiar figure around Kansas City and Cheyenne where citizens thought he left the troupe because he had been driven away. "[O]n his return he had to shoot two or three of them to re-establish things on a peace basis."[55] In March 1876, he married Agnes Lake, widow of a circus owner; shortly thereafter, he organized a band of gold prospectors to the Black Hills. Drifter Jack McCall assassinated him while he was playing poker in Deadwood, Dakota Territory, on August 2, 1876. Eventually, McCall was found guilty and hanged.[56]

Following Hickok's departure, the combination's route took them along the coast of Lake Erie, moving them through Lockport, Buffalo, and Dunkirk, New York. Cody and Omohundro would miss their pard, but Cody was relieved of dealing with Hickok's antics. Statements Cody made later in the season hint at his intentions to continue in show business and to take it very seriously. What began as surrender to Buntline's nagging turned into a full-time, no-turning-back occupation for the former buffalo hunter.

CHAPTER FOUR

Border Life Onstage

❧

From the rising of the curtain in the first act, until the final drop,
the audience were wild with enthusiasm.
—*Dayton Daily Journal*, March 6, 1875

WILD BILL HICKOK'S UNEXPECTED DEPARTURE HAD NO EFFECT ON THE popularity of Cody's combination. Publicity prepared in advance continued to advertise his presence, but most reviewers failed to notice he was not onstage. Did it matter that only two scouts saved the damsels in distress? Some critics mention Hickok in their reviews as though he were still with the troupe; one of the supporting actors may have assumed his role and made himself up to look like him.

Continuing the circuit along the Great Lakes, the troupe filled Erie's Park Opera House in mid-March. The melodrama "would fall far below mediocrity" were it not for Cody and Texas Jack, assumed the reviewer. Another asked by what critical canon they were to analyze its construction? "By none," he answered himself, because "it has no likeness to anything else, it is unique, *sui generis*, and 'naught but itself can be its parallel.'"[1] *Scouts of the Plains* eclipsed all previous melodramas in sheer number of incidents. Where the others had one death, *Scouts* had twenty; "where they used their popping iron in the cause of crime, this fires a whole volley in the interests of virtue." The nearly constant firing kept up from first act to last impressed one critic, who worried that "[t]he drain on the treasury for gunpowder must be fearful."[2] No reviewer ever complained of boredom. "[T]hrilling incidents, blood curdling situations and harrowing details" kept the audience on the edge of their seats. The scouts mete out justice to Daws and his cowardly cohort Tom Doggett and many Comanche braves bite the dust, while "the apportionment of the girls among their lovers is satisfactory."[3]

When the Indians tie Texas Jack to the death stake, he defies his tormentors, laughing as Buffalo Bill shoots down each brave attempting to light the fire around Jack's feet. Playgoers thundered their response to the Indians' antics. One critic believed that after all the war dances, fires, and deaths, the entire company must have been killed three times over. His tally of the slain reached thirty-seven before he ceased counting. Yet, even with the incredible slaughter, he advised that, because "the proprieties are never outraged, and many a fashionable play has more immorality in a line than could be educed from the whole performance," "ladies need not fear to go."[4]

In the nineteenth century, men considered middle- and upper-class women "endangered" and warned them away from the theatre and the kind of people who attended it and performed in it. Proper ladies, reassured of the wholesomeness of Cody's drama and able to afford frequent theatrical amusements, were seated in the parquet. On the other hand, wives of working-class men led confined lives. After household and child care chores, they had little time or money left for leisure, so their attendance was limited. Single working women, who reveled in their autonomy and splurged on theatre offerings, participated in the sense of community prevalent in proletarian theatres, where everyone joined in the hissing or cheering and in warning the scouts of impending danger.[5]

Frequent Indian conflicts and failure of the government's Indian policy provided fodder for playwrights. Strewn among the bloodied scouts and Indian characters was Quaker Jebadiah Broadbrim. Most often played by Alfred Johnson with his "true nasal twang," the Quaker role incorporated humor into the otherwise serious business of annihilating the redskins. The burlesque role of the government peace commissioner Ebenezer Langlank also received his share of plaudits. The satirical role placed the government's peace policy in a well-deserved ridiculous light.[6]

Of all government departments, the one most ridden with corruption was the Bureau of Indian Affairs (BIA). From early in the century, lawmakers had reserved large tracts of western lands for the exclusive use of Indian tribes. After the Civil War, policy goals had been to imbue Indian people with European manners and values, then integrate them into mainstream American life. Understandably, Indians never budged from their position that they were a separate people with rights of cultural and political self-determination. By 1870, however, hordes of prospectors, cattlemen, and farmers had invaded their lands, resulting in wars and raising questions about the government's policies. Many BIA agents were irresponsible or corrupt in their tribal dealings. Westerners and army officers contended that the only satisfactory resolution was the removal of the tribes from all lands coveted by whites. Policy was changed to specifically focus on breaking up reservations by granting land allotments to individual Indians. If he adopted white men's ways and learned to farm, he would gradually drop his intrinsic culture and could be assimilated into the population, or so it was hoped. Then there would be no more need for government to oversee Indian welfare in the paternalistic way it had been obliged to do or to provide meager annuities keeping the Indian in a subservient position.

However, the legislation, "generally quite liberal, has been sadly perverted in administration. Good intentions of law-makers were never more signally nullified by inefficient or rascally agents." With the exposure of the problem, reforming Quakers, who demonstrated enthusiasm for "anti-slavery activity and aid to freedmen," found a calling in working with the Indians. They insisted the Indian be treated like anybody else and that the white man had no more inherent rights than he. One editor reminded his readers of the true policy of American nationality, which was to "discourage rather than foster distinctions among the people under its protection."[7]

Finally an astute someone noticed Hickok was not among the players and started the rumor that the other scouts would not be onstage either, resulting in only a fair-sized audience on hand in Quincy, Illinois. A few days later, confusion arose over whether the actors were the real Buffalo Bill and Texas Jack, so the *Peoria Daily Transcript* urged doubters to contact General Sheridan to substantiate their claim. "But to our mind the most positive proof of their being the original scouts was their natural easy manner on the stage, being free from all rant and mouthings, so frequent in old actors."[8] To validate their authenticity, Cody offered biographical details, telling how he freighted for Russell, Majors, and Waddell before becoming "the *first rider who started on the route* of the Pony Express." The

riders "were noted for their daring and endurance. They were lithe as pan-
thers, cunning as Indians, and afraid of nothing." His first experience with
Indians occurred when he was fourteen years old, he told a reporter, and in
the employ of Simpson and Poole, emigrant guides and cattle drivers. He
then served in the army under General James G. Blunt, glad to accept the
opportunity "to *avenge his father's death*."[9]

He boasted that his rifle, which he named Lucretia Borgia, "*never failed
a shot*." He said "nothing of the number of Indians to whom Lucretia has
spoken," but it was "well known on the frontier" that he was "one of the most
successful Indian fighters now living."[10] Once, a Binghamton, New York,
Democrat reporter coerced Cody into confessing he had killed forty-one
men, "but as he is very modest the real number of his victims is supposed
to be an average of one a week for eleven years." In his heyday, Cody didn't
kill that many buffalo, let alone men, but such sensational reports helped
to sell newspapers.[11] Instead of crowing about Indian lives he had taken
during his many scouting assignments, Cody said, "I have always noticed
that the man in an Indian fight who does the most hollering does the least
killing." After the season ended in early June, he explained, he planned to
return to the plains. He anticipated "a lively time there this summer" and
thought the Sioux and Cheyenne would be rebellious in Nebraska, Dakota,
and Wyoming territories.[12]

Cody wrote in his autobiography that this theatrical season closed in
Boston on May 13, 1874, but again his memory proved faulty.[13] Ads for the
scouts' production appeared in Massachusetts, Michigan, Illinois, and
Canadian newspapers for over a month after that date with the last performance being on June 30 in New York City, though the Chicago critic
reported waning interest in the production. The "real live Indian scalping,
buffalo shooting and redskin-whooping drama" engrossed only those in the
gallery, while the lower portion of the house found Mlle. Morlacchi's introductory dances far more pleasing, a situation the critic found heartwarm-
ing.[14] Critics, particularly those in cities with extensive theatrical activity,
"marginalized audiences at frontier plays by labeling them 'ignorant,'
'ingenuous,' and 'unwashed.'" However, the popularity of frontier drama
eventually led lowbrow taste to triumph. Sheer numbers of the "unlearned
over the educated, of the popular masses over the critical establishment, and
. . . the 'unwashed' over the aristocracy of the well-dressed" led to the legiti-
mizing of frontier subjects.[15] The *Atlantic Monthly* distinguished between
"false culture" and "real culture" and chided its readers to remember that

not everyone was in the position to acquire refinement. "Any wood may be varnished, but not every sort receives polish; and so it is with men and women."[16] In only a few short years, however, lowbrow theatre themes so prevailed that the highbrow was forced to recognize and adopt them.

Cody hinted to the press that he planned to take the troupe to England "at no distant day."[17] However proud and confident in his newly discovered acting ability, his anticipation proved premature; more than a decade would pass before he crossed the Atlantic as star of his own company.

Citing the upcoming end of season, the *Lawrence Daily American* supposed the "thin house" was due to the "thin entertainment." The scouts generated high spirits, but "the show is of no account and could only be tolerated by gallery gods." Cody, it briefed, planned to remain in the area for a short time. During the summer, Jack was to guide a hunting party; his wife would retreat to her farm in Billerica, and "the local Indians . . . [would] retire to Common street and the 'Plains,' never ceasing to steal into a dime novel show when occasion offers."[18]

Appearing in Boston June 15–20, in some of the season's last performances, Cody and Omohundro promised to "awaken memories of past excitements among the boys, and lead the elders to seek illustration of what has formed the subject of many a tale of adventure since the East began the work of peopling the great West." Walls of the Boston Theatre rocked with the crack of rifles, savage whoops, and women's lamentations. Nevertheless, to the sophisticated crowd, the inevitable appearance of the scouts to the rescue

> dulls the interest after the second such happening, and the audience calmly awaits the denouement of otherwise blood-curdling preparations for a prisoner's doom or a maiden's even more horrible fate. . . . [T]hat the two men should escape unscathed in a dozen deadly combats with foes outnumbering them ten to one is too much for even an upper-tier auditory to swallow without a giggle.[19]

With the theatrical season finally over in late June 1874, Texas Jack left for a hunting expedition with the fourth Earl of Dunraven around the Yellowstone region. The earl further popularized Jack's reputation in three books he wrote about his adventures. The "diamond shirt-studs and breast-pin shining on [Jack's] snowy bosom" led him to wonder "if he were in the vicinity of a comet," but Jack proudly wore the jewelry bought with proceeds from their successful season.[20] Cody returned to New York City's Wood's Museum to continue the run of *Scouts of the Plains*. The play, which had been through so many roastings it was well done, held all with "absorbing interest." After all, it was not merely a drama "evoked from the imagination of a sensation [*sic*] dramatist"; its success was also due to its basis on true incidents in the life of "the remarkable man who fills the chief role."[21]

While in New York, Cody met wealthy Londoner Thomas P. Medley who offered him $1,000 to serve as his guide for a hunt on the plains.[22] It's likely Cody appreciated the opportunity to briefly return to his former occupation, and the significance in maintaining a link to his past was not lost on him. His reputation of being a true frontiersman, only mimicking onstage what he did in real life, was important to preserve. His remark, "I was now on my old familiar stamping ground, and it seemed like home to me," typified his feelings.[23] After the constant travel and stress of managing his troupe, he reported that since he'd left the states for the territories, his health had improved. A month after the hunt broke up in North Platte, Cody boarded a train to Fort McPherson where Captain Anson Mills hired him to escort an army expedition whose objective was to scout the Powder River and Big Horn country.[24]

In July 1874, General George A. Custer led an expedition of twelve hundred men through Dakota Territory's Black Hills to verify miners' reports of gold and other mineral wealth. A reporter for the *Chicago Inter-Ocean* observed rather scornfully that "It has not required an expert to find gold in the Black Hills, as men without former experience in mining have discovered it at an expense of but little time or labor."[25]

Mills's expedition through the Big Horn Mountains was "more to reinforce Genl. Custer's command, or to draw the Indians away from him than for any other purpose," Cody wrote in a letter to his relatives in West Chester. "We are directly in the stronghold of the Indians, and I anticipate a lively time. I will not get East for some time."[26]

Anticipation proved greater than actuality, however; the expedition encountered no Indians.[27] The tour lasted from August 7 until October 2 for which Cody received $150 a month in pay, less than one night's receipts for a performance.

By the time Mills released Cody from duty, after commending him for sustaining "his old reputation as an excellent and invaluable guide," the next theatrical season had already begun.[28] However, he seemed in no hurry to resume his stage career, and besides, Texas Jack was still engaged out West. Cody used the interim to hire a professional company and to prepare publicity highlighting his recent adventures. By November 1, he was back onstage at the Bowery Theatre in *Scouts of the Plains* as the solo star supported by Johnson's Dramatic Company. New advertisements proclaimed, "This popular hero has just returned from the BLACK HILLS, where he acted as Guide to the famous BIG HORN EXPEDITION, establishing his popularity greater than ever."[29]

He reached Williamsport, Pennsylvania, on November 16, when the press reported the Rochester Opera House Company, under the management of John B. Schoeffel, would act as his supporting characters. Many Williamsport citizens were convinced this version of *Scouts of the Plains* was identical to the one he played the previous winter, but Schoeffel quickly assured them that, despite the myriad similarities, it was "entirely different in plot, and more interesting, presenting more vividly the scenes enacted upon the frontier." Nevertheless, the references to Indians, a blundering Dutchman, and a sanctimonious Quaker left some doubts.[30]

Between performances, a *Gazette & Bulletin* journalist queried Cody about his most recent frontier adventure. He recounted the Big Horn expedition, describing how the army commands had covered five hundred miles. He prophesied events would be heating up in the area when miners headed for the gold regions in the spring. "The Indians do not care for the march of United States troops through their country, but when they see a miner with a pick and spade they know he comes to stay, and they will scalp him if possible." Cody knew the miners were "devils to fight," intent on claiming the hidden gold, and they would give the "red skins" a run for their money unless the Indians overpowered them first. Cody realized that, having spent the summer scouting, he could easily revert to his plains lifestyle and that "show business seem[ed] unnatural for him" now. But Cody was still a relative novice in the theatrical world. A few more years would pass before he jumped in with both feet and even then, he considered the West his true home.[31]

Cast members of the Rochester Opera House were still serving as supporting cast when the combination played Elmira on November 17. The troupe's Indians were "perhaps not real ones, but such counterfeit presentments as will stir up one's blood sufficiently by the manner in which they act." Many of them were killed during "plenty of fighting, all meaning something and having to do with the story."[32] The tableaux at the end of the acts were so pleasing that the audience demanded they be shown twice. Had photographs been feasible in theatres, these would have been perfect scenes to capture on film. Created by simply posing still bodies in a frozen moment, the tableau represented an event, an idea, or an emotion. Some critics considered the tableau too static, suggesting it offered visual tensions of a scene but failed to explore them. In a melodrama such as Cody's, tableaux underscored the significance of a moment—an Indian killing, the heroine's rescue, the horror of a prairie fire—by stopping the action of the narrative and inserting, or ending with, a momentary and static picture.[33] Invariably, Cody held center stage during such scenes. After all, as the Elmira reporter gushed,

> Mr. Cody . . . commands your respect the instant you have
> shaken hands with him. You know he is a Man, and brave
> as he is and has shown himself to be, he is as gentle in voice
> and manner, and as pleasant spoken as a woman. His face is
> a kindly one, and he looks out at you through eyes clear and
> sharp, truthful and honest as the sun. He is one whom, we
> venture to assert, under almost any circumstances in which
> a man could be placed, it would be entirely safe to "tie to."[34]

Auburn's *Daily Advertiser* found that, as a general rule, patrons who attend the production of dramas like *Scouts of the Plains* are "those whose peculiar tastes lean in that direction and hanker for an experience of the sensational, and are bound to be satisfied with the entertainment so long as the requisite number of persons are murdered in the drama, enough hairbreadth escapes occur and blood and thunder generally prevail." Because of this, Cody, who played to the dime-novel crowd, never failed to give "unbounded satisfaction. As a scout and heroic frontiersman 'Bill' was, and is, doubtless, unexcelled, but he possesses very little dramatic talent or ability." His acting, the critic concluded, is "crude and unnatural."[35]

John Burke jumped to Cody's defense, reminding the press that,

> Men who have criticized Buffalo Bill as an actor forget wholly
> that he is the only man who is *playing himself*. He plays his
> part as he knows it, as he has acted it upon many a field, acting
> naturally and without bombast and forced tragic effort. Be the
> motive what it may, love of lucre or the gratification of pride, the

fact still remains that in his delineation of border life, Buffalo
Bill educates the people to seeing the hated and ever-dreaded red
men in another light.[36]

Not everyone came to the theatre expecting to be overwhelmed by his
acting. The combination's popularity derived not only from the melodrama's
rough-and-tumble action but sometimes simply from Cody's good looks.
"Buffalo Bill will undoubtedly cause some cases of emotional insanity on
the part of his female auditors at the Opera House," enthused the *Danbury
News*. His fans included boys, girls, and adults—the latter envied his plains
reputation, and the youngsters just wanted to be like him when they grew
up. Men would most appreciate his character and how he heroically extri-
cated himself from various scrapes, but his fine bearing attracted the ladies.
James Monaghan concluded that Cody's "appeal was not to the intellect but
to the eye—mainly to women who made up the matinee crowds." *Chicago
Daily News* columnist Amy Leslie agreed:

> Cody is one of the most imposing men in appearance that
> America ever grew in her kindly atmosphere. In his earlier days
> a hint of the border desperado lurked in his blazing eyes and
> the poetic fierceness of his mein [*sic*] and coloring. Now it is all
> subdued into pleasantness and he is the kindliest, most benign
> gentleman, as simple as a village priest, and learned as a savant
> of Chartreuse.[37]

Remarks about Cody's and the other scouts' eyes, long hair, and stature
were not unusual. However, one reporter had noticed Cody's and Texas Jack's
unusually small feet, commenting how Jack, "with the solid weight of over
190 pounds, wears a number five boot, and Buffalo Bill has a thin, small foot,
excellently shown off by the beaded moccasins he wore on the stage."[38]

When Texas Jack returned from the West, he decided to join his wife
in Massachusetts, so Cody replaced him with Kit Carson Jr. If Carson had
been with the troupe since its opening in New York City, no mention of
him surfaced in reviews or advertisements. His name first appears in the
Wilmington, Delaware, *Every Evening* Amusements column on December 4,
1874. Carson portrayed Ebenezer, the missionary, while John Burke, a former
Wilmingtonian, played Antelope Ned for a few of the performances.

The press guessed that Kit Carson Jr. was related to the famous scout

Kit Carson Jr., Courtesy Buffalo Bill Historical Center
(P.71.1269.1), Vincent Mercaldo Collection, Cody, WY.

when, in fact, he was not but was most likely William A. Carson from Wheeling, West Virginia, who left home at an early age for a career in theatre. As Cody progressed through the theatrical years and particularly in his Wild West show, he insisted on authenticity, but at this stage in his career, he seemed willing to overlook a bit of deception in a less-than-authentic frontier character.[39] Carson was soon being billed as "The Renowned Texas Ranger," further enhancing his reputation and prestige.

The January 2, 1875, *Spirit of the Times* observed that "[t]raveling companies are faring very badly during the present season, and a careful overlook of all on the road shows a great falling off in numbers during the past few weeks. Only those of strong merit or those presenting some popular star meet with paying patronage."[40] Combinations, like most businesses, were contending with the domino effect of the Panic of 1873 that had bankrupted nearly ninety railroads and closed 18,000 businesses. The unemployment rate reached nearly 14 percent, and so when it came to buying food or theatre tickets, people bought food. But since Cody's troupe supplied if not "strong merit," then at least an overwhelmingly "popular star," his combination survived.

A thousand "unterrified" people thronged city hall in Lawrence, Massachusetts. Nearly half were boys consigned to the gallery's upper tiers by their twenty-five cents, a considerable sum for youngsters to pay, roughly equivalent to over $3 in today's currency. Mandatory school attendance had not yet been adopted in all states, so many of the youngsters helped support their families by working as bootblacks or by pitching newspapers on the street. In coal mines, "breaker boys" as young as seven sorted coal from rock for ten hours a day; girls might work in factories cutting or hemming fabric. Such unskilled work typically paid ten cents per hour or about $5.50 a week.[41] Doling out their hard-earned cash to see Cody's combination entitled them to issue the catcalls with which they greeted their hero.

To promote the combination's upcoming engagements in Rochester, J. Clinton Hall of the opera house asked Cody to prepare a new play. To comply, Cody hired longtime cast member J. V. Arlington to arrange a drama titled *Life on the Border*. Biographers date the play to 1876, but contemporary newspaper ads confirm a play with that title premiered as early as January 11, 1875. The *Rochester Union & Advertiser* of February 10 credited Hiram Robbins of Cincinnati as author. However, the *Union & Advertiser*'s reference was to *Wild Bill; or, Life on the Border, a Sensational Drama in 5 Acts*.[42] Possibly the new play by Arlington was a slightly rewritten version of Robbins's play with the first three words deliberately left off, since Buffalo Bill would be the protagonist, not Wild Bill.

Life on the Border received one of its first congratulatory reviews from the Worcester, Massachusetts, *Evening Gazette*. Unlike many frontier dramas, the lines were "free from the stilted twaddle of the dime novel," and the action was "toned down within the range of human probability, while preserving all the dash, danger and devil-may-care elements of the traditional life of the backwoods." Pleasantly absent were the "rivers of gore" onstage and the "suffocation from burnt powder" in the theatre.[43] All in all, it was much better than previous dramas Cody had brought to the city.

Because he had proven himself the genuine article, at this point, Cody thought about how the dramas reflected his personal experiences. He was becoming a more professional actor who could remember his lines and who no longer had to resort to a rip-roaring display of all-out Indian massacre to hurry the drama along. Consequently, appreciating that slaughter was not a daily occurrence on the plains, he encouraged the writer to mitigate displays of it in the drama as well.

Nevertheless, the plot of *Life on the Border* ran true to melodramatic form. Government scout Jim Reynolds goes missing, and Buffalo Bill promises to return him to his wife and daughter Emma. The villain, Captain Johnston Huntley, schemes to marry Emma during her father's absence. In his role as protector, Buffalo Bill intercepts and kills a grizzly bear. Meanwhile, Huntley sneaks in with Wolfy Dick and Grasshopper Jim, his white cohorts disguised as Indians, to burn the Reynolds' cabin. Buffalo Bill rescues the women from the blaze. Foiled, Huntley demands that fort commander General Duncan arrest Buffalo Bill. Ignorant of any charges, Cody informs Duncan about counterfeit money found on Wolfy Dick's body near the burned cabin. While bloody encounters with Indians do not make up a majority of the scenes, all the same, the general blames his troubles on them, giving Buffalo Bill an opportunity to take their part in a speech echoing Cody's own changing philosophy.

> [I]t is not they who are to blame for these difficulties. . . . [T]here's a class of bad white men on this border who disguise themselves as Indians and commit depredations for which the Indians are, of course, blamed. Then away goes your military after them, and that brings on a war. The Indians are not the first to start it, I assure you; but when it is started, they do try to protect

themselves. I have no love for an Indian, but I swear they are not to be blamed at all times, no, sir.

The general sees his point and promises to guard the Reynolds women while Buffalo Bill searches for the counterfeiters. He finds George Reed guarding Jim Reynolds in a prison, providing the opportunity for Cody to use disguises to fool the audience. After he successfully uncovers a secret, he "un-disguises himself" and then together the men head back to the fort. While they're gone, Huntley convinces Emma that her father is alive but is being held for $10,000 ransom. He'll pay it if she will marry him; reluctantly, Emma agrees. As the ceremony commences, Buffalo Bill rushes in to stop it and to reunite the young woman with her father. George Reed identifies Huntley as a train robber, murderer, and counterfeiter. Mr. Reynolds offers Emma to Buffalo Bill for his wife, while Jebadiah Broadbrim, the Quaker peace commissioner, urges them to "go west and raise a family."[44]

Standards in dime-novel literature were evident—disguises, fake accents, and the last-minute rescue of the innocent young woman. Depending on any one critic's perceptions, the "assortment of bloody encounters with demoniacal savages, noble rescues of captive maidens, and narrow escapes from torture and death" in the drama was thrilling or revolting. The Lewiston, Maine, critic found that even the "most exacting and gory-minded spectator cannot grumble." However, he implied that those who favor extermination as the only solution to the Indian question were happy with "the manner in which Buffalo William dispatches aborigine after aborigine to the happy hunting grounds."[45]

In true combination tradition, when the company played in Troy, New York, on two successive nights, they performed *Scouts of the Plains* one night and *Life on the Border* the next.[46] A week or so later, Cody magnanimously donated the proceeds from his Rochester performance to the "grasshopper sufferers," some of whom had lost everything when the insects swept in from the Rockies to the Missouri River during the previous year.[47] Reports of lakes of insects three inches deep were not uncommon. After losing their entire crop, some disillusioned families packed their belongings into wagons and headed east. To help those who stayed, the federal government offered financial relief, but funds quickly ran out. Charities stepped in to defray additional expenses.

Because early impressions are the most lasting, a Columbus, Ohio, reviewer speculated, it is no wonder that old and young have a more vivid recollection, perhaps of pioneer stories read and heard in childhood than of almost any general topic of early local history outside of the Revolution. Almost every grand parent in the States can remember incidents of pioneer life. These incidents have been repeated time and again to children. Those children, now grown to early manhood, are curious to see men who have shot bears and met Indians in deadly conflict.

The next day, after having seen both of the combination's plays, the same reviewer thought "*Life on the Border* . . . has more body than *Scouts of the Plains*, but less comedy." The former, he added, more fully illustrates "what we conceive to be a perfect picture of life on the plains."[48]

Meanwhile, events were happening that in due course would have significant ramifications for Cody. The project for the government purchase of the Black Hills held by the Sioux under a treaty agreement assumed definite form as their representatives headed to Washington. The Indians were asking $4 million, but a deal was by no means signed or sealed. In the theatre world, revitalization translated into cautious spurts in the building of opera houses and music academies. The combination system, so recently emergent but fast growing, forced even scenery painters out of stable company staffs. In the drive for increased profits, managers often hired the lowest-bidding freelance artists.[49] Instead of settling for whatever scenery or wardrobe was available, Cody began to hire his own scenic painters and costumers. Transporting the new scenery drops or set pieces ran up transportation costs and, because they were bulky and unwieldy, they often arrived the worse for wear.[50]

Cody's particular stamp on frontier dramas had many imitators. Likewise, he too read the trade papers and observed who was popular and what specifically about their presentation was attracting audiences. Frank I. Frayne was a relative newcomer to theatre, but as an expert shot, he was able to incorporate shooting tricks and animal stunts into his drama. His marksmanship display included shooting apples off an actor's head and extinguishing a candle with a shot. In just over a year, Cody would introduce the same attractions. He waited until he had a drama in which a shooting exhibition would fit and also brought not a small dog such as Frayne's but, in true Cody "bigger is better" style, a donkey and horses onstage. As with all stunts involving guns and live targets, accidents were a constant risk.

In 1882, a freak explosion tilted Frayne's rifle barrel downward and resulted in the death of his leading lady in front of a full audience.[51] Fortunately, Cody never experienced that horrific a tragedy, although he would come close.

Near the end of the third season, advertisements for the performances listed Cody as proprietor and manager. This was done for legal purposes, but it also demonstrates Cody's complete control over the combination by that time. In any one town in America, a theatrical "season" consisted of a scheduled series of plays that would last as long as the performances were profitable. Some combinations terminated their seasons following one or two poorly attended productions, sometimes leaving town under cover of darkness with bills unpaid. Aside from the "star," many actors in the companies received little or no credit for their support, even though, in addition to playing a role in the drama, they often headlined the introductory pieces or, occasionally, doubled in the orchestra. In the years following the Civil War, beginning actors' salaries ranged from $3 to $6 per week; support players earned $15 to $30 a week; and lead actors were paid anywhere from $35 to $100 for a week's work. Traveling stars, like Cody, could command $150 to $500 for a seven-to-ten-day engagement, but this was unusual except in very large cities like New York. The salaries were good for the period, especially for women, even though they received less pay than men in comparable roles.[52]

Because he played an extra week in New York City in late June, Cody wasn't free from the combination until July 1875. With no scouting demands from the army and weeks to go until the next season, he returned to Rochester. The previous summer, upon his return from the Big Horn expedition, Cody pronounced he was really happy in the West and had been glad to return, even if only for a few months. When he promised Louisa at their wedding he would give up the plains for her, she surely took it to mean he would be a stay-at-home husband and father. No doubt she was surprised to find herself losing him to theatre, an allure ostensibly as strong as the western frontier.

Summer 1875 proved to be some of the few months Cody had much time to spend with his wife and children. After the strain of one-night stands, of keeping audiences happy, and of managing his band of troupers, he appreciated the time off.

CHAPTER FIVE

First Scalp for Custer

> *It didn't make much difference how many shots were fired; the
> number of Indians that toppled over was always more than the
> number of bullets, which chased them to their death.*
>
> —Louisa Frederici Cody and Courtney Ryley Cooper,
> *Memories of Buffalo Bill*

TEXAS JACK OMOHUNDRO AND HIS WIFE GIUSEPPINA MORLACCHI
rejoined Cody at the end of summer 1875 when Kit Carson Jr. left to form
his own combination. The newly organized troupe opened in Albany, New
York, on September 2 and toured around New York State. At the end of the
month in Rochester, they once again were performing in combination the
two plays of the previous seasons with which Jack was familiar—*Scouts of
the Plains* and *Life on the Border.*

When the combination appeared at Easton, Pennsylvania's opera house,
they had the best house of the season. Receipts compared favorably to the
$800 profit in Scranton and the $900 taken in Wilkes-Barre. Easton's *Free
Press* reported that one day when Cody was talking with friends at West
Chester's Green Tree Hotel, a young lawyer "chipped in, anxious to have
Bill talk about his exploits, something he never does except on Sundays

after church." The barrister asked if he ever shot anyone "under necessity, of course." Cody frowned "as black as a whole troop of corkologians" and "thundered: 'No! what do you ask me such a thing for?'"

The lawyer, under the mistaken impression that Cody enjoyed a reputation as a gunman, assumed he believed in "that kind of thing a little." Cody growled, "No, sir, emphatically I don't. But see here, my friend, I'll tell you something. If you ever find some thunderin' fool mixing into your business and trying to insult you, and you feel that that man's brain is suffering for want of ventilation, always *shoot quick*." At that, he suddenly grabbed at his hip pocket, "but before he could get his paper of 'Solace' out the young lawyer was on the other side of a two-inch door."[1]

For all his claims of reenacting actual events, Cody may not have realized that his act onstage translated into a perception of himself as violent in the public mind. Early in his career, he boasted he and Jack would clean out the Modocs. Months later, he had been goaded into a "revelation" that he had killed dozens of men. Now he was being taken more seriously as an actor, and the idea of appearing as a bloodthirsty gunfighter did not sit well.

Despite the legend, a gunfighter was not the "heroic lone crusader who fights evil in order that good may prevail." Instead, according to Joseph G. Rosa, "the gunfighter invokes a sinister image" of a man who "arouses controversy and stirs emotions."[2] But even though Cody's stage persona embodied the frontier spirit where skill with firearms was a necessity for both hunting and self-defense, he vigorously protested being regarded as a brawler or gunman. Some years before, he responded to a story in the *New York Herald* about another "Buffalo Bill" in Pensacola, Florida, who had stolen the sheriff's horse and then been shot by the lawman. Cody clarified, though the name was the same, it was not he. "When I die it will be maintaining honor—that which constitutes the safeguard of society, whether it apply to man or to woman."[3]

In previous seasons, the troupe had confined its travels to eastern states, but in November 1875, Cody headed for the Deep South, to Alabama, Georgia, Louisiana, even as far west as Texas. Unlike the North where the Civil War brought expansion and redistribution of wealth, the first years of the war closed a number of southern theatres, and only some reopened.[4]

Frontier stories of triumph over savagery did not appeal only to eastern audiences. The southern man was not that different from his northern counterpart. Both expected to expand their province for agriculture and speculation by claiming Indian lands. When Cody came south, the Civil War had been over for over ten years. His service as a Union soldier did not detract from southerners' acceptance of him, if indeed it was common knowledge. One journalist admitted, "[W]e know nothing of the company other than that they are highly complimented by the press of other cities."[5]

Besides, Cody's style was very appealing to southerners. His stature as a gallant, brave, and modest hero fulfilled that of chivalric codes with which they were familiar. In dime novels, he was often regarded as "a knight of chivalry" or "the prince of reins." Rosa also suggests the gunfighter, such as Cody was perceived, was viewed as "the New World's counterpart of the knights in armor. . . . His sword was a Colt .45, and his armor the ability to outdraw and outshoot any rival."[6] Southerners could relate to his mission as a mounted warrior in the cause of civilization. After the war, when the South was warily reconciling with its northern neighbors, along came Cody, the Yankee, traveling with Texas Jack, the Rebel. Their friendship emphasized consanguinity and the rejection of separateness. Therefore, it's no wonder that southern reviewers echoed the acclaim Cody received elsewhere.

During the evening's entertainment in Mobile, ovations called him to the footlights several times to receive "Niagaras of applause."[7] In one scene in which he fought the stuffed bear, an enthusiastic spectator, thinking the contest real, cried out, 'Shoot him, Bill! Run in on him and kill him!'"[8]

The *Savannah Morning News* remarked that the "very exciting and intensely interesting" drama Cody brought "was in most striking contrast with the miserable performance given by the frauds who, last winter, swooped into this city under the name of the Buffalo Bill Combination." The known itinerary does not suggest that the frauds were Cody's troupe in an earlier, less polished, performance. Two prominent residents of Savannah who had known Cody for some time—Surgeon Dickson with the Federal garrison and D. H. Elliott, a Kansas Railroad worker—verified him as the "redoubtable personage." If any doubts lingered about their authenticity, the scouts had "letters from distinguishing personages to this effect, and their actions and the manner in which they handle rifles, revolvers, bowie-knives, etc. corroborate[d] this claim."[9]

Such questions arose because their popularity spawned imitators and drama pirates—men who sat in the audience, took shorthand notes, and later transcribed them into dialogue. If the bootlegger could prove in court that he had only witnessed a play, then memorized it, he had the right to present it as original.[10] In the days before ubiquitous photographs, too, anyone calling himself "Buffalo Bill" could easily pull off the deception.

One such imitator was Julien Kent who was producing the play titled *Wild Bill, King of the Border Men*. Outraged, Cody, who considered the drama his, specifically targeted Kent in a *New York Clipper* front-page announcement. On January 1, 1876, this warning appeared:

Notice
is hereby given to
MR. JULIEN KENT,
OR ANY PARTIES
producing a drama called
WILD BILL,
as it is none other than the drama of
LIFE ON THE BORDER,
purchased and solely owned by us. Having paid the author
Hiram Robbins for all rights to the titles, etc. of
WILD BILL AND LIFE ON THE BORDER,
managers and others will be legally proceeded against
who produce or assist in producing the same.
[signed] W. F. CODY, "Buffalo Bill;"
J. B. OMOHUNDRO, "Texas Jack."

Kent retaliated by admonishing managers to disregard Cody's protest. S. J. Simmonds, Kent's manager, "purchased the manuscript copy of Mr. Robins [*sic*], the author who alone has the right to sell. [I have] searched the records of the Librarian, and find that Mr. Robins has made no transfer of the copyright to Mr. Cody or anyone else previous to the date of my purchase." According to the Library of Congress listing, *Wild Bill; or, Life on the Border* was copyrighted by Robbins in 1873.[11] However, Kent could have obtained a pirated version, defending its use with the argument that it was not identical to the original. For several years, Kent, undaunted by Cody's threats, continued to tour with the drama. In act 4 where Cody fought a fake bear, Kent fought his real trained bear. Cody did not follow through; the legal threats were simply a bluff on his part.

The critic for one of the Quincy, Illinois, papers, the *Daily Herald*, referred to Cody and Jack as the Damon and Pythias of the western wilderness and was surprised when the combination did a better business than expected. Even the already numerous dress circle patrons "increased very perceptibly as the week went on."[12] Both lower- and upper-tiered crowds unanimously cheered the villain's humiliation. "Don't you do it," called one fellow to Emma, when the villain asks her to marry him. Every now and then, young boys yelled at the wrong place, "but they were promptly put down by the majority."[13] Instead of the bemused, sometimes confused, language of traditional reviews, the Springfield critic used coarse dialect to give the impression of a lower class when he remarked how Cody's troupe took "many old roosters" by the hand, then led them "out on the illimitable prairies, showed 'em Ingins, [and] made 'em feel for their scalps." Back in Springfield, they were turned loose from the opera house "to go home gulping a Comanche yell in their throats, and to bed to dream of buffalo tongues, jack rabbit ears, sage brush, alkali water and tamarack swamps."[14]

Rationalizing that superior drama serves up less blood and guts, critics continued to regard *Life on the Border* as superior to *Scouts of the Plains*. A certain subtlety in presentation was emerging, and reviewers repeatedly pointed out that *Life* was devoid of the slaughter distinctly characteristic of Cody's early productions. "We believe but one shot is fired in this drama and even that, we presume, would not be admitted were it not absolutely necessary."[15]

In April 1876, just as he was about to go onstage in Springfield, Massachusetts, a telegram summoned Cody home with the news that his five-year-old son was ill with scarlet fever. Somehow Cody survived the first act, then rushed to catch the train to Rochester. "I found my little boy unable to speak but he seemed to recognize me and putting his little arms around my neck he tried to kiss me. We did everything in our power to save him, but . . . my beloved little Kit died in my arms."[16]

His absence when the troupe played at Worcester led to "a rather tame presentation" of the drama. John Burke, "the long-haired business man of the company, who looks like a backwoodsman," took Cody's part. The troupe performed the best it could under the sad circumstances. Nevertheless, the Worcester *Daily Spy* observed, "Without Buffalo Bill the play, which is not a high order in itself, is a poor affair."[17] His border dramas alone were not the draw; they required the personality and presence of Cody himself. After laying the child to rest in Mount Hope cemetery, Cody returned to the stage subdued, relieved the season was nearly over.

Helen Cody Wetmore wrote in her biography of her brother that, though he played to crowded houses, his heart was not in it, and he was glad for the army summons at season's end.[18] Following their final bow in Wilmington, Delaware, on June 3, Cody broke up the combination, being eager to participate in the impending Sioux war.[19]

Before his departure, in an amicable split, Cody and Texas Jack decided to see how each would profit with his own combination. The Kansas City *Journal of Commerce* reported later that while Cody was "making Rome howl!" in the West, Texas Jack was "splitting the ears of the groundlings" in the East. It was a toss-up as to which of the scouts was more effective. "Texas Jack makes the most noise, but Buffalo Bill gets the most scalps."[20] Jack and his wife toured with their dramas until June 1880 when, at age thirty-three, Jack contracted pneumonia and died in Leadville, Colorado. Giuseppina never performed again; she retired to Billerica where she died six years later of stomach cancer.[21]

On June 18, the *St. Louis Times* reported Cody visited friends in Buffalo before reporting to Cheyenne. Seven years previously, in 1868, the government had signed a treaty with the Sioux recognizing their right to the Black Hills. Custer's 1874 expedition confirmed the territory's large gold deposits. Once the news spread, thousands of hopefuls headed for the Black Hills, ignoring the treaty and infuriating the Sioux and Cheyenne who joined forces to drive out the whites. Even though the government had ordered them to return to reservation lands before the end of January 1876, tribes had spread all over the region. Government officials appointed Lieutenant General Philip H. Sheridan to coordinate the army campaign. He sent Major Generals George A. Custer and John Gibbon and Brigadier General George Crook to deal with the Indians.

Cody signed on as chief scout of the experienced Indian fighters of the "Dandy Fifth" Cavalry led by Colonel Wesley Merritt. From scattered posts along the Kansas Pacific Railroad and in the Indian Territory, companies headed to Fort Laramie to organize for the campaign. In mid-July Merritt learned that Morning Star's Cheyenne band, some eight hundred strong, had departed Red Cloud Agency headed for the Powder River country. Intercepting them became his immediate purpose, and the subsequent march took them to Warbonnet Creek. Near dawn on July 17, 1876, Cody and others spotted a small band of Cheyennes. Soldier Christian Madsen, posted on a hilltop, testified that he saw Cody riding in advance of the party:

> One of the Indians was preceding his group. . . . The instant they
> were face to face their guns fired. . . . There was no conversation,
> no preliminary agreement[.] . . . Cody's bullet went through
> the Indian's leg and killed his pinto pony. The Indian's bullet
> went wild. Cody's horse stepped into a prairie dog hole and

stumbled[.] . . . Cody jumped clear of his mount. Kneeling, he took deliberate aim and fired the second shot. . . . Cody's bullet went through the Indian's head and ended the battle. Cody went over to the fallen Indian and neatly removed his scalp. . . . There is no doubt about it, Buffalo Bill scalped this Indian, who, it turned out, was Cheyenne sub-chief called Yellow Hair.[22]

Ever the showman, or at least always anticipating how he could dramatize an event, that day Cody wore one of his theatrical costumes—what could only be described as a bizarre Mexican vaquero suit. The scarlet silk shirt had billowy sleeves and silver buttons on the placket; black velvet trousers, decorated with a crisscross braid, flared below his knees. The Indians too, it seemed, had come dressed for show in trailing warbonnets, with silver armlets, necklaces, beaded leggings, and their faces stained "most vivid vermilion."[23]

The irony was not lost on Cody. Plays had demonstrated his real life in theatrical terms. This day he was "performing" on a stage of history. Cody recounted the event in his autobiography: "As the soldiers came up I swung the Indian chieftain's top-knot and bonnet in the air, and shouted: 'The first scalp for Custer.'" Soldiers trooping by heard the vengeful cry, not guessing how the story would make for good theatre in subsequent years of Cody's combination.[24]

Two weeks before the skirmish, America had celebrated the nation's centennial with an ongoing exhibition celebrating the country's progress. The underlying message was one of white domination. While American Indians were on display as the vanquished in Philadelphia, the Sioux defeat of Custer in Montana Territory shocked sensitivities and brought to the forefront the realization that perhaps America had not progressed as much as it liked to think. If "savages" could wipe out the Seventh Cavalry led by the illustrious boy general, no one was safe. Before Cody took "the first scalp" in revenge, he was, self-admittedly, only a second-string actor. However, the summer's event furthered Cody's status as, if not a hero in shining armor, at least one in buckskin.

Cody wrote to his wife about his exploits and promised to send the Indian's war bonnet, shield, bridle, whip, arms, and scalp for his old friend Moses Kerngood to put in his cigar store window.[25] In early August, the grisly package arrived before the warning letter, and poor Mrs. Cody fainted when she opened it.[26] A braided switch of straight black hair nearly two feet long

Cody, dressed for war or melodrama, 1876. Courtesy Buffalo Bill Historical Center (P.69.30), Cody, WY.

was attached to the three-inch-square piece of scalp. The headdress, five or six inches wide and that many feet long, was made of buffalo skin and set with eagle feathers. Several scalps hung from the shield. As publicity tokens, they attracted the attention of large numbers of people. "The old man with his spectacles and the street gamin with his wonderment gazes in admiration."[27]

The rest of the 1876 campaign was anticlimactic. For all of the troops in the field, the Great Sioux War did not end at Warbonnet Creek. Though he was discharged on August 22 and collected his pay of $150 a month, Cody delayed returning to the stage, spending a few more weeks carrying dispatches between camps. He finally left General Terry's corps on the Yellowstone River on September 11.[28] A reporter for the St. Paul, Minnesota, *Dispatch* caught up with him two days later as he passed through to Chicago. "You understand that Crook is short of rations?" queried the reporter, hoping for an explanation of the military's failures.

"Crook is undoubtedly having a hard time, and there is much anxiety about him. His rations are out, men sick, and everything seems to be in a bad way," replied Cody. "Comparatively few of the men knew anything about a gun; in fact it is dangerous to trust some of them with loaded arms, and altogether the campaign was very lame."

The reporter continued, "What do you think of what is said by some newspapers about Custer's rashness?" Cody answered, "There's no use talking about Custer's rashness. Mistakes are common, and if Custer made a mistake in his dash, there are many who think the mistake could have been better remedied by another dash."[29] Years later, he would expound on this theory:

The defeat of Custer was not a massacre. The Indians were being pursued by skilled fighters with orders to kill. For centuries they had been hounded from the Atlantic to the Pacific and back again. They had their wives and little ones to protect and they were fighting for their existence. . . . In nine times out of ten, when there is trouble between white men and Indians, it will be found that the white man is responsible. Indians expect a man to keep his word. They can't understand how a man can lie. Most of them would as soon cut off a leg as tell a lie.[30]

The summer's events intensified the government's enthusiasm for subduing the Indians, but Cody's comments indicate a man who was accepting of them and who understood their sufferings. His speech in *Life on the Border* defending them against preying whites synced with his personal beliefs. In later combination seasons and, more particularly, during the Wild West years, Cody hired Indians and promoted their way of life, hoping whites would come to understand them through education. Increased public attention focusing on the situation also brought Cody more approbation.

He arrived home in Rochester to a hearty welcome. To the Rochester press, he spoke about his plains adventures, first giving some history. Lieutenant Colonel Carr had had control of the Black Hills in June; then, in early July, Lieutenant Colonel Merritt replaced Carr in command, much to Cody's dismay, who believed that the Fifth had acquired its fighting reputation under Carr. Shortly, reports of Cheyenne warriors headed toward Sitting Bull's band of Sioux began to circulate. Cody guided the force of five hundred soldiers who arrived ahead of "the reds." Yellow Hair singled out Cody, he said, but Merritt's command rushed the main body of Indians, saving him and his men. On August 3, Brigadier General Crook took control of the whole force and met Brigadier General Terry's campaign coming from the Yellowstone region. When Terry took command, he "wasted a day and a half in council," affording the Indians the opportunity to head to safety in the mountains.

Cody compared the generals' personalities. Whereas "General Crook slept on his blanket, made his own coffee and broiled his own bacon[,] General Terry had a bed brought with him, a portable cooking range and an extension table. 'We could not travel fast enough to catch the Indians as we would break the dishes,'" Cody criticized. He also guessed that "the end of the war will be in the coming winter or next summer." He had no doubts about Sitting Bull's combat skills. "To prove how good a commissary Sitting Bull is . . . in to-day's paper I see that the soldiers have found whole wagon loads of dried beef and berries, while at the same time our boys were starving. An Indian will keep fat and fight you forty years on dried beef and berries."

The reporter reminded Cody of Hickok's death just a month before and repeated the rumor that the two scouts were bitter enemies. Cody disagreed, saying they had always been friends. "There was but one time when he felt hard towards me, and that was from jealousy, when I was appointed chief of scouts over him by General Sheridan. I used to be under him as chief, and naturally he felt it a little."[31] Cody, perhaps not knowing the true story, repeated the trumped-up adventures of the Hickok-McCanles fight from *Harper's Magazine*, giving Hickok credit for having stood his ground when eight men conspired to knife him.[32] He acknowledged,

> [Hickok] had been in a great many fights and killed a
> great many men, but I never knew of his killing a man
> when the law and justice were not on his side. I met him
> on his way to the Black Hills just before he was killed and
> he said he did not expect to come out again alive. He was
> killed at Deadwood; but I don't know the circumstances.
> When I met him we were nooning on Sage creek, and
> we I [*sic*] talked for two hours telling of old times.[33]

Confirmation of one last amiable meeting between the two old friends is noteworthy. According to Joseph "White Eye" Anderson, the pair ignored each other. But if Cody was right, Hickok's premonition of death suggests it was an emotional parting for both of them.[34]

After speaking with the reporter, Cody left for New York to arrange for a new drama embodying the Indian campaign. Custer's death ignited interest in newspaper readers all over the country and made it a popular topic for the next season's plays. *Custer and His Avengers* and *Sitting Bull; or, Custer's Last Charge*, and *Custer's Oath; or, The Hero of the Yellowstone* were all in production.[35] Cody commissioned J. V. Arlington to script a story by Prentiss Ingraham for the stage that would slightly modify the truth. The simple warrior, Yellow Hair, was promoted to subchief, and the long-range rifle fire became a more impressive hand-to-hand duel.[36]

By December, *Red Right Hand; or, Buffalo Bill's First Scalp for Custer*, was ready to debut. This drama and this season embody Cody's theatrical career. Up until this point, the themes of his melodramas had emphasized westward expansion and victory over Indians. Over the summer of 1876, he played himself in a real Indian battle down to the suit of clothes he wore. Now he was about to reenact onstage an important historical event in which he had participated. "The audience was getting 'reality,' if not specific truth. They could almost *smell* it on the stage."[37]

The drama is "founded on the contest between Black Hills miners and Indians, complicated as frontier romance ever is with outlawry and black-guardism. There are numberless combats, single-handed and *en masse*, in which the immense bowie knife, the short repeating rifle, and the big silver pistol of Buffalo Bill invariably do tremendous execution."[38] Cody realized

One of many illustrations of Cody's "First Scalp for Custer."
Courtesy Buffalo Bill Historical Center (MS6.S6.A.1/3), Cody, WY.

the drama was not sophisticated, logistically planned, or well written. "It was a five act play," he wrote, "without head or tail, and it made no difference at which act we commenced the performance. Before we had finished the season several newspaper critics, I have been told, went crazy in trying to follow the plot. It afforded us, however, ample opportunity to give a noisy, rattling, gunpowder entertainment, and to present a succession of scenes in the late Indian war, all of which seemed to give general satisfaction." And that, after all, was the point.[39]

Theatre managers prominently displayed the battle's gruesome artifacts until protesters condemned them as obscene and barbaric, serving to further popularize the program. In any event, "[j]ust what the Red Right hand had to do with the play never was fully determined," it was only necessary for someone to pull out a pistol and start shooting when the action lagged.[40] That Yellow Hair had had nothing to do with Custer's death or that there had been no duel didn't make much difference. Audiences willingly sacrificed reality in favor of Cody's version.

On the Big Horn and Yellowstone expedition, Cody had encountered a fellow scout, Irish-born Captain Jack Crawford. During his recuperation from a wound suffered in his service with the Volunteer Forty-eighth of Pennsylvania, Jack had learned to read and write and used the skills prolifically in seven books of poetry and over one hundred stories. After the Civil War, he worked for the *Omaha Daily Bee* as a Black Hills correspondent, then set himself up as chief of a volunteer company of scouts. At the end of July 1876, he joined the Fifth Cavalry. One day, Jack amazed Cody with a bottle of good whiskey sent from Colonel Jones. "Jack Crawford is the only man I have ever known that could have brought that bottle of whiskey through without *accident* befalling it, for he is one of the very few teetotal scouts I ever met."[41] When Cody left the Yellowstone region, he recommended Crawford succeed him as chief of scouts. In September Crawford was fired for leaving the command to deliver dispatches to the *New York Herald*, but the *Herald* furthered Jack's reputation by publishing the exciting story of his ride. Cody invited Crawford to join his troupe and even allowed him to play the title role.

By January 1877, the combination was performing *The Red Right Hand* almost exclusively in cities where they played one-night stands. For longer stays, they alternated between it and *Life on the Border* to entice repeat patronage. A Boston critic raved about the "truly extraordinary attraction" and remarked that "the ideas obtained of these terrible fellows in this play make them out much less formidable characters than the sort of free-shooters with which the city populations at the East are acquainted." He added, "Buffalo Bill has a pleasantly frank and open countenance and speaks very 'bad grammar' in a high nasal key, while his long and curling locks and his somewhat unmasculine figure, gait and manner convey the notion rather of a 'gentlemanly' hotel or dry-goods clerk than of the shooting, riding, scalping hero of a hundred fights."[42] Just as Hiram Robbins described Wild Bill Hickok as having an effeminate voice, this reporter perceived Cody's voice and bearing as less than strong and masculine.

Critics' perceptions tempered their reviews. The *Worcester Evening Gazette* reviewer, who had seen both of Cody's earlier dramas with their "sensations of all kinds," decided *Right Hand* "had more of it than both of them." His opinion concurred with many who believed readers of "blood-and-thunder romances demand a blood-and-thunder drama occasionally," and Cody did not disappoint.[43] Conversely, Worcester's *Daily Spy* reporter thought it required "the liveliest kind of a lively imagination to make head or tail out of the collection of rubbish" that was Cody's production. The scouts "face dangers of a most appalling nature as calmly as they pocketed the handsome receipts from last evening's entertainment. Of course, there is a maiden or two in the—well, the bills call it a drama"—who frequently and strongly declare, "He saved my life, and I will save his."[44]

A month later and miles down the railroad line, any resident of Cleveland who believed manners were foreign to Cody, that his "contentment only could be among red savages," did not know the scout. Once introduced to him, that person would find himself greeted with a "salutation in a mild, pleasant voice, completely dispel[ing] all thoughts of a frontiersman or Indian fighter." Cody "appears fully conversant on all topics of interest and debatable matters of the day, and on politics he carefully observed a neutral position."[45]

Beginning in the winter of 1876–77, a temperance movement known as the Murphy wave swept the country. Francis Murphy, a destitute alcoholic, experienced a religious conversion in prison that led to his sobriety. After his release, he became the foremost temperance orator throughout North America. The Parker City, Pennsylvania, press reported that Cody joined thousands of others who signed the Murphy pledge promising to avoid intoxicating liquors.[46] If Cody, in good faith, did sign, no evidence exists of his having done so.

Newspapers rarely covered any Buffalo Bill Combination performer extensively besides Cody, but the *Kansas City Times* detailed one journalist's acquaintance with Jack Crawford, "a genius very seldom met with." Jack was

> shot and supposed to be mortally wounded at Gettysburg.... As soon as he was able to get out of hospital he met with a friend in the present Governor Hartranft of Pennsylvania, and by his influence was promoted to a suitable position in the army.... [A]t the end of the war he became a pupil of Ned Buntline, the novelist. It was under the patronage of this distinguished romance writer that Crawford the drummer boy went West to study Western life and habits. He was one of the first of the white men to break through the military cordon surrounding the Black Hills and reach the gold mines. He was one of the original founders and incorporators of Custer City, and the leader of the company of scouts which protected the miners and cabin builders from Indian inroads and forays.[47]

Prior to curtain time, Crawford's duty was to prepare blank cartridges with which Cody blasted away. For the Nebraska City performance, Crawford gave the job to a property man, telling him to "stop the end of each shell with parafine [*sic*]." The man thought a tallow candle would do, so he prodded candle grease into the cartridges and placed six in each gun. The first shot melted the wax and sparks set off all the other cartridges. Frank Helvey, a youngster at the time, heard and saw the explosions. He rushed into the street and hollered that Cody was "massacreing [*sic*] the whole audience."[48] The *Daily News* reported the combination had earned $20,000 from their performances. They might have "a snug little sum left," reported the editor, if they purchased the gunpowder wholesale.[49]

Early in spring 1877, Cody contacted the North brothers, Frank and Luther, in Sidney, Nebraska, about going into the cattle business. Purchasing several thousand head, he set his sights on retiring as a wealthy rancher. Until then, he arranged for the combination actors to gather in Omaha. In mid-June, he transported them at his expense to his North Platte ranch where they would be free to do as they pleased but would be on call for a California tour.[50] After day-tripping for several years all over the eastern seaboard and into the South, Cody had received an offer to perform at San

Francisco's Bush Theatre. He decided to take the show there "against the advice of friends who gave it as their opinion that my style of plays would not take very well in California." Yet, why not?

The 1849 discovery of gold in California prompted a huge transcontinental migration. The first variety theatre—San Francisco's Bella Union—already needed rebuilding by 1869 when theatre design and technology were changing. Renovated interiors included ornate decoration, comfortable seats, excellent visibility, and good ventilation, encouraging attendance by more middle- and upper-class patrons. In the 1870s, the hub of theatrical activity shifted to Bush Street. "I opened [*Life on the Border*] for an engagement of two weeks . . . in a season when the theatrical business was dull," he wrote. "I expected to play to a slim audience on the opening night, but instead of that I had a fourteen hundred dollar house."[51]

Ten days later, the troupe wowed San Francisco audiences all over again with the first performance of *The Red Right Hand*. The *San Francisco Chronicle*, after praising *Life* as one of the best of its kind, stated that Cody's newest play was "well worth seeing, not alone by the gallery, which admires them merely for the blood and thunder element that runs a sensational vein through them, but by all for their pictures, sometimes overcolored, of a life that is novel to most, and before long can be seen by no one except through the medium of the drama and historic fiction." Comparing both, the critic preferred *Red Right Hand*. "Its plot moved quicker, its incidents are more naturally arranged and its climaxes more startling and sensational."[52] Cody's success was so great the troupe stayed for five weeks.

After the first two weeks of watching the unmitigated enthusiasm theatregoers displayed, folks at the *Chronicle* pondered the combination's popularity: "[t]heir plays and themselves are without art; they only make pretense to amuse in an humble way" and so "if they are to be judged at all it must by their own standards." Just as there is a difference between readers of classical literature and readers of "gaudy fiction with thoughts as cheap as its covers," so there is high drama and then there is Cody. To judge either would be to

> bring the stage within very narrow limits and seriously diminish
> our genuine amusements. . . . Mr. Cody's second play is a little
> livelier than his first, fuller of movement, and more wasteful of
> gunpowder, and much more bloody, otherwise it would have
> a less sanguinary name. . . . Buffalo Bill and Captain Jack both

Captain Jack Crawford and actress Gertie Granville onstage in
1877. Courtesy Tony Sapienza, DMD, Ridgewood, NJ.

do some good acting, not considered as acting merely, but as representations of real personages and of life on the frontier.[53]

The following day a similar evaluation appeared, as though the *Chronicle* reporters were still scratching their heads in bemusement.

It were easier to make bricks without straw than to construct an elaborate critique from such material. [*Life on the Border*] has had the advantage of a strong cast, stronger than it has merited. . . . The two great exemplars of frontier honesty, virtue and pluck have been [Cody] and Captain Jack. . . . Both are free from stage artifice; they speak their lines in a manly way, and walk through their parts with a naturalness and a realism which go far toward suplying [*sic*] the place of art itself. The border play will probably last as long as the border fiction, that is, until there ceases to be a border, and if we are to have it we may be well satisfied to have it in so good shape as this.[54]

For his share, Crawford asked for $100 pay per week and, when Cody counteroffered with $40, Jack threatened to leave. They compromised on $50 a week plus expenses, a good deal of money at the time.[55] A letter Crawford wrote to Cody many years later may explain his reluctance to leave. He admitted he had believed "you were the real genuine hero Buffalo Bill that Ned Buntline and other writers had glorified."[56]

In early June, Cody presented yet a third play from his repertoire: *Scouts of the Plains*. Californians found it

fairly bloodthirsty in its murderous purport, death being hardly pacified with a score of soupers [*sic*] and the amount of gunpowder expended would suffice to carry on the Turko-Russian war for a twelvemonth. There is a slender thread of a plot, which fails, however, to give the piece sufficient continuity to enable the observer to remember, having left the theater, what it was all about.[57]

During their final days in the Golden Gate City, Cody attempted even more realism to demonstrate how he had killed the hapless Indian by introducing onstage "two very frightened horses and the worst shooting ever witnessed." Cody, whose horsemanship on the plains proved faultless—Bat Masterson wrote that Cody "was an expert horseman and could shoot a pistol with deadly accuracy, while riding his horse at full speed"—was upstaged when "'Yellow Hand' (Crawford) in riding, mounting and dismounting and on the ground, in every way showed himself superior in agility and artifice to 'Buffalo Bill.'"[58] Adding live animals to the stage show moved Cody closer to the future days of his Wild West show and its numerous livestock. And, after they settled down, the horses even performed their parts well.[59]

For its four-night sojourn in Sacramento, the troupe gave a combination of plays in the truest sense of the word. The actors performed *Scouts of the Plains* for the first couple of performances and then switched to *Life on the Border*, combining it with the last act of *Red Right Hand*. Advertisements teased how the heroes, mounted on horseback, would engage in "deadly combat, at the close of which Buffalo Bill . . . [would] take the scalp off Yellow Hand (Captain Jack) without dismounting."[60]

Bright and early, on the morning of June 23, the *Daily Bee* editor dispatched a journalist to the Golden Eagle Hotel where the scouts were staying to confirm a rumor that Cody and Crawford had been called to the service of the Idaho government. The Nez Perce, forced to leave their ancestral homelands, moved to a reservation east of Lewiston, Idaho. During the journey, hostilities broke out between white settlers and the Indians. When the army arrived, the resisting bands headed east across the Rockies for refuge in Canada. They eluded capture for months, traveling through Yellowstone National Park and out onto the Great Plains. Just short of reaching the Canadian border in Montana, most of the party was overtaken.[61]

Crawford, his long hair floating about his shoulders, invited the reporter in. From his restless manner, the reporter inferred Jack was "satiated with the dull drama of life as enacted in the cities, and that he long[ed] to be on the boundless prairie." He responded to questions "in an affable, pleasant, and gentlemanly manner, showing that a life on the plains cannot wipe out native courtesy" but contradicted the rumor that he and Bill had been "officially requisitioned to the front." Both plainsmen had heard the news about the Nez Perce, and Crawford had requested a position as scout on the Salmon River. If no reply came, he intended to start for the Black Hills. Neither he nor Cody knew much about the Salmon River country or the Nez Perce, but they "had no doubt that they could make things lively if they once got up there."

The reporter then hunted down Cody. Finding him leaning on the hotel desk, the reporter repeated his questions. He had also telegraphed Lieutenant General Sheridan about a position as scout. "He is satiated with the mimic drama, and longs for the wild life," inferred the journalist, though "he wasn't 'one of those fellows who go off half cock,' and . . . he did not intend to do anything in the matter until he first saw which way the land lay." If Cody did not go to Idaho, he planned to retire to his Nebraska ranch. In contrast to Jack, Cody appeared "more cool and nonchalant. . . . He is as desirous for action as the other, but he is not so headstrong as the younger and more hot blooded Captain Jack."[62]

The attitude marked a more mature Cody who did not plan to rush into the melee and "clean out every one of 'em" as he was previously known to have promised. The reporter was observing Cody's true nature, a temperament his commanding generals had also noticed. Lieutenant Colonel Carr wrote in July 1878 that "Mr. Cody . . . was very modest and unassuming. . . . He is a natural gentleman in his manners as well as in character and has none of the roughness of the typical frontiersman[.] . . . [H]is temper and disposition are so good that no one has reason to quarrel with him. . . . Mr. Cody is never noisy, obstreperous or excited."[63] The model for Cody's behavior, as well as for a generation of plainsmen, was the modest and gallant Kit Carson. Cody thought so highly of him that he had named his son after him.[64]

No army orders arrived, so the troupe headed eastward to fulfill engagements in Nevada. *Life on the Border* opened in Virginia City for a five-day run on June 25, 1877. As other critics had observed, *Red Right Hand* was more exciting than *Life on the Border*. "There is an air of reality about it. . . . There is also any amount of fun in connection with the play, as well as much that is thrillingly sensational." The critic describes how after Yellow Hair and Cody meet in a fierce conflict, and "Buffalo Bill snatches the reeking scalp from the head of the chief, and holds it up, the tableau represents Custer dashing at full speed into the thickest of the fight. It was encored vociferously."[65] Cody acted "naturally and splendidly." Jack Crawford's "salute" to women he encounters in the hills was "one of the neatest tricks ever executed with a gun. The motions . . . [were] as quick, precise and clear-cut as saber strokes."[66]

On June 28, during the final act on horseback, Cody and Crawford were to exchange shots. Jack, before mounting up, had cocked his pistol and placed it in its holster. During the draw, it snagged and discharged, sending a blank cartridge into his groin. When he unceremoniously fell from his horse to engage Cody in hand-to-hand combat, blood soaked his pants. "Still, but few persons in the audience seemed to know that anything was amiss for, notwithstanding the injury which he had evidently sustained, and with the *esprit de corps* characteristic of all true actors, he continued to play his part." After the manager quickly lowered the curtain and Crawford was carried to his room, a doctor ascertained the wound was "large, ragged and painful, but not necessarily dangerous."[67]

A week later, the *Black Hills Champion* reported Jack had recovered and would "soon launch out in the theatrical world on his own hook."[68] The animosity building between the two men had peaked. The dispute over salary and the question of how and when to introduce horses onstage were problematic. Perhaps the circumstances surrounding the shooting will never be known for certain, but as a result of Jack's blaming Cody, the rift between them intensified and was responsible for his departure. When the combination reached Reno in early July, Cody gave no scheduled performance. However, according to the *Clipper*, his agent, Charles E. Locke, "being one of the sharpers," complained about his conduct and accused him "quite wrongfully." He attempted to swindle Cody out of $200, "being money deducted from Bill's salary for being in a hilarious condition on the stage." The men exchanged angry words, and Cody, "playing [that] the agent was an Indian, went for his scalp. Parties interfered and prevented an interesting performance."[69]

Crawford headed back to California with his own combination. Over the following years, he abandoned his family to prospect for gold in Arizona, New Mexico, and Alaska, occasionally opening supply stores to finance his ventures. By 1885, he was back onstage, giving lectures and poetry readings about frontier life. While he could bring audiences to tears with heartrending soliloquies, it wasn't lucrative, and he was left with a reputation as a "poet-scout" but no money. He railed against Cody's Wild West, denigrating him as an opportunistic fictionalizer. Crawford's plays faulted yellow journalism and sanguinary border dramas for leading young boys into lives of crime and poverty and luring them into a West with which they were unprepared to deal.[70]

An unidentified clipping in Cody's scrapbook offers a rebuttal of sorts. A journalist wrote:

> Whatever may be said against this class of literature and
> performance, it certainly is highly relished by the self-reliant

Captain Jack Crawford. Courtesy Tony Sapienza, DMD, Ridgewood, NJ.

members of the masculine sex; and the fact stands that it does much towards inculcating freedom and independence in boys who seem to have a natural "hankering" after this style of thing. There is no vulgarity, no bad or immoral sentiment advocated in the piece, and we are unable to see wherein the evil lies in such productions. . . . Good stories of adventure are much more natural and healthful than the average Sabbath school narrative, and when their morality is good, there can be no harm emanating from them. If Buffalo Bill and his confreres have done any good from this standpoint, they deserve the approval of all level-headed citizens.[71]

The men continued adversarial contact for over thirty years. The two scouts' philosophies were far apart in life, but their deaths came close together. Crawford died in February 1917, a month after Cody.

Disbanding the rest of the company in Omaha in July 1877, Cody exuberantly kissed the actresses good-bye. Unfortunately for him, his wife was on hand to witness the fond farewells. Twenty-eight years later it became an issue in their divorce suit, though Cody didn't understand what the fuss was about. His fellow troupers had become family. He spent more time with them than with his wife and children and couldn't understand her indignation.

I think [she] would have been rather proud of a husband who had six or seven months work with a party of people who were in his employ, to know and feel that they were on a kindly footing with their late manager, that they were sorry they were going to be separated from a good, kind manager who had always paid their salaries himself.[72]

After a summer spent establishing a cattle ranch on Nebraska's Dismal River with Frank North, on August 5, 1877, Cody telegraphed Crawford asking if he would open with him in September.[73] Not in a forgiving mood, Crawford declined.

Two days later, Cody fired back an angry response.

My Dear Jack, . . . People have flattered you until you think as many others have done that you are a great man Jack go ahead You will find out that all that glitters is not gold. I told you last

fall allso Texas Jack wrote that you would in a short time think
that you were the attraction and would want to branch out for
your self like Kit Carson Jr. I wish you success and will never do
a thing to hurt you. . . . I am very sorry the accident occered and
you know it was nôt my fault as I never wanted to put the horses
on the stage. but had the accident not occured I think you had
made up your mind to start out for your self. So good Luck. . . .
You are way off in lots of things. Yours as ever. Bill[74]

The gregarious Cody did not understand; to him the combination was
more than a business. Ned Buntline created the theatrical Buffalo Bill from
dime-novel stereotypes but William Frederick Cody took the fabrication
and made him real. Reviews applauded each of his fellow scouts, but Cody
was definitely the star. Perhaps his inflated ego led him to think everyone
shared his enthusiasm and dedication to the combination and its semi-
mythical world, but where Hickok, Omohundro, and Crawford saw simulation, Cody envisioned an innovative and authentic narrative.[75] From here
on, he would be the lone frontiersman in his combination.

— CHAPTER SIX —

Incidents and Accidents

*Buffalo Bill . . . surrounded with defunct Indians, and standing
stalwart in a cloud of smoke and dust . . . was sublime.*
—Craig Nieuwenhuyse, "Six-Guns on the Stage"

IN THE EARLY FALL OF 1877, CODY HEADED TO THE RED CLOUD AGENCY
in Nebraska to recruit Indians for his combination. Most Americans had
regarded the Indian policy of Ulysses S. Grant as a failure, primarily because
of the bloody battles it produced. With the succession of Rutherford B. Hayes
as president and the appointment of Carl Schurz as secretary of the interior
came a change in policy allowing Indians eager to leave reservation confine-
ment to take jobs in traveling shows. With the Indians and his family in tow,
Cody headed east; Louisa and their daughter Orra had opted to travel with
the troupe. Daughter Arta was enrolled in a Rochester school.[1]

He opened at the Bowery Theatre in New York City on September 3,
1877, in *May Cody; or, Lost and Won*, a drama by Captain Andrew S. Burt.
An army career soldier, Cincinnati-born Burt had proven his gallantry
in the Civil War. During the Great Sioux War, he was stationed at Fort
Laramie, the anchor for military operations, communication, and supplies,
at which time he and Cody almost certainly met. Reviewers often judged

the play "realistic," which it was, owing to Burt's experiences on the plains with wild bears, road agents, and outlaws. From these, he had arrived at "conclusions which an unbiased judgment must necessarily draw."[2]

Cody's proclivity for incorporating current frontier events into his dramas assured timeliness and easterners' continued interest. The Mountain Meadows Massacre in September 1857 provided the basis for *May Cody*. At that time, convinced the Mormon Church in Utah was flouting the authority of the territorial government, President James Buchanan decided to replace Governor Brigham Young and dispatched a sizable military force. Expecting persecution, the Mormons went into high alert. Meanwhile, a band of 140 non-Mormon emigrants on their way to California from Arkansas reached the territory. With no military to resist federal authority, Young authorized, if not commanded, his Paiute Indian allies to attack the emigrant party to show the nation the cost of waging war with Mormons. According to historian Will Bagley, Young's manipulation of the Indians before the massacre makes it seem he was "directly responsible for the tragedy."

After a few days, during which the emigrants put up a valiant resistance, the commander in the field, John D. Lee, realized "the Indians could not do the work and we were in a sad fix." He needed to persuade the emigrants to surrender their arms and then to convince the Mormon militia to murder them. Some participants claimed they only killed the emigrants to avoid an Indian war that would have destroyed their own families but, in fact, the Mormons did not regard the Paiutes as a military threat. Moreover, most of the Indians had already left the scene.[3]

After the Arkansans surrendered, Lee's treacherous scheme was compounded when, under the guise of a white flag, he and his men approached the wagon train. Along with a group of Mormons disguised as Indians, they separated out the "innocent blood" of children under eight, led the rest away, and executed them.[4] The surviving children later recalled seeing the "Indians" washing off war paint, exposing white faces.

Days later, Young had mixed feelings about the massacre. It would prove perilous to his sect if word leaked out that Mormons had joined Indians in the slaughter. Needing to distance himself, Young ordered Lee to write an account blaming the Indians. The sect was well aware that the actions of the few did not reflect the philosophy of all its members, but previous harassment at the hands of non-Mormons convinced them denial was the best course. Most Americans, however, laid the responsibility for the massacre at the feet of the Mormons. Federal officers believed Young was responsible, but they could not get enough evidence to make a case in court. Instead, Lee was made the scapegoat until, by March 1877, he had composed at least four accounts ranging from "the Indians did it" to the "Indians made us do it." All the while he was convinced he had done nothing wrong. Still protesting his innocence, he was tried and executed by firing squad on the spot where he and his "avenging angels" wrought the devastation.[5]

Throughout the second half of the nineteenth century, most Protestant Americans perceived Mormonism as an alien and threatening force, its adherents "un-American" outsiders at odds with "native" American beliefs. Its tenet of polygamy headed the list of contentions. One columnist compared the religion to a "noxious weed" that "thrives best by neglect." He feared that "like a weed it will overrun the fairest portions of our territory and choke out all pure and useful life unless it is plucked up by the roots." Many years passed before the country forgave the entire sect for the actions of a few. Mormon violence provided fodder for melodramas, complete with innocent victims and outrageous villains. Anti-Mormon literature and drama enjoyed much commercial success, most of them portraying Mormons as lying, stealing, murdering hypocrites.

Burt's drama opens in a New York City drawing room where May Cody, Buffalo Bill's sister, serves as secretary to Mrs. Stoughton. In the second act, a reenactment of the Mountain Meadows massacre in Echo Canyon occurs. Somewhat historically accurate, John D. Lee's band enters the emigrants' camp as friendly Indians, then attacks the luckless wagon train after which the curtain descends on a "thrilling tableau," representing Lee's abduction of May Cody. Buffalo Bill, at times disguised as White Wolf, rescues May from Brigham Young, who is about to force her to become his wife. Finally, at Fort Bridger, Buffalo Bill is charged with being a spy and condemned to death. The sentence is about to be carried out when he proves his innocence and everything ends happily.[6] A reviewer thought the play a vivid illustration of "Mormon iniquity, perfidy and crime" and believed it did more to show the "hideous and monstrous practices of those strange and deluded people" than could be learned by lectures, books, or speeches.[7]

Harry Ellis played the nefarious John D. Lee; George C. Charles the ever-present melodramatic Irishman Darby McCune; and popular actress Constance Hamblin May Cody. The production also included a Mexican burro named Jack Cass. Mules served the purpose better than horses because "any mule sufficiently gifted in histrionic arts" would, unlike a

Chicago, IL, ad for the January 7, 1878, performance.

horse, "be able to climb three flights of steep stairs unassisted."[8] Two genuine Sioux chiefs—Man-That-Carries-the-Sword and Two Bears—filled the Indian roles, adding a *"performance* verisimilitude."[9] The former had guided General Sheridan on his journey from the Union Pacific railroad to the Yellowstone River that summer.[10] Fifteen years previously, Two Bears had headed the Yanktonai Nakota tribe and was one of the signers of the Black Hills treaty.[11] As a go-between for American Indians with the U.S. government, he was knowledgeable in white men's ways, having traveled with Father Pierre-Jean DeSmet and met with General George Custer.[12] W. S. MacEvoy (or McEvoy) played General Harney, patterned after Major General William S. Harney, commander of the Utah expedition. One journalist who knew the general credited MacEvoy with good acting, but "he wasn't tall enough, or slender enough, or jolly enough or spry enough, to deceive the eyes of the old friends of that glorious old gentleman."[13]

Mindful of Frank Frayne's popular marksmanship demonstration, Cody introduced the sharpshooting Austin brothers, Ike and Charles. They shot potatoes from each other's heads then snuffed a candle and cigar from a man's hand. Reviewers rarely failed to mention their marksmanship prowess and praised their efforts. The camping scene in the canyon set up the reason for the Sioux and the Austins to display bullwhip cracking and more rifle marksmanship.[14] The result gave them an increased edge over the competition.

Few extant items remain from the combination years. However, one ledgerbook for several months of the 1877 season has survived with details of the troupe's expenses and income. The take on most days was about $400, double the daily expenses. Cody's managers paid out money for posters, billboards, hall rentals, ushers, licenses, supers, advertisements, hotels, and meals. Weekly salaries for the managers, advance men, and actors averaged between $12 and $30 a week, with the Austins receiving $100. Considering theatre seats ranged from twenty-five cents to $1.25, such payouts indicate capacity houses. Neither Cody's share, nor what he paid the Indians, was listed.[15]

Rent for an opera house might average $43 per night, and hotel rooms might cost $31. Incidental expenses such as city tax ($2.50), a doctor bill for agent Josh Ogden ($5), and cigars (ninety cents) were added to the bills. They bought two buffalo robes as props for $10, a whip for $6.75, and a bearskin for $2. Travel was high on the list of expenses—Cody paid a bill of $125 for five hundred miles. A steamboat trip cost half that.[16]

From New York, the troupe boarded the train to Baltimore where the *American & Commercial Advertiser*'s editor assigned a reporter to interview the Indians. Hesitantly, he knocked on their door at Guy's Hotel. Cody introduced him to fellow scout and Indian interpreter, Cha-sha-sha-o-Pogeo, which translates as Red-Willow-Fill-the-Pipe. His given, more pronounceable name was John Young Nelson. Ironically, Nelson had guided Brigham Young to Utah twenty years before Cody met him, when they both were scouting out of Fort McPherson. Cody thought him "a good fellow but [he] had few equals and no superiors as a liar."[17] Nelson no doubt facilitated Cody's acquisitions of Indians for the show and, along with his Sioux wife and family, followed Cody into his Wild West.

The younger of the two Indians, Man-That-Carries-the-Sword, had battled Custer and said he enjoyed traveling through eastern cities and learning the "ways of the pale faces for his own good." When the journalist asked if he were eager to talk to the Great Father in Washington, he indicated that, as a U.S. soldier who had fought for the government, he was indeed looking forward to it. He said he would fight his own people if he were told to. Two Bears added that he too was "a fighting chief and thought only of war." His wife had died, leaving him with five children whom he would bring up "like white people."

When the reporter asked Cody how the Indians took to acting, he replied he was happy with their performance. His increased sympathy for the Indians' plight and regret at the wholesale slaughter his previous dramas portrayed prompted him to remark, "[t]hey were supposed to be his friends in the play; indeed, it would hardly be politic to use them in any other way."[18]

Travel with Indians was not unique to Cody's combination. In the 1830s and 1840s, American painter George Catlin found the public eager to see re-creations and trappings of Indian life. Seeing firsthand the devastation of tribes by men who exploited them with forced migrations and ravaged them with foreign diseases, Catlin hoped to educate through his paintings while he entertained. He brought along Indians to demonstrate native dances at a showing, so that in a sense the artwork came to life. If Catlin's was, in effect, a primitive Wild West show, Cody also matched Catlin in his empathy for the Indians' plight, but he expanded Catlin's idea by showcasing them in a dramatic narrative. Because the horrors of Indian warfare were familiar to soldiers, immigrants, and prospectors, they tended to view the tribes as abhorrent, but to easterners with no direct contact, they were the "noble savages." Cody launched them as dramatic entertainers in his combination, and they became indispensable in his Wild West show. When problems arose with the commissioner of the Bureau of Indian Affairs, John Burke told him it was Cody's "honorable ambition to instruct and educate the Eastern public to respect the denizens of the West by giving them a true, untinselled representation of a page of frontier history that is fast passing away."[19]

Door receipts confirm the play with its realistic demonstrations was lucrative. The evening's show in New Bedford, Massachusetts, added $428.10 to the coffers; in Lynn, Cody counted $448.63. According to the account book, between Gloucester and Lawrence, he took in nearly $750. A large audience also attended the Manchester, New Hampshire, performances on November 2–3, which brought in $853.45.[20] We may never know what happened in Waterville, Maine, on November 12 causing whoever was keeping record to note—"God Dam the Town. Never to be played again. Blacked Bill," but Cody garnered only $118, a quarter of his usual take.[21] Publicity was not at fault—the *Waterville Mail* commended the combination as "one of the most attractive dramatic companies that travel the broad road to amusement and mirth and money . . . ; it makes its own noise, and its own fun, and those who get a ticket get both."[22]

Each time the company played in Worcester, Massachusetts, a flurry of newspaper activity announced its arrival and subsequent goings-on. Cody's ability to draw the biggest houses ever at the local theatre was one reason. The troupe's November 20 visit was special because a sportsman's club had arranged a shooting match between Cody and Lincoln C. Daniels, a local marksman. Each man would get ten shots at the target—a three-foot square with a four-inch bull's-eye—from fifty yards. The victor would walk away with $100.

Before the contest, however, Cody had a show to do and, as predicted, filled the theatre. The lack of obscuration by powder smoke, as well as the dearth of rifle shots, afforded the audience a clear view—a special treat for the eyes, given his appearance not only in buckskin, but in evening dress as well. Other popular attractions included the "meek-looking squirrel-gray donkey" and the Austins using Frank Wesson rifles. Another of the characters wielded a mule whip "with which he kept the nervous ones in anything but a happy condition by the rapidity of the cracks, loud as musket reports, he discharged over their heads."[23]

The next day, several hundred people were on hand at Worcester's

Sportsman's Club to witness the Cody-Daniels match. Despite the clear day, the men put in rather unremarkable shooting; both were using new Wesson rifles with which they were unfamiliar. Cody's lack of opportunity to practice was a factor, but even so, the "man from the Plains" triumphed with Daniels facing defeat good-naturedly.[24] The appeal of the contest gave Cody the idea to introduce yet another new feature onstage—a target-shooting match between himself and Charles Austin.[25]

Rumors were flying as a result of Cody's comments to the press that this would be his last season as a theatrical star. He wanted to retire to his ranch as a cattle dealer and gentleman farmer. But in the *New York Clipper* of November 23, 1877, business manager Josh Ogden reported business with the troupe was great, so Cody would not be retiring as planned.

Despite most critics' wholehearted enthusiasm for the new drama, the *Cincinnati Daily Gazette* reviewer pointed out, "The story ends somewhat lamely in the escape of Mormon Lee. . . . In view of the fact that Lee was executed at last, there seems to be no good reason why a regard for chronology should stand in the way of a natural and appropriate denouement to the play."[26] Modern filmmakers who disregard historical accuracy are, it seems, following a precedent playwrights like Andrew Burt set over a century ago.

Toledo, Ohio, police working during the Christmas holiday encountered a problem with Two Bears. He charged into police court demanding a warrant for Cody who he claimed had violently struck him. Officer McMahon, who "talk[ed] Indian," had a difficult time understanding him but thought that was the gist of his complaint. Finally Cody appeared and explained, "Two Bears awoke cross as one bear this morning. He wanted to go home on the towpath," and he thought he could pull this off "by telling a story of some sort to get Mr. Buffalo arrested and then flee to his own western wilds." Cody proved he never struck Two Bears, and finally, persuaded by a fresh cigar, the Indian left, grumbling, "I dam heap mad."[27] Two weeks later, Two Bears "made up his mind that Bill was making him 'do all the work,' at which his noble nature rebelled, and he left the party for the luxurious comfort of his own community on the plains."[28]

From time to time Cody had to defend himself against like allegations of cruelty to his show Indians. The Bureau of Indian Affairs and vigilant reformers were engrossed in making sure traveling Indian exhibits were legitimate and that unscrupulous managers were not exploiting them. Near the end of the century, the Indian Rights Association pointed out how such

Cody in Indian headdress and moccasins, c. 1878. Courtesy Buffalo
Bill Historical Center (P.69.1655), Cody, WY. Gift of William W. Giles.

shows, failing to convey any idea of the Indians' progress toward civilization, led whites to see the Indian only as a savage.[29] Reformers argued that their being part of traveling shows fostered idleness and brought the Indians into contact with people of low character from whom they would learn bad habits. Upon returning home, they would likely share the bad examples they had learned. Their families, it was feared, suffered from lack of care during their absence. Managers who deviously lured Indians from the reservation were apt to be unprincipled and would not hesitate to abandon their charges far from home.[30] Such accusations against Cody could be not be corroborated or proven.

During the coldest part of winter, Cody took the troupe north into Wisconsin, then about-faced to Illinois where they appeared in Chicago at Haverly's Theatre beginning January 7, 1878. The *Tribune* praised the troupers in *May Cody* for their lack of stage business and the freedom afforded by their not following convention. The drama, the press judged, appeared to have been "dashed off . . . in a kind of frolic by a careless genius, who builded [*sic*] better than he knew . . . an addition to our dramatic literature. . . . It is not as wildly improbable in incident or situation as one-half of the drawing room dramas which pass current in these days, and it has the immense advantage of dealing with unfamiliar occurrences." The subject of the Mormon massacre "had never before been handled by a competent artist and so it has been left for artisans to deal with." Burt's "rough-and-tumble picture" contained more realistic scenes than the "most patient polishing could have accomplished." Scenic artist Frank Skiff painted the backdrops, and his "acquaintance with the localities . . . lent a vigor and freshness to his brush."[31] At the sight of Cody, "the boys roar over him with delight, and all the girls are 'mashed.'" Five months into the production, even Cody thought *May Cody* was the best drama he had produced when it became "a grand success both financially and artistically."[32]

A correspondent for the *New York Clipper* attended the performance during the mid-January tour of the central states and reported that Charles Austin and Ada Forrester, the combination's leading lady, were married in Chicago on January 13, 1878. They made the third couple to meet and marry on Cody's watch.[33] Texas Jack Omohundro found a bride in Mlle. Morlacchi, and Walter Fletcher and Lizzie Safford tied the knot shortly after joining the company in 1873.[34]

Despite their celebrity, or perhaps because of marriage arrangements, by the end of January, combination ads no longer listed the Austins. Cody, a keen observer of the popularity of their marksmanship exhibition, was left to pick up the slack and inaugurated a display of his own remarkable talents with a rifle. Standing at a distance the width of the stage, he shot potatoes out of property man John Howard's hand, "shooting with the rifle held over his head, between his legs or in almost any position." He extinguished a lit cigar in Howard's mouth and snuffed a candle by shooting the wick. "The men who so coolly stand up to hold the targets seem to have the greatest confidence in Bill's skill, and thus far he hasn't abused it," reported the press. Howard said Cody "never used buckshot on the stage. He used real bullets" and, because he always shot cleanly, "we never had an accident."[35] Doubters abounded, so the *Terre Haute Daily Express* exhorted its readers to "let him try it," if they didn't believe the claims.[36]

Most reviewers gave *May Cody; or, Lost and Won* plaudits for the diminished amount of smoke and gunpowder produced, but the Louisville, Kentucky, newspaper called it a "folly to tone down a wild Western sensational drama. [The play] needs a few ounces of gunpowder to quite realize the expectations of the youth of the land."[37] In Fort Wayne, Cody engaged eleven amateurs from the ranks of local citizens to take the parts of soldiers, Indians, emigrants, and peasants at twenty-five cents per head, as he had done at least one other time in Massachusetts.[38] The practice of hiring local amateurs allowed volunteers with histrionic aspirations to join the cast onstage in supers' parts. The press berated friends of the chosen for distracting him with shouts and whistles; in those circumstances "he cannot be expected to carry his part well—whether he be a painted 'Injun,' a knight in armor, or a black-corked and slouch-hatted villain. . . . Give them bouquets," advised the editor, "but don't overwhelm them with too much other recognition." When no one paid the Fort Wayne locals, disagreement arose between combination managers and the head of the opera house as to who ought to bear the expense. Lawyers brought a suit against Cody and routed Justice Hoagland out of bed. The judge ruled that Cody should pay the claim of $13, "over which Buffalo William was quite indignant."[39]

Lydia Denier, a professional actress formerly associated with Robinson's opera house of Cincinnati, joined Cody in Ohio and remained with the troupe as leading lady almost continually for the next eight years. When the troupe performed in Erie, Pennsylvania, on March 13, the *Morning Dispatch* declared *May Cody* "one of the most thrilling border dramas that was ever placed on the stage." The press credited Cody with being "really a good actor" and a "most remarkable marksman." Miss Denier "is not only a fine actress, but a lady of unusual nerve." In the camping scene, she coolly faced his unwavering rifle and allowed the "modern William Tell" to shoot potatoes from the top of her head. At this, "the hearts of the auditors stand still with fear, and a sigh of relief escapes as the smoke clears away and the plucky woman stands unharmed."

Allegedly, Cody had signed the Murphy pledge promising to temper his drinking, but the Wilkes-Barre audience viewed a rather tipsy scout who ruined the production. The critic hoped he would take better care of himself; his fancy shooting was "a dead failure" with shot after shot missing its mark. The critic judged Darby McClune's bit with the donkey the most successful part of the show; the animal's acting "was a redeeming feature of the play—and he was sober, too."[40]

In the index to his biography, Don Russell lists thirteen references to Cody's drinking. To be fair, some of those include quotes from Cody's acquaintances wondering at his *not* drinking on a particular occasion. Russell also states that no military officer officially registered a complaint about his being drunk on duty.[41] However, that Cody enjoyed a drink now and then is undeniable. Allowing for the strain of managing his combination, and that, in general, actors often endured a reputation as vagrant lowlifes, it is to Cody's credit that he got drunk as seldom as he did. Also, judging a critic's ulterior motive in belittling him with scornful comments is impossible.

The *Brooklyn Daily Eagle*'s drama critic attempted to draw "a highly important lesson" from the western drama. After comparing it to trying to "extract sunbeams from cucumbers,"[42] he convolutedly expressed his amazement at Cody's thespian improvement: "To appear natural upon the stage involves art. To be natural is to appear unnatural. To appear natural involves study, dramatic talent and a great many other things, and this is why amateurs who look pretty and dashing in private life, appear insipid or affected the moment they are seen on the stage." If one supposed that all Cody had to do onstage was to personate himself as the frontiersman he really was,

> then his audience would [have] see[n] a very natural and
> consequently a graceful actor. When Mr. Cody made his first
> appearance on the stage we have no doubt that he shared this
> common and fallacious belief. . . . But his first appearance
> was a failure. He spoke in his natural tones, and the effect was

ridiculous. He moved about the stage like a bull in a china shop, he failed. Since then he has learned that acting is an art to be studied and learned, and that to be natural on the stage is the highest attainment. Now, by constant study and the exercise of intelligence, he has succeeded in appearing natural.[43]

Twenty-first-century audiences might wonder at the prominence the critic gave Cody's naturalness, but at the time, a melodramatic acting style still dominated, and so Cody's naturalness would have struck audiences as unusual. Cody acted naturally because he knew no other way; six years into his career, his acting style still reflected his frontiersman persona. But as realism was beginning to influence dramatic arts, Cody, albeit inadvertently, once again, was on the cutting edge. Still, even if he wasn't consciously trying to be avant-garde, he did make refinements on his natural style. Whereas previously he acknowledged audience applause for a particular scene or broke the "fourth wall" by addressing theatre patrons as if they were personal friends, now his progression as an artist was evident. The key was credibility, and that, as much as anything else, contributed to his success as an actor.

When the theatrical season ended—"the most profitable one I had ever had," Cody wrote—he headed for his Nebraska homestead. By the time he arrived, Frank North and the cowboys had organized the spring roundup. During six weeks of demanding ranch work, Cody wondered, after "having to be in the saddle all day, and standing guard over the cattle at night, rain or shine . . . where the fun came in, that North had promised me. But it was an exciting life, and the days sped rapidly by."[44] He practiced fancy shooting at glass balls and when he ran out of those, he "shot most of the potatoes from his garden on the fly." The summer's activities included visits from two of his sisters and in August, on the way to secure Indians for the next season, he stopped in Kansas to visit his other sisters.[45]

On August 14, he left Omaha for Baltimore to organize his company for the 1878–79 season, one of the largest he would end up taking on the road.[46] Frank North, who commanded a regiment of Pawnee scouts for over ten years, facilitated Cody's contacts with the Pawnees as John Nelson had done with the Sioux. The Indians included in the combination were Follow-the-Sun, a tall, dark-looking Nez Perce; Eagle-That-Flies-High, a Pawnee; Little Warrior, another Pawnee; and Young-Grass-That-Sprouts-in-the-Spring, his wife. Only one of the four could speak English. Besides the Indians, Cody hired the Burgess brothers—Charles, a government interpreter, sometimes called "the Napoleon Interpreter," because of his resemblance to the French emperor, and Ed (also known as Willie Burgess or Was-each-asulla, the Lone White Boy), the eighteen-year-old "Boy Chief" of the Pawnees. Raised among the Indians, they understood native language and customs.[47] The *Clipper* on August 31 pointed out that Cody was the sole proprietor of the show, C. E. Blanchett the business manager, Josh E. Ogden the general agent, Chas. J. Thorne the assistant agent, J. H. Harvey the master of transportation, and Harry Melmer the superintendent of stock. The combination having grown significantly, several managers were needed to keep things in line.

In mid-September 1878, the troupe opened in Baltimore in *May Cody* under the management of John T. Ford with Lydia Denier in the title role. Foreshadowing Cody's Wild West show, after the drama, the performance concluded "with Part Second: Thirty Minutes among the People from the Plains; Introducing the Pawnees and Nez Perce Indians in their native pastimes, Archery, Breaking Glass Balls with the Bow and Arrow, Fancy Rifle shooting, War Dances, Religious Rites, Nuptial Ceremonies &c,." In addition, theatre managers could display the combination's "Frontier Museum of Interesting Collection of Indian paraphernalia, War Equipments and Hunting Utensils"—Cody's souvenirs from Yellow Hair.[48] John Burke's press agentry may have been involved in referring to the Indian accoutrements as a "museum." However, considering a museum's mission is to acquire, conserve, and exhibit items for study, education, and enjoyment, his usually flamboyant phrasing hit the mark.

Word of Cody's outstanding marksmanship displays got around theatres fast, and other performers attempted similar feats. The Pawtucket, Rhode Island, press reported the incident of Mlle. Volante, who was killed when costar Jennie Fowler aimed her rifle at an apple on Volante's head and missed. Newspapers immediately railed against such exhibitions. That marksmen like Cody could handle a gun "in a masterly manner" "by no means gives immunity from accident, which might occur at the critical moment." A law prohibiting the pointing of firearms at people should be enforced, demanded the press, as "[l]ives are too precious to be sacrificed for the mere exhibition of a marksman's skill." The *Newark Daily Advertiser* rebutted irreverently, "Human life is cheap and the excitement of trapeze performances and others cannot be foregone merely because a woman's skull is occasionally smashed by a fall or riddled by a bullet."[49]

In Baltimore, Cody faced a consequence of his using firearms onstage. Fortunately, unlike Mlle. Volante, his victim survived. With safety in mind, any weapon Cody used in the play contained only blank charges. But near the close of the drama while riding a pony up an imitation mountain, he fired several shots at his Indian pursuers, "and by some grave mischance one barrel was loaded with ball." The stray bullet hit a boy named Michael Gardner sitting in a front seat in the gallery. A doctor's examination found that the ball had penetrated his lung. The next day the boy remained in critical condition with a very slight chance of recovery, and Cody directed he be given every attention money could provide.

Journalists sought explanations for the calamity. "Owing to want of practice, short range, or the way in which the rifles were loaded, he did not strike the [glass] balls as often as was expected and this circumstance seemed to disturb him. During the shooting he missed six balls in succession and misses appeared to be the rule and hits the exception." This poor performance could have so upset him that he then perhaps loaded the wrong cartridge in his rifle by accident (of the two kinds of rifle cartridges, some were blanks and others, used to shoot at the glass balls, contained bullets that were underloaded with powder so that the bullets wouldn't travel far). The contest over, Cody then charged up the fake mountain and fired the errant shot. Later that night, the press reported Cody's genuine regret and added that "He had no idea the charge of powder was sufficient to carry the bullets from one side of the theater to the other. He had tried them yesterday just to satisfy himself and found that the bullets did not even penetrate a piece of wood as thin as the side of a cigar box."

He told the reporter that

[t]he Indians of his troupe had not been doing as well as usual, as it was the first night, and they had not been properly stirred up. They are a very excitable people, and the least little thing starts their enthusiasm. For the purpose of stirring them to such a show of wildness as would make the close of the performance exciting to the audience, he shouted as he urged his pony forward and fired two shots in the air.[50]

Cody needed to move on. He kept up a correspondence with the boy, however, and when Michael recovered, the Cody family invited him to their North Platte home.

After that, the use of live ammunition onstage became an issue. The previously cited incident where a stagehand loaded Cody's and Crawford's blank cartridges and then substituted candle wax for paraffin shows how careful one had to be—and why the actors themselves usually took care of their own ammunition. Black powder, even used in blanks, is unstable and dangerous. Hickok's habit of venting his frustration on the unfortunate supers by shooting at their legs may have amused him, but it was not something he would have done had his pistols not been charged with underloaded ammunition.

Following the Baltimore engagement, Cody headed for Washington, D.C., where he learned that the Bureau of Indian Affairs was apprehensive about his employment of the Pawnees. Secretary Schurz told Cody the Indians, now wards of the government, were off the reservation without leave, and he ordered them to return immediately. When the Indians learned this, "they executed a terrific war-dance, held an excited pow-wow, and finally concluded not to go." Cody maintained that

> Indians were frequently off of their reservations out west, as I had
> a distinct remembrance of meeting them upon several occasions
> "on the war path," and furthermore I thought I was benefitting
> [sic] the Indians as well as the government, by taking them all
> over the United States and giving them a correct idea of the
> customs, life, etc. of the pale faces, so that when they returned
> to their people they could make known all they had seen.

He notified Schurz that, if the order were carried out, it would cause him "considerable pecuniary loss" because the combination advertised appearances twenty days ahead of time. In consideration of Cody's past valuable service as chief of scouts, Schurz acquiesced with the stipulation that Cody be appointed an Indian agent and pledge to return them safely to their reservation. According to the *Clipper*, the "dusky chiefs of the forest sang O-be-joyful! and will indulge in deeds of daring and blood-curdling horror upon the stage, instead of living upon Government rations at their agency. This is the first instance of an appointment of an Indian Agent East of the Missouri River."[51]

With the troupe intact, he moved it on to Norfolk, Virginia, where, in order to advertise performances on September 23 and 24, the Indian chiefs walked about the streets, thrilling "the boys and colored people."

The *Richmond State* observed that, as an actor, Cody was "a failure, though in real life a big success; but he went through his part in an off-hand don't-me-care sort of manner that took immensely with the boys in the gallery, who were all 'well up' in the history of his numerous scouting adventures and perils in the far West." His rifle exhibition was well done but he failed in the glass-ball shooting due, he said, to the light. "[T]he bow-and-arrow practice of the Indians rather shamed his efforts in that line. . . . [T]he whole performance was rather rough and disjointed." Cody was having an off day, but the next evening, "the performance went off much more smoothly and was received with even greater delight."[52]

The *Spirit of the Times*, however, contradicted any notion of good houses, reporting Cody encountered poor business, particularly in Charlotte, North Carolina.[53] This may have been due to yellow fever sickness widespread across the South at the time. Business manager C. E. Blanchett advised the *New York Clipper* that "he does not think it safe or wise for parties to venture into the afflicted States before December."[54] According to the memoirs of Dr. H. A. Gant, the plague struck the mid-South from August to November. Casualties in Memphis, Tennessee, the hardest hit community, numbered over five thousand. Lack of knowledge about the fever or how to properly treat it produced terror in a community when a case was diagnosed, and citizens stayed in their homes, fearful of contagion.[55]

After the "well received and highly enjoyed" appearance in Savannah, Cody anticipated "a big harvest of silver" during Atlanta's fair week. His troupers, however, fearful of the disease, refused to travel any farther in the South. "Bill argued, stormed, persuaded and threatened in vain."[56] Reluctantly, he canceled the remainder of his southern dates and headed northward to Wilmington, Delaware. Even though the crowd was "the largest of the season," and the $963 in ticket sales prove it, the critic dismissed the play as "trashy." After the drama, the Indians showed their dexterity at bow-and-arrow shooting. "If the plains Indians could shoot no better than those who appeared on the Opera House stage, the buffalo was in no danger of extinction," sniffed the critic from the *Every Evening*. Live demonstrations depended on a number of variable factors—lighting, equipment, and performers' moods and health. Cody gave an exhibition of rifle marksmanship for the finale, "which young and old agreed was really wonderful, the best feature of the whole show." No one could ascertain with certainty why, for some performances, Cody's shooting was off the mark and why, in others, he consistently hit the bull's-eye. His rare misses could be chalked up to ill health or audience distractions. On the occasions when he did not shoot well, a critic was likely to scoff at his marksman's reputation.

During the early months of the season, Cody had commissioned author Prentiss Ingraham to write another new play for him, and by November 2, it was ready for production. *Knight of the Plains; or, Buffalo Bill's Best Trail* debuted on the New Haven stage. The brand-new play deserved bigger and better billing, so Cody now advertised his troupe as a "Monster Combination of 22 Artists." Professor J. G. Rampone's Silver Cornet Band and Orchestra supplied the music and led a "Grand Street Parade" on the morning of each performance. Everyone walked except Cody who rode at the head of the marchers in a barouche. The Indians always drew large crowds, looking "Indiany enough, . . . painted like a new barn, frescoed and trimmed in different colors, with ornamental cornices, and all that sort of thing."[57]

The cast of *Knight of the Plains* included a villain "aided by minor rascals, a mercenary father, a distressed maiden, (which the villain still pursued) and a champion of right and rescuer of innocence," none other than Buffalo Bill. He assumed four different characters, portraying all of them in perfect disguises. In the melodramatic tradition, "[t]here was much drawing of revolvers and general denunciation of scoundrels and sundry impressive tableaux of manliness triumphant. . . . The gambling house scene included robbery and all sorts of playing and cheating and terminat[ed] in a duel. In the last act the villain is disposed of in a bowie knife fight."[58]

Details are scarce, but we can somewhat piece together the story. The curtain rose on a scene representing a prairie sunset. A herd of buffaloes stampede into an Indian camp where Buffalo Bill's friend Red (or War) Eagle is mistaken for a bitter enemy and held prisoner. Pawnee and Nez Perce Indians add a "spice of reality" by performing war dances "and other antics." Cody makes his entrance and "compels the rapt attention of the audience." The second act takes place in an urban drawing room and introduces the heroine, Rose Melton, whom Buffalo Bill had met and fallen in love with some time previously. Villain Ralf Royston plans to kill Buffalo Bill to assure his own safety and fortune. The scene shifts to a Cheyenne gambling house for the third act and features Cody's shooting. At the finale, a "lifelike" representation of a gang of robbers stopping a stagecoach "adds much to the effect of the scene." Royston suffers a knife wound to the heart at the hands of Buffalo Bill. Forgetting her hatred of her husband, Nellie flings herself on him and cries, whereupon Royston rises on his elbow and, cursing her, plunges a knife into her heart. The two lie side by side in death.

Near their bodies, Buffalo Bill and Rose Melton pledge their love. At that tender moment, the old Jew cries out, "Mowly Hoses!"

"The scene is extremely extravagant, and really ridiculous," thought the *Dubuque Herald* critic, but Nellie Jones acting as Rose Melton was superb and Lydia Denier "could hardly be improved as Wild Nellie. Being the wife of 'Royston,' wronged and deserted by him, her strong love turned to hate, and living the same wild life as her male companions, she carried the sympathies of the audience with her until her tragic death at the hand of her husband."[59]

Cody, by now savvy in stage ventures, realized though blood and thunder plays are apt to be satisfactory, even youths fresh from reading dime novels could not condone the indiscriminate slaughter of villains. So his plays "are seldom seriously overdone. The plots, the expressions, the dress, the gambling scenes, are all natural."[60] Another journalist surmised the audience was disenchanted with *Knight of the Plains* because they expected to see western men in buckskin; instead Cody walked the stage in disguise much of the evening in "the habiliments of Eastern civilization." The audience wanted "blud" in their border dramas and, since Cody stabbed and shot fewer than a whole tribe of Indians, "the people did not get what they expected."[61]

One critic commended individual actors, but in the end, Cody was the "whole show in himself."[62] Ten months down the road, another reporter would criticize him for that very thing, affirming the old saw about not being able to please all the people all the time. "The play is too much of a one man production to suit the public. . . . He does not allow his support to make any hits, which is to be regretted."[63] Bookings next led him to Watertown, New York, in mid-January 1879, but snowstorms prevented trains from running. Cody may have just sat back, waited out the weather, and counted his money. He had so far "made $135,000 with his blood and thunder drama."[64]

Drama critics had adopted a well-ordered format in their reviews. They usually mentioned the audience first, commenting for newspaper readers on whether patrons filled the house, including the dress circle and parquet, or if it mainly consisted of youngsters in the gallery. The next item was a description of the drama itself. Words like "sensational," "incongruous," and "thrilling" described the play; additional details illustrated specific scenes or tableaux. "Well-placed" and "above average" portrayed the action for those unable to attend. Supporting cast came in for their share of plaudits and then the writer usually proclaimed Cody to be the "finest example of a frontiersman scout" or "not a very good actor." Along the way, the reviewer might drop an unexpected tidbit revealing for the reader just a little more about the production.

The following tidbits demonstrate the point. A Wilkes-Barre journalist, in commenting on the marksmanship exhibition, noted he was "pleased to see that the objects being shot at were no longer placed upon the head and in the hands of a human being." The accident in Baltimore had unnerved Cody enough to resolve not to fire where a person might be harmed. Also, the *Titusville Morning Herald* revealed that not only were the scenery and props made especially for Cody, but also that he included a Concord coach and four horses onstage. Cody recalled they hired an authentic coach at times but generally used a light and portable property coach that could be taken apart and put up readily yet still look real.[65]

When the combination performed in Cleveland, Ohio, in February 1879, Cody talked to a reporter about the city being the home of his father's family. He answered several questions about his home in North Platte where his wife and children waited for him. The journalist also inquired about his cattle ranch and then about the Indians.

> Well, lately they are becoming rather troublesome[.] . . .
> [I]t is a mistaken idea to think the Indians are a treacherous
> race; they are peaceable and true if let alone, but they know
> that in fighting with the white men they are outnumbered
> and therefore they seize any advantage they can. The fact is,
> the Indians have not been treated rightly by the American
> Government: they have had promises made them that were
> never fulfilled, and this has angered them. . . . The Indians
> should not even be blamed for these cattle and horse raids we
> hear so much about, because they are merely retaliating. . . .
> Although I have had many a tough fight with the red man my
> sympathy is with him entirely, because he has been ill-used
> and trampled on by those whose duty it was to protect him.[66]

In his autobiography, Cody clarified just how much he identified with the Indians' sorrow at their loss of freedom. He believed the Indian was the "real American." No "scheming politician" or "short-sighted administration of law" should infringe upon his rights; therefore men who desire to share Indian land should see that he is dealt with "justly and fairly." In his public pronouncements, Cody displayed a more enlightened attitude; he abandoned the dime-novel posturing he had earlier adopted and more closely reflected the view of contemporary reformers.

The annual Lake Mohonk Conference of Friends of the Indian, which held its first meeting in 1883, served as a forum where liberals discussed methods for improving the Indians' condition. The assembly moved to change federal policy, beseeching the government to abolish reservations and distribute tribal lands to individual Indians. In 1887, Congress passed an act proposed by influential politician Senator Henry L. Dawes that provided for the allotment of lands to reservation Indians and extended the protection of United States law over them. However, much of the land found its way into the hands of white speculators, while Indians were left with inadequate compensation. Like many good intentions, the Dawes Act failed to produce the result for which it was designed: the assimilation and "civilizing" of the indigenous people.[67]

Other "Assorted Indians" along with "Scouts and Trappers" were the combination's most recently formed competition. In its February 8 issue, the *New York Dramatic Mirror* reported that six boys living on the west side of Erie, Pennsylvania, wrote and performed a four-act drama, *Last of the Pawnees; or, Buffalo Bill's Best Shot*. Aged eleven to thirteen, they were the youngest of the Buffalo Bill Combination imitators. Their mothers, after paying entry fees totaling $2.82, gathered to watch the youngsters in their first thespian roles. Meanwhile in Chillicothe, Ohio, in *May Cody*, the real performers failed to satisfy audiences, and the Indians left Cody and returned home.[68]

For the most part, Cody proved to be the strongest drawing card many theatres had seen in several seasons. Nearly all audiences and most critics wholeheartedly praised the production. Despite occasional lukewarm reviews in Pennsylvania and Ohio, Cody had contracted to take the program once again to the West Coast. In mid-March, he left the eastern stages and headed for the sunny climate of California.

CHAPTER SEVEN

*Sir Cody, Knight
of the Plains*

How the boys' eyes gleam and shine from the gallery; how their
young hearts swell and long for Injuns and highwaymen, and the
punishment of villains; how, in fact, they all yearn to be Buffalo Bills.

—*Fort Wayne Daily News*, October 17, 1879

"CALIFORNIA OR BUST!" MAY HAVE BEEN THE MOTTO OF GOLD-SEEKING
forty-niners, but the gold Cody had in mind lay in the pockets of theatre
patrons. Characteristically, his intuition about where his plays would attract
audiences proved as much on the mark as his sharpshooting.

May Cody drew excellent business at the California Theatre in San
Francisco. At first, the proprietor was angry when manager Barton Hill
signed Cody, thinking he would be a poor draw, but first-night receipts
totaled $2,300, and the week's run brought in over $9,000.[1] Typically, the
overwhelming majority of any audiences were the "gallery gods." Hill
remarked to two newspapermen during intermission at one first-night
performance, "I don't care much what you chaps say about the new show
tomorrow. It has already made a hit with the gods." Frank Mayo, the popular actor who played Davy Crockett for nearly a quarter century, knew that,

in many theatres, "[t]he owners are those d— little rascals in the gallery, of whom, however, I say not one derogatory word." Some producers considered the "small boys, street cleaners, rag-pickers, plug-uglies and ragamuffins" essential to the success of the play. The "ascent of the gods to Mount Olympus" before each performance was a trek, beginning about half an hour before curtain time. Like the actors, the youngsters used a special entrance. Up a long stairway, they trooped uncomplainingly to the highest galleries where friends wrangled with friends for front seats.[2]

Regardless how the gods cheered, the critics would fill their columns with personal judgments. "Although this style of drama may not tend to elevate the standard of the stage, the management would be foolish not to cater to such public taste if it can fill his coffers with the presentation of Buffalo Bill and his Indians in their thrilling feats, rather than lose money with a Union Square or any other excellent and talented combination that fails to draw," wrote the *San Francisco Chronicle*.[3] The *Daily Alta* pointed out technical errors in the script: "For John D. Lee to address Brigham Young as 'Holy Father,' is simply ridiculous. The scene in the Endowment House has not the least semblance to the truth. . . . But to go into any real criticism on *May Cody* is like breaking a butterfly on the wheel, and we desist."[4]

One editor titled a column "Across the Continent Comes the Testimony of the Greatest Attraction of the Season" and filled it with critics' comments from New York to Oakland. One noticed that, even as star, Cody took the part of the grizzly bear and "makes an excellent bruin." Another compared him to Othello who "gained in the eyes of Desdemona when he recounted his tales of danger by flood and field."[5]

After seeing Cody's handsome looks, the *Argonaut*'s female journalist wondered what Frank Mayo wouldn't give for the "genuine frontier accent which hangs upon the lips of Buffalo Bill and will not away." She marveled at "how transparently the consciousness of the man shows all through it. When he shakes his head like a young bison, you felt that he is conscious of his Absolom [*sic*] locks; when he sits on his horse and strains his eye to look over the prairie, you can realize that every detail of the costume, every pose of the figure, has been studied." However, she worried that such pandering to an audience makes him an "apostate of nature. But the gallery likes it, the people like it, and I know Buffalo Bill likes it."[6]

The San Francisco stringer for the *New York Dramatic Mirror* reported that audiences packed the theatre to the roof every night. According to the write-up, a California audience was a hard one to please; even celebrated actors often played to meager houses. "To the winds with boasted aesthetics, to the marines tell the story of Juliet"—what the public wanted was "poetic Buffalo Bill with his handsome figure, his natural grace, supple form and ignorant ease."[7] The critic couldn't understand it. However, the female journalist could. She admitted she had "looked on many a play" and had concluded "we had never met with such a wealth of incident in any one of these plays as in 'May Cody' nor any actor who so thoroughly played con amore as Buffalo Bill."[8]

The *Chronicle* seemed surprised by the "tone of art . . . given to it by its surroundings and accessories. Nobody needs to be told that Mr. Cody has sufficient opinion of himself, his reputation and his talent, to assume the heroic on his own responsibility." He is "the exciting exponent of chivalry, of grace, of heroism and indomitable courage. He blanches no more before the *haut ton* of the first circles in New York society than he does when General Harney's army of supers present their carbines at his manly breast."[9]

An actor named Bock played John D. Lee "mavelously [*sic*] as a Protean artist" and showed "a facility in changing himself that one scarcely credits to the Mountain Meadow massacre Mormon." In one performance, the revolver Cody used did not go off. Bock, his intended victim, fell "dead" anyway, and no one thought more about it until the curtain came down. Cody, "who was 'a little off,'" explained he had inadvertently replaced his stage revolver with the "howitzer" he carried in private life. Just as he was about to fire, it occurred to him there might be a ball cartridge under the hammer, so he decided not to shoot. Bock was not amused and refused to play the part thereafter "unless he could be allowed to personally examine the pistol."[10]

In another instance, when H. Thompson's role as officer called for him to arrest Buffalo Bill, he exuberantly seized Cody as though he were an "obstinate drunk, and marched him away in a manner not compatible with the star's dignity." Cody berated him behind the scenes, whereupon the "rather exhilarated" Thompson claimed he would "clean out the *Knight of the Plains*, Indians and all." Management, fearing his devotion to the role a bit too realistic, asked him to leave.[11]

Pleased with their West Coast success, the combination headed to Carson, Nevada, where Cody penned a letter to Jack Crawford detailing his accomplishments and barely resisting the impulse to boast.[12]

My Dear Jack, . . . I would have answered at once from Frisco but I was on a hell of a toot. . . . I have just finished a big engagement at the California Theatre My share was nearly $6.000.00 I am playing to fine business on the road. . . . Am glad you have such fine prosperity. but realy I think you had better stayed with me when I offered you $200.00 a month and all expenses. But I hope you will come out rich. . . . Wishing you success, I am as ever your friend W. F. Cody. Buffalo Bill[13]

By early May 1879, Buffalo Bill's combination was wrapping up the season. They played *Knight of the Plains* in Salt Lake City where the *Deseret News* did not recommend the performance because at times the audience could not hear what was said, "and the play 'dragged' considerably as well." If the journalist was aware that Cody's alternative drama portrayed Mormons in an unfavorable light, he did not remark on it, but it is significant that Cody repeated *Knights* for the second performance rather than switch to *May Cody*. The critic thought the "points of merit will be brought out better when the actors become better acquainted with their parts." However, being the end of the season, they would likely not improve much. The actors were not unfamiliar with their parts but perhaps merely tired of them.[14]

Throughout the season, Cody had been working on his autobiography, *The Life of Hon. William F. Cody, Known as Buffalo Bill, the Famous Hunter, Scout and Guide*. At the end of June, it was published by Frank E. Bliss of the American Publishing Company in Hartford, Connecticut, whose father, Elisha Bliss, was Mark Twain's publisher. The book sold for $2 in cloth and $2.50 in leather and claimed prominence as one of the first sold by subscription method, that is, by book agents going door to door. Scholars have speculated on its authorship. Prentiss Ingraham, with whom Cody was associated around this time, may be a possible ghostwriter, but Cody's biographer Don Russell does not think so. Too many embarrassing stories are included for it to have been written by an admirer, one being Cody's joining the army while intoxicated. Errors in dates and spellings also point to it being Cody's own work; the errors also could have resulted from the printer not being able to read his handwriting. In a few instances, he exaggerates or uses melodramatic language in telling a story, easy enough to do for someone involved daily in melodrama.[15]

Cody's book was sold at all performances of his stage show. A month after publication, the *Cheyenne Daily Leader* called it "a most reliable and succinct history of the later Indian wars of the north. . . . It is unusually interesting to read of the deeds of one who lived in our day and generation, and who may be called upon at any time to again take the field against the

Indians as a scout."[16] On the last page, Cody wrote of his expectations to take his plays to England, "where I purpose to go next season on a theatrical tour, having been urged to do so by my many friends abroad." The time had not yet come for Cody to take his program across the Atlantic, but his repeated assertions to do so prove he was certainly thinking about it.[17]

Despite the book's revenue and his remuneration as combination star, Cody was juggling finances, or at least he wanted friends to think so. Past acquaintances emerged from the woodwork to ask for money and some share in fame now that his theatrical star had risen and his coffers were fuller than they had ever been. Cody was a charitable man, but after generous loans and gifts, even he had his limits.

On June 24, he replied to Crawford who had written to ask for a loan. "I am hard pushed for money just at present," Cody wrote. "[M]y expenses this summer have been heavy and more I have lost heavy in cattle. besides losing 61 head of horses stollen by the Indians. I bought 100 head of mares the other day and it straped me of funds for the present. But as soon as I can get hold of some money. am not afraid to trust you." On Independence Day, he wrote to Jack again: "[L]oosing our horses and so many cattle this season its crippled us considerable. but we don't loose our grip. although we will be pressed for funds until we ship beeves. Or I get to playing to some big houses."[18]

Another old pal, Major "Buckskin Sam" Hall approached Cody about a job in the combination. Cody and Ingraham had met him in New York and persuaded him to write up his Civil War and Texas Ranger experiences for Beadle, the dime-novel publisher. After the publication of his first story, "Kit Carson, Jr.; or, The Crack Shot of the West," Hall's novelettes and short sketches were somewhat successful. Cody, however, reiterated his decision to be his combination's sole plainsman. All the other frontiersmen he had partnered with soon left to start their own companies after seeing how profitably it was done Cody-style. He replied to Sam,

> In regard to you going on the boards again. I must think of it I have no part in either my dramas that would be suitable for you to play as I did say that I would never again have another Scout or western man with me. . . . For just as soon as they see their names in print a few times they git the big head and want to start a company of their own. I will name a few. Wild Bill Texas Jack John Nelson Oregon Bill Kit Carson Capt. Jack all busted flat before they were out a month and wanted to come back.[19]

Even without Sam Hall, the combination had grown larger, and by mid-July 1879, it had twenty-four performers. Cody started his theatrical season a few months early and was appearing to sold-out crowds. After Denver, where N. C. Forrester's dramatic company took the stock parts and then accompanied the combination on its tour, the troupe played in Colorado Springs and Pueblo. The Burgess brothers—Eddie, known as Pe-risk-y-la-shar, and Charles who served as interpreter—continued their affiliation. White Eagle, a Pawnee chief, called white men "tekittowe" meaning "boss" and invented a new word after riding the railroad from Denver to Georgetown. As near as anyone could interpret, "temarecksty" meant "poison."[20]

The troupe alternately presented slightly modified versions of *May Cody* and *Knight of the Plains*. Scant details record the opening scene with War Eagle. There's "[a] report, a blinding flash and several feathers are clipped from his headdress," then Cody makes his entrance. Such a histrionic effect set the critics scribbling. The *Pueblo Chieftain* predicted the citizenry would turn out en masse to greet this "first-class entertainment." Those who did not would be missing the "rarest treat of the season."[21]

Central City's *Daily Register Call* saw it through different eyes:

> As might have been expected, the opera house was filled to
> overflowing last night to see the great scout of the plains, his
> wild Indians, black bears, buffaloes and jack rabbits, all of
> which the flaming posters on the dead walls announced would
> be present. But the small boy and the lover of western romance
> were disappointed. There were no buffalos, no black bears,
> no wild Indians; but instead a third-rate dramatic company,
> playing at some sort of a sickly play without point or pith.
> There was not a passable artist in the crowd, and if there had
> been there was nothing in the play to bring him or her out.[22]

"The flaming posters" refer to the colorful publicity announcing the upcoming performance. In 2002, during restoration of a building in Jamestown, New York, workmen uncovered an extraordinarily large billboard Cody's publicity team had pasted onto the wood sheathing. The ten- by twenty-six-foot color advertisement had been bricked over soon enough that the poster advertising the March 14, 1878, performance of *May Cody* was relatively intact. At its first exposure to weather, however, the 124-year-old paper began to disintegrate and blow away. Volunteers quickly and carefully collected the fragments, some as tiny as jigsaw puzzle pieces, for preservation. The colorful images recreate the narrative, showing Cody on horseback waving his hat to enthusiastic crowds who are waving back. Images of Indians and other scenes from the drama depict the Mountain Meadows Massacre, while John Y. Nelson stands close by, rifle in hand.[23]

The Jamestown discovery provides us with a fine example of how Cody's narrative posters had become increasingly sophisticated, and the impact on potential audiences was no doubt well worth the probable $15–$20 printing and posting cost. Even had the poster only showed Cody alone in a scene, it would have told a story of the Wild West. After his death, the *New York Times* realized "there was something essentially poetical and artistic about the man." The various businesses Cody worked with over the years had one factor in common—"the indomitable will and presence of Cody himself." It was this will and presence that accounted for the magnificent posters.[24]

Cody arrived in Davenport, Iowa, at the end of August where he expected new cast members to join him. Besides the professionals from New York, a band of Indian chiefs from the Ponca and Pawnee reservations were coming. While he awaited them, he took a drive out to his old home at Walnut Grove to visit his brother's grave, then returned by way of LeClaire and explored the place where he was born.[25]

Although Cody could rely on his competent management team, the responsibility of successful, money-making tours was his. Decisions about the drama, the supporting players, and even the tour circuit and the size of publicity posters were his to resolve. Gone were the amateur productions resembling *Scouts of the Prairie*. Gone was his association with fellow scouts who turned vainglorious after a few months. Whether the critics praised or roasted the performance, audiences were crazy for him. He was trouping with professional actors, genuine American Indians, a staff of publicists, advance men, and stock tenders. He had performed in the East, the South, and the West and had considered more than once taking the show abroad. As a result of his popularity, border dramas became more acceptable to cultured audiences. In the years after the Civil War, the status of actors also grew; they were now often redefined as "gifted artists."[26]

Consequently, when men like Buckskin Sam wrote again pleading to be part of his success, Cody had to turn them down. By mid-career, he realized an artist projects a good stage presence, and references to his needing to "brace himself up" with drink or of bellying up to the bar are rare. From Davenport, Cody wrote to Sam. "I was about to place you in a very

A Buffalo Bill Combination poster, recently uncovered in Jamestown, NY, advertises the March 14, 1878, performance. © 2007 Reg Lenna Civic Center, Jamestown, NY; photo credit: Robert Knobloch.

responsable position. But I would have made a fearful mistake as I see you are like most of the prairie boys. Tangle foot gets away with you. And I will have no one with me thats liable to let whisky get away with him in this business a man *must* be perfectly reliable and *sober*."[27]

A few years down the road, Cody would be on the receiving end of a similar slight. In the early months of the Wild West show, his partner, Nate Salsbury, traveled to St. Louis to assess the show's preparations. Even before they met, Salsbury had watched Cody's career and recognized something special in him. But now he may well have turned on his heel, disgusted when he found Cody "surrounded by a lot of harpies called old timers who were getting as drunk as he at his expense. . . . He had taken a plug hat from someone in the crowd, and jammed it on his head, and as his hair was long

and thick in those days, a more ridiculous figure could not be imagined."[28] In plainsman style, Cody admitted he drank as freely as the next fellow, describing euphemistically those times "I had been partaking too freely of 'tanglefoot'" in the "biggest beer jollification I ever had the misfortune to attend."[29] With responsibility for the show resting on his shoulders and the realization that as a star he was accountable, Cody sobered.

Fifteen hundred people attended the September 4 performance in Clinton, Iowa, prompting the *Daily Herald* to ask, "Why is this thus?" Contemporary Emile Zola, "the French apostle of realism," argued that "the masses care more for sensation than for art of any kind." Zola's philosophy suggested a play should be "a fragment of existence."[30] Though melodrama dominated late nineteenth-century theatre, realism as a critical aspect of characterization and performance had begun to emerge. Realists objected to the simplification and idealization of melodrama. They insisted drama "could and should deal with issues of vital interest in a natural and honest manner" and employ the language of real people. Critics lauded Cody's dramas for being realistic, but the truth of western life was that white men did not go around shooting dozens of Indians at every opportunity. Realism also demanded a different, "more understated, more nuanced, and more evocative" acting style. Cody got it, and critics noticed his improved elocution and stage presence. When he appeared, he "gave some natural bits of acting that eastern professionals would do well to copy." Unlike professional actors who "throw too many 'stage' attitudes into their business to make their acting of western life natural," Cody, one critic found, is "a very natural and quiet actor."[31]

While the same moral melodramatic choices remained, the goal was to have "ordinary characters engaged in normal daily lives rather than . . . extraordinary characters caught up in an idealized world."[32] Cody's newest drama headed that way. His ambition was for audiences to leave the theatre believing they had witnessed authentic frontier encounters. All the time he was acting he was aware, and the audience was surely aware, that he was dramatizing deeds he had actually done. By bringing in *real* Indians, *real* horses, *real* plains life, Cody transmitted a sense of the West no other actor in a border drama had been able to do. Zola claimed he was

> waiting for someone to put a man of flesh on the stage, taken from reality, scientifically analyzed, and described without one lie. I am waiting for someone to rid us of fictitious characters, of these symbols of virtue and vice which have no worth as human data. I am waiting for environment to determine the characters and the characters to act according to the logic of facts combined with logic of their own disposition.[33]

Zola need wait no more.

The *Daily Arkansas Gazette* grasped Cody's role in the myth of the West. "Every nation has an actor—a play which represents itself." As western frontiersman, he nicely fulfilled the need for a homegrown, mythic hero. "England has her dramatic dukes and kings, and Austria her Philips. All nations have plays and characters peculiar to themselves. The true—the original representation of America is wild plains and uninhabited forests. A hero of these scenes is purely American and his name is Buffalo Bill." Cody was called "one of nature's noblemen"—he was not only the hero of the play but also the hero of the "broad drama, written by nature and by fate." A paradigm of realism, his defining moment had come in 1876 with the reenactment of events in which he had actually participated. It didn't hurt that he possessed "style, independence and the reckless gesture."[34]

Cody could only shake his head and wonder at what one Clinton journalist thought. Playing against circus man Dan Rice, Cody showed profits double the amount of Rice's three performances. Yet the critic condemned the play, speaking of "Indians being sacrificed, horrid scenes, blood curdling deeds, and other things" not even part of the play. Cody assumed the reporter had not attended the theatre at all, but had "written the criticism from his fertile imagination."[35]

The full houses the combination had that autumn, the brisk trade, and rich fall fairs led Cody to observe that "the dark days are over and prosperity rests upon the face of man and nature." Having more money in their pockets did not deter some from attempts at freeloading. Railroad men, to whom traveling troupes paid huge annual sums, thought free admission their prerogative and brought along their extended families. If refused tickets gratis, the "baggage smashers" got even. Young boys, often "ragged dirty and saucy," claimed to be members of the press sent to scoop a story. One urchin arrived at the ticket seller with one eye closed, asking to be admitted for half price since he could only see half the show. So great was the desire of "the bummers" for free admission that some improvised a ladder and raised it to the windows. One boy tried to get in with a glass of water, saying it was for a lady who had fainted. Cody had a soft spot for them and let the imaginative fellows in free—and they "were given good seats too."[36] But, before each performance, management searched the hall, backstage, and dressing rooms for concealed, nonpaying adults.

Knight of the Plains was an apt title, one columnist decided, because no one held a better right to the phrase than Cody, having long been distinguished as the "Prince of Prairiemen."[37] The cavalier tradition was alive and well on the frontier. Cody belonged to a society of scouts who lived by a chivalric code of honor—fierce in battle but honorable to their foes and courteous to and humble before those under their protection. As a fearless and competent chief of scouts, he earned the respect of the men he led as well as that of the officers under whom he served, many of whom singled him out for his intelligence, endurance, and coolness in battle. His familiarity with the natural surroundings enhanced his leadership. Like many of the plains brotherhoods who adopted eccentric or ostentatious attire, Cody had once showed up on the first day of a hunt "dressed in a new suit of light buckskin, trimmed along the seams with fringes of the same material," wearing with it a "crimson shirt handsomely ornamented on the bosom" and a soft broad sombrero. As Cody knew well, sometimes clothes did make the man. Mounted on a white horse, his long hair flowing in the wind, Cody looked and felt every bit the knight of old when the horse had been an integral part of chivalry—indeed, the word itself derives from the French for horse: "cheval."

American novelist Mark Twain recognized the air of a chivalric hero in his 1906 story titled "A Horse's Tale":

> I am Buffalo Bill's horse. . . . He is over six feet, is young, hasn't an ounce of waste flesh, is straight, graceful, springy in his motions, quick as a cat, and has a handsome face, and black hair dangling down on his shoulders, and is beautiful to look at; and nobody is braver than he is, and nobody is stronger, except myself. Yes, a person that doubts that he is fine to see should see him in his beaded buckskins, on my back and his rifle peeping above his shoulder, chasing a hostile trail, with me going like the wind and his hair streaming out behind.[38]

Playwright Prentiss Ingraham, who bestowed the descriptive label of "knight" on Cody, was a Mississippi-born gentleman. He grew up imbued with the southern chivalric code, which included dueling as the most public expression of a man's honor and courage. After the Civil War, Ingraham began his literary career in London writing satiric sketches of the British social scene, but success eluded him. Returning to America, he continued writing and completed over six hundred novels and four hundred novelettes; more than two hundred of these works featured Cody as hero. His ability to get words down on paper extremely fast "did not allow for niceties of plot, neither did it permit subtlety of character. Indians are invariably treacherous, foreigners foolish, beautiful women good." Nevertheless, after reading his books, real cowboys began to act and dress the way he described them.[39]

Because easterners read a lot of the yellowbacked books churned out by sensationalizers like Buntline and Ingraham, authors based western

Prentiss Ingraham. Courtesy Buffalo Bill Historical Center (P.69.143), Cody, WY.

adventures on eastern preconceptions and expectations. Writers romanti-
cized characters according to established conventions, often exaggerating
a few biographical details of a real person, like Davy Crockett, Kit Carson,
or William Cody, to create a man of heroic proportions. Idealized western
heroes did not smoke, drink, or swear. They excelled at the frontier skills of
trailing, marksmanship, and hand-to-hand combat with wild animals and
Indians. The fictional frontier character was very clever; his enemies were
never able to outwit him, though literary convention required they out-
number him in unreasonable ratios. The stories created an overall impression that, west of the Mississippi, disputes were resolved violently, and only
the intelligence and superior strength of the handsome hero could rees-
tablish order. Despite its being no more dangerous than the slums of many
eastern cities, easterners still believed the West was a "dangerous, untried
place, where violence was the norm."[40] Newspapers were full of reports of
ongoing Indian wars; the legendary gunfighter Wild Bill Hickok had himself been assassinated; the James gang and other outlaws like them flirted
with death by committing brazen daylight armed robberies. Violence flour-
ished in the wilds of the West, but also on the eastern stages with some of
the same participants. Indians in war paint who had killed soldiers on the
Little Bighorn battlefield now decorated their faces with grease paint and
fought sham battles in front of footlights.

For all of his censure of Cody, Jack Crawford had been in touch and asked
his permission to produce one of his dramas. Arriving in Cincinnati, Cody
found the letter waiting for him and immediately sat down to reply. "My
Dear Jack, I will write to Texas Jack about 'Life on the Border' Drama for my
part you are welcome to it to play it where you please and its the *boss* border
drama. . . . My business this season is something wonderful larger than the
first seasons with Buntline. I cleared $1,800 last week in St. Louis."[41]

Permission granted, Crawford now needed money to produce the drama.
He did not want to throw in his lot with Cody again but was not above repeating his request for a loan. On October 5, from Philadelphia, Cody, despite his
claim of large profits, refused him again:

> My Dear Jack[,] . . . I can't just now spare $200.00. I am doing
> an immense business. But I go back to New York to one of the
> leading theatre and I furnish company Costumes and propertys
> and am going to a big expense to have them all got up new and
> put on my new Drama in grand style. I have made a tremedious

hit in Major Burt's drama. It is far a head of anything of the kind ever produced. Wishing you success I am yours truly Bill[42]

The combination arrived in Fort Wayne, Indiana, at six o'clock in the morning on October 18, 1879, for a performance that night. There was not much time for the actors to catch up on sleep before one of the first scheduled parades with Cody and the Indian chiefs was due to begin. Realizing the advertising potential of having his actors walk about the streets was one thing, but Cody, with his knack for knowing what people wanted and giving it to them, appreciated the impact circus parades had as "massive moving show windows" and copied them as one more publicity medium. One of his partners in the Wild West, "Pawnee Bill" Lillie, recognized that Cody's "two big fort[e]s in the show business was his personality and his ability to capitalize it from an advertising standpoint." Cody understood early on how the performers were their own best advertisement. Posters and newspaper ads promised genuine scouts and Indians, and here they were.[43]

The *Ohio State Journal* observed that the quiet Indians might actually be responsible for the levitation of drama. Because the "Aboriginal" would rather act than talk and, because he values the influence of dress, "he seldom regards [this] as the full duty of man." He impresses spectators with an air of tranquility of which some other artists "are lamentably deficient." While not averse to makeup, he "never attempts to make art take the place of nature." If he should volunteer for a benefit, he is not likely to play Romeo, thus saving the audience from a familiar tale; when he appears, it will be in a definite novelty. "[Make r]oom for the Indian," recommended the journalist, "even if he should draw the scalping-knife upon the histrionic battle-field, it is not certain that he will hurt the public as much as he may benefit it."[44]

As Catlin had proved with his traveling exhibit, ritual and art were complementary aspects of an Indian's makeup. Foreshadowing their role in the Wild West show, the combination Indians acted as themselves in traditional performances. But, perhaps the question is not, after all, how well did the Indians *act* onstage, but how did Cody manage to *get* them onstage at all? Aside from their roles as his friends in *May Cody*, their main duty was to serve as foils for Cody's vision of the West, which, for most audiences, abounded in Indian war dances, bow-and-arrow shooting and, in the end, white conquest over red savages. Yet, only thirteen months after Cody had reveled in his revengeful killing of Yellow Hair, he was able to

Akron, OH, ad for the October 28, 1879, performance.

hire real Indians to travel with his combination. Nightly, they performed as paradigms of those the white man defeated on the western plains. Without reflecting negatively on their culture, they were able to present themselves being defeated in the drama.

Biographer Bobby Bridger believes the answer lies in Cody's youthful experiences with Indians, how some of them became his lifelong friends even when circumstances of the Indian Wars cast them as mortal enemies. "Cody shared a destiny with the buffalo and Plains Indians"; the three "are symbiotically related both metaphorically and in reality." The Indians had been victorious warriors at Little Bighorn and recognized that Cody warranted the same honor. That they willingly participated in his melodramas implies, as Bridger suggests, "either the skill of a master salesman, or complete Lakota confidence in a trusted friend." They realized instinctively that Cody had their best interests in mind.[45]

The journalist's opinion that the Indian would not hurt the public did not quell one man's fears. An Englishman of the *H.M.S. Pinafore* troupe, which was staying in the same hotel as Cody's combination, was "'just over' and wholly green as to American ways, Indians and such like." He shared a room with a practical joker who persuaded Charles Burgess to "play Injun." Burgess threw a blanket over his shoulders, tiptoed into their room after they had gone to bed and swept his long hair into the victim's face.

"'It's one of those d—d Indians! . . . Murder! Help! Murder!' he cried.

"'Will never play Pinafore no more?'"

"'Never!'"

When Burgess shouted for his tomahawk, the Englishman screamed so loudly, the jokesters were alarmed and fled. In the end, the Englishman took the joke kindly but requested a new roommate.[46]

After Ohio and Tennessee, the troupe wowed crowds in the central regions of Arkansas. Cody steered his combination south, westward into Texas, then turned around and headed through Louisiana and Alabama. The combination showed phenomenal success—so much so that Cody took out ads calling for "satirical managers [to] pause and meditate."

"Behold and Wonder!!!" the ad read.
Figures Never Lie! Read One Week's Receipts!
Wheeling, W. Va. Matinee and Night $1,092.80
Zanesville, Ohio 614.00
Newark, Ohio 435.00

Columbus, Ohio 1,240.90
Springfield, Ohio 664.35
Dayton, Ohio 936.75

_____

Total for Week 4,983.80
Expenses for Week. 1,480.75

_____

Profit from Week 3,503.05
Ten Weeks on the Road and Total Receipts. . . $31,985.00
Total Expenses for Ten Weeks 13,474.00

_____

Cleared on Ten Weeks. . . . . 18,511.00[47]

The ostentatious announcement of wealth was one feature of the Gilded Age. Cody's boasting of his profits may be exaggerated for effect, but his Nashville, Tennessee, profit of $1,080, "the largest by nearly $100 taken in for two seasons past," should come as no surprise as "the galleries were black with people. . . . What the traveling agents would style 'im-mense.'" Nashville critics thought the play lukewarm; but the striking tableaux brought down the house. Even the "superb charger" Cody rode in on acquitted itself "with as much credit as any of the rest of the company. Buffalo Bill has a fine stage presence and, with the exception of a little of the stiffness and elocutionary deficiencies which mark the amateur, is not a bad actor."[48]

A Little Rock, Arkansas, *Gazette* reporter caught him in the wings between acts. "This stage business was no doubt harder to learn than the more natural dash of the plains?" he asked. Cody's positive reply was followed with a question about how many Indians he had killed. In evasion, Cody deferred to General Sheridan who "says that I have killed more than any white man living." Comparing the salaries of scout and actor, Cody, again enhancing the numbers, mentioned he "got $5 a day while in active service. I was always poor, and never able to raise as much as $500. I managed to make about enough to support my family." In fact, Cody, as chief scout, did fairly well for a man in his situation at the time. Still, the stage was much more profitable, he found, "in ten weeks, at one time, I made $18,000."

The journalist then asked Cody, "Do you expect to go back to the plains?" He replied, "Yes; . . . I may go out there some time in the future. I don't believe very much, however, in killing Indians. They have been very badly treated.

There has never been a treaty but that it has been broken. Whenever a gold or silver mine is found on land belonging to an Indian, he is shoved further on." There was no time for elaboration; Cody had to change for the next scene.[49]

While the troupe played in Austin, Texas, Cody did some crack shooting with Ben Thompson, a gunfighter turned marshal. Using Thompson's rifle, "he struck six half dollars out of seven that were thrown up." The informal marksmanship contests established a firm, albeit short-lived, friendship between the men, and two years later Cody sent Thompson an engraved target pistol as a gift. Despite their familiarity with western life, Texans were thrilled with the show at Millett's Opera House from the opening farce, *Turn Him Out*, to the scenes depicting the life and times of Buffalo Bill—"A synonim [*sic*] for a mighty, far-famed Western chvalier [*sic*], a man whom honor loved and cowardice abhorred . . . the hero of a thousand tales." Dime-novel readers who pictured him "in all the amplified and varied forms that imagination will ever bring before the gigantic multiplicity of human minds" were not disappointed to see the man in person.[50] Between acts, J. G. Rampone led the orchestra in "some excellent music, a claironette [*sic*] solo being particularly admired."[51] When Cody arrived in San Antonio, its citizens hoped for an exhibition of his shooting outside the one given onstage. The *Daily Express* mentioned that Cody might show himself at the springs; instead, he spent time between shows as tourist, visiting the missions and the Alamo.[52]

Cody may have felt a kinship with the Alamo's defending hero, Davy Crockett. Like Cody, Crockett was a frontiersman, familiar with Indian people, and one who reveled in adventure and confrontation with danger. Crockett was also a politician, having been elected to Congress from his native Tennessee, just as Cody had been elected to the Nebraska legislature, though he never claimed the seat after the final vote tally. Crockett had decided to explore Texas and move his family there if prospects were good, but he had no plans to join the Texans fighting for independence. However, his fame and reputation preceded him, and he was offered a leadership role. When the attacking Mexicans outnumbered the Texans by nearly eight to one, Crockett was everywhere, "animating the men to do their duty." His bravery struck an echoing chord in Cody's breast. He remembered Indian battles during which the best thing one could do was one's duty. Cody and Crockett, "men of the west," Paul Fees eulogizes, "born in the wild, yet endowed with natural grace and intelligence of civilized gentlemen."[53]

Over the next few weeks, the troupe performed in the Carolinas and

Virginia and then in Pennsylvania and Maryland. The combination's publicist flaunted the impressive responses with more ads in the *New York Mirror*.[54]

BUFFALO BILL BOOMING!
A SPLENDID WEEK AT THE
WALNUT STREET THEATRE, PHILADELPHIA
DRAWING THE ELITE OF THE CITY.
THE KNIGHT OF THE PLAINS!
BUFFALO BILL AND HIS STAR COMBINATION

According to the February 28, 1880, issue, Cody would tour the country next season as usual. He "looks sharp after his own interests, and arranges early in the spring many of his important engagements." During the summer, the article continued, he accompanies distinguished sportsmen on their trips over the plains, and it was likely the coming summer would be no exception. In the meantime, Ingraham, who was also the combination's treasurer, had been writing another new drama, but one has to wonder when the troupers had time to rehearse and perfect a new play mid-season. The Baltimore press announced that *Buffalo Bill at Bay; or, The Pearl of the Prairie* "resembles the one the company is now playing, but is much stronger and presents the hero in new characters" so perhaps it wasn't a matter of learning the lines and action for a completely different play after all. In the newest drama, presented in four acts with sixteen characters, Cody attempts "to drive out road agents which infest the borders imperiling the lives and property of settlers and travelers." The lawless hate him and plan to convict him of collusion with Indians and to implicate him in crimes they have committed. The heroine is Buffalo Bill's sister, beloved of Guy Woodbridge. Captain Hart Moline, the villain, is a U.S. renegade officer. He schemes against the happiness of the heroine, and the plot hinges on a kidnapping and a rescue. If Cody's "sister" May had it rough as a prospective bride of Brigham Young in *May Cody; or, Lost and Won*, his other "sister" Nellie, "the pearl of the prairie," has it as bad, if not worse, in having to contend with Moline's romantic aspirations.

Moline connives to outlaw Buffalo Bill, who "in circumventing the designs of his enemies and vindicating himself . . . assumes various disguises, among them that of an old trapper, a captain of cavalry, an agent of the secret service &c. He finally unravels the difficulties surrounding the situation and the drama ends in his triumphant vindication and the confusion of his accusers." Included in the drama were the familiar Indian dances and the "intelligent donkey Jerry." New additions, including Cody's Negro servant and an "old quack doctor and pretended naturalist," added "zest and variety."[55]

The troupe produced the new drama at the Bowery's Windsor Theatre for two weeks beginning March 1. From New York, the combination traveled to Connecticut, where Duprez and Benedict's minstrels were appearing at the New Haven Opera House at the same time Cody's company was in the city. An Indian appeared at the door, signing he wanted to go in and see the show. "Me Ingin. Me don't have ticket. . . . [M]e professional." Mr. Duprez teased him for awhile and figured out he belonged to Cody's troupe, then gave him a front seat for the show.[56]

Ladies who attended Cody's productions made no attempt to hide their admiration for the star. Titled "A Woman's Opinion," an article in the Rochester press advised anyone who "wishes to behold one of the most perfect and handsome specimens of manhood in existence" to go see him. He is "[t]all, straight, well-knit, supple and commanding" and "he adds to a complexion fair as a woman's, the dark eyes, hair and mustache of a man." Each time he appears, "one notices an improvement in grace and refinement of manner." When Cody steps onstage, dressed in suit and kid gloves, "he is the last person you would select as the brave, daring, dauntless Indian scout but, as the play progresses, and his skill, markmanship [*sic*] and strength become apparent, we no longer wonder at his famous reputation."[57]

It is a wonder his marksman's reputation didn't deter the next reporter who attempted to push Cody's leather satchel out of the way so he could put his hat on the hotel desk. The russet-colored bag was heavy with coins from the Comstock Theatre performance the previous evening, but the reporter hardly noticed it as he sized up the scout. He took in Cody's "magnificent breadth of chest, small hands evidently of great power, [and] a remarkably handsome though almost girlish face." Cody's voice, capable of broadcasting throughout a full theatre, was "soft" and "melodious." The outlines of his face are "delicate, and speak rather of a gentle character; and the gentleness crops out in his conversation."

Usually, when an interviewer approached Cody, the talk turned to Indians; in this case the reporter was interested in their prowess and endurance. The Indian is "neither as large nor as strong as the white man of the West," Cody commented, but "he is full of courage, and his vitality is wonderful. He can't lift as much as a white man, but he is fearfully quick with his weapons and without weapons; if you fight him he'll stay with you all summer. . . . When you get into trouble with one of these hostiles, the only means of personal safety is in killing him at once." Familiarity had taught Cody, "[W]hen you promise him anything you must keep your word; break it, and the trouble commences at once. . . . Treat him honestly, guide him firmly and trouble would end by their all becoming farmers and stock raisers."

Then he continued in a sadder tone.

> While I have been in the East I have heard men say 'You ought to exterminate the whole lot of them.' And I have invariably replied, 'Did you ever take an Indian by the hand and make him a friend?' Of course they had not. Just as after the civil war everyone but the men who fought wanted to keep it up, so now those who know nothing of Indian war clamor most loudly for it. I have fought Indians since I was a boy and God knows I've killed many; but I never sighted a rifle or put my knife in one that I didn't have a feeling of pity for the man and regret at the act.[58]

Finally, in mid-May, another touring season ended. When he closed at Buffalo, New York, with a $50,000 season behind him, Cody gave a wine supper for the cast and invited guests at Gerot's restaurant. The Indians entertained with speeches and native songs, then toasts were drunk and more speeches made appropriate to the occasion. A week later, an ad appeared in the show business press proclaiming the past season with an eye toward publicizing future performances and bringing in more revenue:

BUFFALO BILL'S BIG BONANZA!
AHEAD OF ALL COMPETITORS
THE BUFFALO BILL COMBINATION A GOLD MINE.
THE SEASON OF 1879 AND '80
CLOSING AT THE
ACADEMY OF MUSIC, BUFFALO N.Y.
AFTER THIRTY-SIX WEEKS
OF
UNPARALLELED SUCCESS
FROM EAST TO WEST AND NORTH TO SOUTH.
Managers will Pause and Read the Record:

RECEIPTS FOR THE SEASON $100,800.57
EXPENSES FOR THE SEASON $50,284.00
NET PROFITS FOR THE SEASON .... $50,516.57[59]

Now that his combination was regarded in theatrical circles as a fix-ture, the end of a very successful season inspired Cody to plan for the next. Another new drama would cost him several weeks' profits but would be worth every penny.

CHAPTER EIGHT

Rescuer of the Prairie Waif

A man, every inch of me.
—Buffalo Bill's line in *The Prairie Waif,*
Manchester Mirror & American, March 20, 1882

DEPICTING HIS CONQUEST OF YELLOW HAIR AND JOHN D. LEE'S RECENT execution for the Mountain Meadows Massacre respectively, Cody's dramas *Red Right Hand* and *May Cody* were deliberately timely. John A. Stevens, author of the successful play *Unknown*, managed New York City's Windsor Theatre when Cody played there in March 1880. Impressed with Stevens's reputation as actor and playwright, Cody asked him to write a play for his combination, but this time, instead of requesting a current topic, he left the subject matter up to the dramatist. Cody was aghast to learn Stevens would charge $5,000 for the work and blustered that he had never paid more than $500 for a play. "But if you had paid $5,000 before, perhaps you would not need a new play now," Stevens retorted.[1]

Reluctantly, Cody parted with a $1,000 deposit; he would remit a further $2,000 when the work was completed. The men agreed Cody would produce the drama for three months, after which time he would either pay the balance or return the script. Rehearsals for Stevens's *The Prairie Waif*, the new drama for the 1880–81 season, began in New York in mid-August.

The drama had four acts: act 1. Prairie Waif; act 2. Home of Buffalo Bill; act 3. Attack and Defiance; and act 4. The Rescue. In keeping with contemporary influences in theatre, Stevens wrote into it more romance and sentiment than could be found in Cody's previous dramas, but he did not totally neglect the sensational violence that played so well to audiences.

The curtain rose on Cody commiserating with General Brown who was marking the anniversary of the day Indians kidnapped his daughter, now in the care of old chief Lone Deer. Jim (or Jack) Hardie, a territorial officer in cahoots with a band of Mormons, plots to steal her away from the chief and marry her, securing any wealth for himself. Buffalo Bill arrives in time to rescue her, but in the ensuing fight, Lone Deer is killed. The waif grieves for her Indian friend. Bill, touched by her sorrow, offers the protection of his home, where his mother will watch over her.

The child develops into a beautiful woman with whom Buffalo Bill falls in love. He tells General Brown he can't marry her, though, because of their difference in station. Brown calls Buffalo Bill a fool and insists he's the noblest man he could have for a son-in-law. Buffalo Bill shows the girl some fancy shooting and, based on this it seems, she agrees to become Mrs. Buffalo Bill. Meanwhile, in their hatred for Cody, the Mormons plan to abduct the waif before the wedding. The villain, whom the Mormons paid to kidnap her, fraudulently introduces himself as General Brown, the father she has never known; then, overcome with remorse for his part in the evil scheme, he seeks out Buffalo Bill and confesses. Cody, disguised as the fake general, enters the Indian camp where the girl is being held and demands they give her up or "rivers of blood will flow." After an exhibit of Indian dances, the chief refuses, so Buffalo Bill "undisguises himself." At his whistle, U.S. troops surround the camp, and the band strikes up the "Star-Spangled Banner."

Several times over the past seasons, Cody had used disguise, a common melodramatic technique. Bret Harte, a Cody contemporary, wrote of one short story character, "I do not think that we ever knew his real name," and it didn't matter what a man was called because in the West, "most men were christened anew." Masquerades and name changes enabled any character to adopt a new personality at odds with his true self. Men with shady pasts could start over, but it was also dangerous in cases where a villain hid behind an honorable name. In Cody's role, a disguise allowed him to penetrate the villain's post and bring about his downfall. Its use kept the audience intrigued.[2]

The cast included some familiar theatrical names. Jule Keen, one of the earliest German dialect comedians, played Hans; Richard C. White, a widely known actor from California, took the role of Mark Stanley; and veteran New York actor Ralph Delmore played General Brown. Lizzie Fletcher of Lynn, Massachusetts, filled the role of Onita, the leading lady. No authentic Indians were on hand, at least this early in the season, but Jack Cass the donkey reprised his role as Jerry. A New York artist developed the scenery, and all costumes for the twenty-four actors were new.[3]

The *New York Herald* listed an "E. Booth" as Lieutenant White who could be the famous actor Edwin Booth. About eleven years earlier, after playing Shakespeare for many years, Booth built a theatre, organized a stock company, and produced Shakespearean dramas. Despite his venture's success, he lacked financial acumen. By 1874, debtors controlled his theatre as well as his entire fortune. Through arduous toil, he built up his wealth again; however, perhaps he was still in the throes of poverty and needed the work or played in Cody's drama for a lark.

A few months after *The Prairie Waif*'s initial production, Stevens telegraphed Cody in Portland, Maine, for his decision about the drama. "The next morning," he recalled, "a messenger boy came to the room in the hotel at which I was stopping and handed me a telegraph order for $100 from Col. Cody." In those days, one could only send $100 maximum in a single order, "so hardly had I received the first $100 than another messenger boy appeared with a second. Surprised, I peered out in the hall and I'm derned if there weren't 18 more messengers all in line, each with an order for $100 making a total of $2,000, as per the word of Col. Cody."[4]

Despite the extravagant cost, when the combination first presented *The Prairie Waif*, the New York press noted the play "was not as well appreciated as the able manner in which [Cody] acted his part." Brooklyn's *Union Argus* added that the Indian who carried off actress Connie Thompson seemed to have more than he could comfortably handle. He suggested Cody "might transfer the job to the donkey, who is evidently stronger than the Indian."[5] The *Daily Eagle* gave it high marks for, though it satisfied the lovers of stage slaughter, there was less bloodshed than usual, "and when some one is shot to the death, or wounded, there always seems to be some reason for it." At least there was a discernable plot, "something never before heard of in any Indian drama. . . . The best compliment that can be paid to piece and performance was that very intelligent people sat the play out with evident interest and enjoyment."[6]

Nebraska City, NE, ad for the October 6, 1881, performance.

After one evening's performance, Cody tangled with Frederick May, a bully much taller and heavier than he, apparently over a three-year-old incident involving *New York Herald* heir James G. Bennett. Not only were Cody and Bennett hunting pals, but Bennett had financed his first trip to New York City. Back then, May had challenged Bennett to a duel because, during a New Year's celebration while courting May's sister, a drunken Bennett "lost his sense of propriety" and urinated in May's fireplace. Afterward, he fled to Paris. Now May asked Cody, who perhaps had defended Bennett at the time, to leave the parlor where they were gathered. Cody refused. "The presence of May was enough to terrorize an ordinary man, but 'Buffalo Bill,' who had met all kinds of animals in the West, was not easily scarred [*sic*]." When May clawed at Cody's long hair, Cody pushed him away. May demanded an apology, but Cody "never apologizes only when he is the offending party." Instead, he rushed him and punched May between the eyes with a blow that knocked him over the sofa. Friends looked on as Cody punished the man "whom so many in sporting circles in New York City dread because of his physical powers and acknowledged willingness to fight." Afterward, rubbing his sore knuckles, Cody denied he was quarrelsome but admitted to being "capable of taking care of himself whenever it [was] necessary."[7]

Violence featured in stage dramas heightened the excitement of an audience composed of a mixture of some who rarely encountered it and others who had survived it. As a part of everyday life in the Old West, violence in the form of gunfights, Indian battles, and personal feuds was also something of a spectator sport. Barroom brawls between men were common, but among the ladies who populated the brothels and dancehalls, catfights also occurred.

Melodramatic playwrights often typified female characters as helpless and weak; however, by the 1880s, real women began achieving professional, legal, and educational equality. Custom still emphasized marriage and family, but more and more women pursued higher education and a career. As a result of society's changes, dramatists wrote stronger roles for the feminine sex. Actors had always been more liberal, and the rigors of the business demanded women be as resilient and determined as their male costars. Audiences booed and applauded them equally. In frontier productions, women could often ride, rope, and shoot as well as men.

At the time the combination was performing in Wisconsin and Minnesota, news of the latest Ute Indian uprising in Colorado circulated throughout the country. In 1853, Mormon intrusion exhausted Ute resources and wildlife; ten years later, continued white encroachment on the gold trails nearly depleted the Indians' hunting grounds, forcing them to steal from settlers to stave off starvation. By 1868, they were situated on a twelve million acre reservation, but Nathan C. Meeker of the White River Agency, in his determination to convert the Utes from "primitive savages" to hardworking Christian farmers, plowed up their racetrack and prime pasture to make room for gardens. In September 1879, the Indians' angry reaction to the intensified oppression triggered a massacre in which a number of Utes, cavalrymen, and agency personnel, including Meeker, were killed. The peaceful efforts of Chief Ouray and Indian agent Charles Adams helped avoid more serious repercussions. Eventually the Utes were forced to move to poorer lands in Utah, opening the favorable Colorado territory to whites.[8]

In early September a reporter for the *Milwaukee Sentinel* braved the prospect of being scalped by one of Cody's Indians to secure an interview. Asked about his familiarity with the Utes' temperament, Cody expressed solidarity with them. "Indians are all about the same in character. I think they have been badly used by whites." He believed that

> [f]or honesty and virtue, . . . the Indians are ahead of the whites.
> They have been robbed by thieving agents, ever since Grant's
> administration. I hope for a change in the Indian policy, with
> a change of administration, which I think sure to come. For a
> hundred years the government has been trying to find out what
> to do with the Indians and they don't know now. I never knew a
> treaty with them but what was first broken by the whites.

Indian affairs had been the responsibility of the War Department since 1789. Sixty years later, Congress transferred the duty to the newly created Department of the Interior. The reassignment resulted in a changing policy that included a plan to expedite their acclimatization into white culture. It removed the Indians to reservations, where disease and starvation were rampant. Unscrupulous agents charged with providing food and other supplies instead caused misery and hostility. To solve the Indian quandary, Cody maintained that a joint government of the Indians by the Interior and War departments made the most sense and was likely to result in the desired "conversion of the nomad into a farmer" and would stop the thieving on the part of Indian agents.[9]

The reporter asked if he thought the army big enough to handle the Indian wars. "Oh, yes! The standing army might be larger, but the militia system is growing so that in a short time a magnificent army could be raised." Cody, however, had some reservations about the quality of training the soldiers received. "Another war, and the privates would pretty much all know which end of the gun goes off."[10]

The troupe traveled eastward to Cincinnati, Ohio, where the *New York Mirror* stringer was dumbstruck trying to describe the "blood-curdling, awe-inspiring (my adjectives fail me) drama."[11] Meanwhile, in Toledo, one journalist predicted a good turnout but differentiated between the classes who would attend the performance. Many Toledo citizens consider Cody "a far greater man than Gen. Grant, Gen. Garfield or Gen. Hancock and all those people will be at the Opera house to-night as high up as they can climb." Others who do not regard Cody as a "a little tin god on wheels" have a "high opinion of his bravery and skill as a scout, hunter and fighter, and appreciate his ability as an actor. All these will be . . . lower down in the house."

After the Toledo performance, a cynical critic reviewed the drama. He acknowledged Stevens as playwright, noting, "[t]he assertion is probably true, or Mr. Stevens certainly would have published an indignant denial of the authorship long before this." He scored Cody as the "worst performer in the cast," with Robert Neil as General Brown a close second.

> Buffalo Bill may be a very great man, but if he were half as great as he evidently imagines he is, he would find it a very difficult matter to move about on the stage of the Wheeler Opera House, or any other. "Buffalo Bill" . . . is no actor. . . . *The Prairie Waif* is said to be made up of scenes that have actually occurred in "Bill's" experience. Were this not so, the probability of one man quelling into submission a band of 12 or 14 ruffians, armed to the teeth, might be doubted. But "Buffalo Bill," of course, is no ordinary man.[12]

In the next interview, after Cody acknowledged the troupe's reception had thus far been good, the journalist wondered if Indians were instinctively warlike. Cody knew that they, like any people, would defend their rights.

> I believe the Indians are more sinned against than sinning. The Indians hate miners. They would rather see ten companies of

soldiers upon their reservations than one miner and the reason for this is that they know the soldiers will not remain long. They simply hang around a few days and then return to the posts, but when they see a miner coming among them with a pick on his shoulder and a spade in his hand, they at once come to the conclusion that he has come to stay, and if they try to maintain their rights and some one happened to be killed the story is at once set afloat that the Indians are on the war-path.[13]

Over the next few weeks, candidates stumping for the upcoming elections cost Cody some business, so he headed to Canada until the political excitement died down, suggesting some flexibility in scheduling. He traveled to Toronto, then zigzagged west along Ontario's southern coast to Hamilton for a presentation on October 25 where over six hundred gallery tickets were sold. Receipts totaled $410; the amount would have been higher had management not been forced to turn away over a hundred people at the door. Cody's combination had gained "a success unparalleled in the history of amusements," a *New York Mirror* story announced, having "[t]he strongest drama, the greatest Star, the finest company and the best drawing card in America." Receipts for past performances proved his popularity— Milwaukee, St. Paul, and Minneapolis, $3,500; Chicago, $3,300 taken in one week; St. Louis, one week, $5,300.[14]

The troupe entertained enthusiastic Canadian audiences, then headed back into the States to Vermont and through to New Hampshire. The newsman for Manchester's *Daily Union* regretted that those who believed Cody merely affected his character were unable to meet him in person. They would, he observed, have found Cody "a courteous, genial gentleman, with an excellent knowledge of human nature in general and of the Western people in particular." A gifted conversationalist, Cody offered his opinion that "the government should furnish Indian agents who have a practical knowledge of the 'noble savage,' his wants, his peculiarities, and his sufferings in the past." He supposed many of the New England agents care for nothing but how much money they can make from their positions. He knew from firsthand experience that the Indians are a "long-suffering race, and have borne many insults at the hands of the authorities and the settlers."

"Nobody could play the part of Buffalo Bill better than Buffalo Bill himself, who makes a very handsome stage picture, and does his love making with the modesty and his fighting with the gallantry and dash of a

Press agents ensure publicity in snowy Ilion, NY. Courtesy Ilion
Free Public Library.

hero," wrote the *Easton Express* critic in mid-January 1881.[15] A year later in
the same city, possibly the same critic, still impressed by Cody's romantic
overtures, quoted the *Omaha Republican*'s review to reinforce his point.
"Bill makes love to [the heroine] just as if he meant it—but he doesn't. The
realistic love-making is only an evidence of his art as an actor." One can
only imagine what Cody's wife surmised if she read these observations.[16]

With so many combinations producing border dramas, audiences
could attend such a show at least once a month. Some critics declared
Cody to be "the best," "the original," or "the genuine article." Newton once
observed that every action has an equal and opposite reaction. So, generally, for each critic who commended the show, another challenged this view.
One Brooklyn reviewer condemned the language of Cody's production as
"mediocre" and claimed that "its characters were performed by a company
no better than the play they appear in." He derided the "tragic comedy" as
inferior even for the gallery's amusement. The only redeeming qualities
were the attractive backdrops and Cody's marksmanship exhibition.[17] But

Despite the prevalence of border dramas, audiences had not tired of seeing the original scout. The *La Crosse Chronicle* explained why:

> Whatever else may be said of Mr. Cody's performance, it cannot certainly be denominated slow. Everything goes with a rush. The conversation is alternately gory and amatory, knives flash in the air continually and guns are liable to go off at any moment. The show fills a want long felt and a field untilled and seemingly heretofore unexplored. Here and everywhere it gets the best of houses.[26]

In his autobiography, Cody wrote that, in one of his plays, there was no telling where the beginning or middle was. Likewise, the audience at the Des Moines Opera House did not seem to know whether the drama had concluded or not. When the curtain fell on the fourth act, many in the audience rose to leave, but "loud cries were made to 'keep your seats, it's not over yet.'"[27]

After the performance in Council Bluffs, Cody left the theatre with his wife and daughters. A man on horseback rode to within a few feet of the family and fired three or four shots, none of which hurt anyone. Josh Ogden, one of Cody's managers, witnessed the shooting and pointed out the would-be assassin, later identified as J. T. Benedict. Public opinion was divided as to whether the perpetrator was a "crazy crank" too much enthused by Cody's fancy crack shots during the play or whether it was a "put up job" on Cody's part to secure free advertisement. Lawmen captured and jailed Benedict, but he would not explain his actions.[28]

The incident must have given Louisa Cody pause and made her think twice about the potential dangers of traveling with her husband. Perhaps brought back memories of their steamboat trip to Leavenworth shortly aft they were married. Men on horseback rode up at one landing, threateni to shoot "the black abolition jay-hawker"—Buffalo Bill. Cody telegraph ahead to make sure that when they landed at Leavenworth, a friendly rece tion would be awaiting him and his bride.[29] No doubt Louisa wonde what she had got herself into.

Perhaps in response to the incident, the *Evening News* of St. Jose Missouri, staunch in its belief that violence begets violence, vociferou condemned Cody's type of show and advised mothers not to allow th sons to view such sensations. The press railed:

There are too many blood and thunder papers and dime novels lying upon the counters of the news stands throughout the country for the good of the rising generation. How many young men have become hard characters and led soiled and desperate lives by reading sensational papers of this character and dreaming of Indian treachery until they become satisfied in their own minds that they are equal to any bloody emergency. The best thing parents can do is to keep dime novels, sensational papers, etc. out of their children's reach and not allow them the privilege of attending plays that will leave a bad impression upon their minds. Mr. Cody himself, is an intelligent gentleman, but his six ignorant Indians are not the people to better the morals of this or any other community.[30]

For many, graphic literature and dramas forecast a decline in the nation's morals. Cody's onetime partner Jack Crawford took up the theme after he left the combination. In an essay titled "A Chapter for Boys," he predicted a bad end for every youngster who persisted in reading the "vile trash" depicting blood-and-thunder situations that seldom occur in the West. Crawford would confine every publisher of such literature to "prison for life" for leading their readers into "ruin and disgrace." His dramas differed from Cody's in being free from blatant violence, according to his biographer.[31] The same biased journalist, who ranted heatedly about the bad impact of Cody's plays, also advised "Negro minstrels and shows of such character" to stay out of St. Joseph.

From Missouri, the combination traveled to Kansas where, in Leavenworth, Cody appeared, "dressed in a blue-tinged suit, with a cut-away coat, and wore his old favorite wide-brimmed, cow-boy hat." The reporter's adjective, "cow-boy," was rarely used. Two years previously, Cody had had to define the word in his autobiography because it was still relatively unknown.[32] Around his neck hung a "heavy gold neck-chain, from which was suspended near his left vest pocket a huge gold horse-shoe set with diamonds. His scarf pin is a solid old gold representation of a buffalo-head with diamonds for eyes." In some ways, Cody hadn't changed much since the old days. "[W]hen among the boys [he] snaps his fingers and says 'what are you going to have?' with the full heartedness for which he was always noted."

Conversing with a Leavenworth reporter, Cody informed him he

Cody looks every bit the successful actor, c. 1876.
Courtesy Buffalo Bill Historical Center (P.6.124), Cody, WY.

would be going out to Pilot Knob with his sisters to find the graves of their parents. After recounting some of his early life, Cody said, "I am now in the stock and real estate business. I like raising cattle and horses better than the stage and will turn my attention to that branch of business after the next two years." Even though he had cleared over $40,000 each of five years and one year made $56,000, he was prouder of his ranch with its sixty-eight hundred head of cattle and four hundred horses. "I have a brilliant offer to go to Europe," Cody repeated, "but I contend that a man can make more money in America than he can any place in the world. I don't play on the stage or do anything else for the fun of the thing; I work to make money."[33]

Such an attitude is not unexpected in a man who had grown up having to work for a living. As a youngster, he'd supported his mother and four sisters after his father's death. Shortly after his marriage, he entertained hopes of an investment in a city he called Rome, on the Kansas railroad, making him a rich man. It failed. Shortly after his second season onstage began, the Panic of 1873 caused unemployment, bank failings, and tight credit. When he finally did have money "to throw at the birds," Cody spent lavishly. He generously gave money to friends and invested in dubious projects. His Wild West partner Pawnee Bill recalled that, once he became accustomed to having wealth, Cody "cared nothing for money, except when he wanted it, or needed it to spend, then if he did not have it, or could not borrow it, it made him sick; he would go to bed."[34]

Critics, at times a tough breed to please, could make it hard for an actor to make money, and few knew this better than Cody. But, aside from toning down the bloody nature of the dramas, he did little to pacify reviewers. Several examples from October 1881 illustrate contrasting viewpoints. The *Leavenworth Times* believed the drama "the best he has ever played here." Across the aisle, the *Louisville Courier-Journal* saw the production "not as strong or as well selected as usual." One newspaperman heard "incessant" laughter, and "at times the actors were compelled to desist for the uproarious applause." The dour Louisville critic disagreed: "The comedy part especially, which should be very strong, is in very poor hands."[35] No one could predict any one reviewer's handling, but Cody would have heartily agreed with the Springfield, Illinois, critic who wrote, "There is something so fascinating about the border drama that few regular theatre goers can resist the inclination to attend."[36]

The *Kokomo Dispatch* thought the play

a miserable jumble of improbabilities [that] does not possess
a single merit from a critical stand-point. The acting was in
perfect harmony with the tone of the play, being poor, trashy, and
decidedly tame. There was positively not a single gleam of genius
in the play nor a spark of talent in the players. . . . The *Prairie
Waif* is no more than a wishy-washy dime novel dramatized and
poorly acted. But . . .

—and there was always a *but*—"it serves its purpose admirably: by its glitter
and novelty, and wildness it is a big catch."[37]

Concurrently, when more Cody imitators were producing border
dramas, many critics believed audiences ought to have outgrown this kind
of entertainment. They disdained the frontier drama and delighted to see
half-empty houses, hoping this was a sign the public was acquiring a taste
for more sophisticated offerings. To the critics' delight, Cody appeared at
Fort Wayne's Academy of Music on November 30 to the smallest audience
he ever "corralled" there.[38]

Several years previously, after seeing a drama like Cody's, a *New York
Herald* critic acknowledged the difference between lowbrow and highbrow
theatre patrons. "[W]e have no inclination to sneer at the thousands of
orderly and decent people who can find an evening's entertainment outside of Shakespeare and the legitimate," he wrote. In Fort Wayne, there
was no such open-mindedness. The press noted with satisfaction that "[t]he
taste of Fort Wayne amusement patrons is slowly but surely improving."
Ordinarily, Cody's combination could fill the theatre to capacity. However,
"in happy contrast last night, any number of vacant seats were visible, . . .
and the house did not represent over $200 or possibly $250."[39]

Cody plugged along despite such criticisms, and advertisements for
his show in theatre papers became increasingly superlative. The *New York
Mirror* for December 3, 1881, for example, publicized him as "The King
of Stars" and rightfully so, as the Buffalo Bill Combination—"a Powerful
Dramatic Company!"—was doing a rousing business. Receipts showed
profits of $485 in Bellefontaine, Ohio; $765 in Springfield; $650 in Dayton;
$855 in Columbus; and $500 in Xenia.[40]

Earlier in the year, Cody reported he would not travel farther west than
Kansas during the current season. Consequently, the combination back-
tracked and issued repeat performances. Only nine months after their last
appearance in Steubenville, the company returned and, in spite of frequent

visits, played to large audiences. However, "there is such a thing as getting too much blood and thunder," observed the *Daily Herald*, "and Steubenville evidently has reached that point, anyhow, as it is served by B.B." The newsman continued disdainfully, "If those who take in this class of entertainments would turn their attention to the better class, our reputation as a 'show town' would be improved, and really good companies would not so often steer clear of us."[41]

The troupers wound their way back to the Windsor Theatre in New York for the week of January 16. Nate Salsbury, with whom Cody would eventually partner in his Wild West, wrote about meeting him in New York City in 1882. If Salsbury recalled correctly, it would have been during this week.[42]

Freeport, Illinois, native Salsbury was born in 1846 and fought for the Union during the Civil War. Following the conflict, he spent several years as an actor, gaining experience and turning into a first-class showman. By 1875, he had organized his "Salsbury's Troubadours," for which he wrote plays, and had become the prince of farce comedy. The next year, while returning from a year's engagement in Australia, he later claimed he had envisioned an outdoor show to comprise a whole realm of horsemanship, with Cody as the show's central figure. According to Salsbury's memoirs, Cody "was about at the end of his profit string on the theatrical stage. I dare say he was pleased at the chance to try something else, for he grew very enthusiastic over the plan as I unfolded it to him and was sure that the thing would be a great success."[43]

However, Cody was not "at the end of his profit string." Discounting the opinions of a few critics, his popularity was as strong as ever. His eagerness at hearing Salsbury's plan was no doubt due to the increasing limitations he found himself laboring under as he added more performers and more authentic displays of frontier life to every season's drama. In addition, he appreciated Salsbury's show business experience. When the two showmen met, they discussed tentative plans each had for creating an outdoor exhibition. Cody may have even mentioned his hopes to take his company to Europe. Neither of them had the money to do it the way they wanted at the time, so they agreed to table the idea and to carry on with their respective shows.[44]

The combination continued to do brisk business. On February 18, 1882, the Dunkirk take was $255, and on February 27 in Auburn they played to a $500 house; they moved onto Manchester, New Hampshire, on March 18 and netted $985.[45] Some of his profits went home to his wife to buy property

Scenes from the drama advertise *The Prairie Waif* in a c. 1880 lithograph by A. Hoen, Baltimore. Courtesy Buffalo Bill Historical Center (1.69.2646), Cody, WY.

in North Platte. This she did, but she put only her name on the deed, aware of Cody's "impulsive generosity and his speculative tendencies."[46] Louisa recalled, "I added to his ranch, and attended to the thousand and one details of farming life that must be looked after, while he was away on the stage."[47] Even though she occasionally toured with the troupe, she had not been happy with Cody since she found him kissing his female costars good-bye at season's end. Cody regularly sent her money, but he found to his dismay that, though he had financed a beautiful house, "I have none to go to."[48]

To someone used to diverse adventures on the plains, a decade's worth of repetitive one-night stands must have seemed a long time. The restrictions of such a life are easy to imagine. His augmenting the drama with increasing realism was, in effect, a way not only to establish authenticity but to amuse himself as well. Cody's frequent talk about returning west to ranch or of taking the combination to Europe is symptomatic of a restless spirit. Nonetheless, anyone could see show business had gotten into his blood, and his future lay in entertainment. For Cody, there was no looking back.

CHAPTER NINE

Exit Stage Right

I'm not an actor—I'm a star. All actors can become stars;
but all stars cannot become actors.
—*New York Mirror*, April 8, 1882

CODY'S BIOGRAPHER DON RUSSELL CONTENDS THAT "HIS CLOSING years on the stage were the most obscure and unadvertised in Buffalo Bill's lifetime."[1] From spring 1882 to spring 1886, Cody shepherded his combination through the eastern states, hardly venturing farther west than Indiana. He stuck to tried and true bookings, often performing in cities only nine months after appearing there last. Audience enthusiasm did not diminish with familiarity; however, many critics had run out of things to say, so increasingly less new information about the dramas comes to light. By now, Cody's ancestry, biography, and philosophy were well known, so fewer editors sent reporters for in-depth interviews.

Nevertheless, Cody's stardom continued on the mark. He improved as an actor and could have continued the stage performances, but he was at a crossroad in his life: the combination with its various extraneous exhibits was outgrowing the limits a theatrical stage imposed. Over the next few years, Cody had to make significant decisions. If he considered abandoning show business for life as a rancher or returning to a career as army scout, it was only with a touch of nostalgia. His decision not to take the troupe to Europe proved, he believed, to "'[l]et well enough alone,' and as long as he continues to harvest money as rapidly as now, he is content to remain in this country."[2]

He had obviously given much thought to a program that would culminate in his Wild West show in only a year's time. He told a journalist for the Manchester, New Hampshire, *Mirror and American* his idea, which "seem[ed] to contain every element of popularity." He would ship twenty buffalo from his ranch and add a number of fearless Indian riders and expert lassoers. "To this combination he ... [would] add his own presence, and then give in some large inclosure [*sic*] an eye exhibition" that would "astonish the natives. There ... [would] be an Indian fight on horseback, a buffalo hunt and other exciting features never yet shown in public."

The reporter found adjectives like "large hearted, frank, courteous and gentlemanly to everybody" described the showman well. The public thought of Cody most often now "only in the capacity of an actor," but when not onstage, Cody went home to the ranch he shared with Frank North, on which grazed six thousand head of cattle. He was also proud of his new investment in horse ranching.[3]

At Whitehall, New York, the troupe played to an audience composed mostly of noisy, drunken workers from the Champlain Barge Canal. When the Indians started their war dance, several of the men rose in imitation. One approached the stage, "interrupted the orchestra, captured one of the instruments, and with it attempted to get upon the stage. Mr. Cody, who had just made his entrance disguised as an old medicine man, called for police assistance, but none could be had at any price, so he took the law into his own hands." The man fell like a dead weight when Cody hit him with the medicine staff he carried in the role. The man's companions, instead of rallying to his rescue, ran from the theatre. The next morning the police summoned Cody before a judge who fined him for assault.[4]

The *New York Mirror* of April 8 reported Cody's "enjoying great expectations just now." His grandfather, Philip Cody, owned fifty acres of real estate on Cleveland's Euclid Avenue valued at $1,600,000. Three years prior to his death in 1848, he, being of unsound mind, deeded away his vast holdings for a mere song. Recently his heirs began suit against anyone who owned property on the land. If a judge sustained the claim, "Bill ... [would] stop starring and live on a couple of cool millions."[5] Cody wrote to tell Jack Crawford that if he received the estate settlement, he would "just have money to throw at the birds. My business is something wonderful this is the worst week so called in the year holy week and I will clear bout $300.00 a day during the week."[6]

Near the end of April, the *Mirror* announced that Cincinnati, Ohio, would be the site of the upcoming Dramatic Festival. To the newsman, the city's name recalled an incident in Cody's life that suggests Cody saw himself as a successful philanthropist and businessman à la Horatio Alger. "Passing through Cincinnati, he met a pleasant-faced lad—a bootblack. Perhaps there was something about the boy that reminded 'Buffalo Bill' of his own early struggles in life." The reporter gave no details, but in some way, "[Cody] insured place, position and an opportunity that made the lad's life a success."[7]

As the lad polished his boots, Cody saw "Doc" Carver, a brother-hunter on the plains, passing by. William Frank Carver had trained as a dentist but proved handier with a rifle than a drill. He headed west after a boyhood in Illinois and, in August 1872, met Cody and Texas Jack at Fort McPherson. Having perfected his sharpshooting skills, he claimed Indians had given him the name "Evil Spirit of the Plains, the Champion Marksman of the World." Carver had recently returned from Europe where he performed brilliantly as a crack shot, challenging any comers and beating them all.

According to the *New York Mirror*, which was perhaps indulging in hyperbole, when Carver saw Cody, he suggested a visit to an old friend. Along the way, they collected other acquaintances, one of whom had lost an arm in an Indian fight. The men soon got down to the business of whiskey and cards. The stakes gradually increased until

> twenty-three thousand dollars had changed hands, and a sorrier-looking party of individuals, whose nerves were ordinarily firm on the trigger, never went into their blankets. Cody is a good deal of a philosopher, and as he tucked himself in bed, he called across the room to Carver, 'Doc, we've all been wiped; but great Scott! If wild John could do that with one arm, what would he have done with two?'[8]

Commiserating on their losses, the discussion possibly turned to Cody's plans to make more money with an outdoor exhibition. Carver may have invited himself in. In February 1883, when the combination played in

Connecticut, they would meet again at Carver's home in New Haven to talk about combining their talents.[9]

At April's end, Cody closed another season with a banquet for the press and members of his company. Business manager Josh Ogden announced that season receipts amounted to $104,000.[10] Cody bragged about his successful season in a large ad in the *New York Mirror* on May 13, 1882:

Echoes of the Conquering March from the Western Plains
to the Atlantic Coast of the King of the Road,
BUFFALO BILL, . . .
HIS CLIENTELE—The People.
HIS RECORD—Satisfaction.
HIS MAGNETISM—Continuous.
HIS RECEIPTS NO "IDLE FANCY"
Veracious Facts And Figures:
Individual Gross Receipts, $104,381.75;
Profits Transferred West, $51,819.40.

The publicity continued with a promotion of his anticipated drama for the next season: *Twenty Days; or, Buffalo Bill's Pledge*. Charles Foster, "a dramatic author of considerable repute," and Prentiss Ingraham combined efforts in a work that would be "[i]nterpreted by an Efficient Dramatic Company, and employ in its vivid realism, A Band of Genuine Redmen, the Handsome Indian Princess, magnificent Scenic Views from the pencil of the celebrated Artist Hughes, of Cincinnati, . . . [and a] Uniformed Silver Cornet Band."[11]

At season's end, Josh Ogden dropped into the *New York Mirror* offices to talk about the combination's success. He boasted that Cody's season was "[t]he best he has ever known. We have played to packed houses everywhere." The editor wondered if his Cleveland legacy would make him eager to quit performing, but Ogden reported that Cody "doesn't want to leave the stage. He has plenty of money; but the million he gets in Cleveland will help him some toward being a rich man." In conclusion, Ogden predicted that, with good dates set for the next season and increased terms, they expected to clear $60,000.[12]

Before heading home, Cody and his family visited his sister May in Denver. Shortly after their arrival, burglars stole his long gold chain and diamond-studded pendant horseshoe that he claimed was worth $500, his

$700 gold watch and chain, and a buffalo head pin with diamond eyes. Two thousand dolloars worth of jewelry and $150 in cash were also missing. The thieves missed Mrs. Cody's "casket of jewels" valued at $5,000.[13]

When the family reached Nebraska, the Fourth of July commemoration presented Cody the opportunity to experiment with an outdoor exhibition. Independence Day, the loudest, most patriotic of American holidays, traditionally called for a grand celebration complete with parades, fireworks, and flag-waving oratory. Overland travelers to Oregon or California considered it nearly mandatory to reach Independence Rock in central Wyoming by the Fourth, to assure being over the western mountains before snow closed the passes. But wherever they were, they celebrated. It seems fitting that Cody inaugurated a new period in his life with such an eventful holiday. Ever the red-white-and-blue American—Theodore Roosevelt called him "an American of Americans"—he proclaimed his patriotism unabashedly.[14] Upon landing at Staten Island after his first trip to England, Cody remarked, "I cannot describe my joy upon stepping again on the shore of beloved America. . . . 'There is no place like home' nor is there a flag like the old flag."[15]

William McDonald recollected that North Platte citizens had arranged for a few horse races by way of patriotic observance. Cody protested the lack of greater festivities, so townsmen nominated him chairman of the event. He proceeded to compile a program with something for everyone, combining elements from the stage shows and his ideas for an outdoor spectacle. Using publicity tactics he had learned from ten seasons onstage, Cody printed announcements of competitions in roping and racing and solicited business owners to donate prizes. His plan for the day turned it into an extravaganza. A street parade included a band, the Grand Army of the Republic (GAR), town children, a long line of carriages, and Cody seated in one, dressed in white corduroy pants and a black velvet coat, acting as marshall. At the racetrack, a program of songs and speeches preceded competitions involving the lassoing of buffalo and Texas steers. Anyone could compete in the horse and foot races. The day concluded with a fireworks display and a GAR ball.[16]

In all likelihood, Cody sat back at day's end and reflected on what he had accomplished. If the idea of a grand Wild West show had occurred to him even before he spoke to Nate Salsbury earlier in the year, the overwhelmingly popular demonstration he had organized for North Platte friends convinced him of the viability and public appeal such a show would have. The "Old Glory Blowout" had been a kind of rehearsal for the grand presentation Cody envisioned. He had seen firsthand how fascinated folks in the eastern cities, as well as in the South and far West, reacted to his portrayal of frontiersman. As ranch owner, his familiarity with the talents and skills of cowboys led him to believe displays of those talents and skills would be worthwhile entertainment. A scant two weeks later, Cody sold his Dismal River ranch to his old friend John Bratt in anticipation of dedicating the rest of his life to performing in one way or another. Cody biographer Nellie Yost states that Cody and Frank North sold the ranch for $75,000, much less than the $175,000 the *New York Mirror* reported, yet another press exaggeration.[17]

Realizing outdoor shows required more capital and development than he had at present, Cody continued with his plans for the theatrical season of 1882–83 but upped the ante. In August, he passed through Sioux City hoping to talk with powerful Sioux chief Sitting Bull, mastermind of Custer's defeat in 1876. Cody was eager "to secure the services of Mr. Bull—as a star, not as an actor—and he claims to have all kinds of official indorsement [*sic*], including a letter from President Arthur, to further his ends."[18] First Cody had to deal with government red tape, which ended up taking three years to unravel.[19] Sitting Bull's people's destitution had forced the chief to give up his exile in Canada and return to the United States to surrender. He was sent down the Missouri River to Fort Randall, where he and his followers were held for nearly two years. Finally, in May 1883, Sitting Bull rejoined his tribe at Standing Rock, but was not willing or able to join Cody until 1885.

The new season opened as promised with Foster's melodrama *Twenty Days; or, Buffalo Bill's Pledge*. A handwritten copy at the Buffalo Bill Memorial Museum in Golden, Colorado, sketches the gist of the play, though only certain lines and cues survive. Occasionally, actors received full scripts, but oftentimes all they had to work with was their own lines and a few words from the previous speaker as cues.

While on a twenty days' leave of absence from his duties as army scout, Buffalo Bill runs into a lynching party headed by Lariat Dan Miller. The villains are about to hang Captain Merton Mortlake, who had been on his way to marry Grace Weldon. Buffalo Bill cuts the rope and frees the captain, then heads off to visit his friend Abner Weldon and his daughter Grace, who tell him that, when Weldon's brother died, he included in his will a stipulation that Grace would receive a fortune if she would marry his adopted son Mortlake. Unbeknownst to Buffalo Bill, the bad guys recapture Mortlake and bury him alive in a mountainous canyon. Buffalo Bill follows

Mortlake's trail and rescues him from the rocky grave. Meanwhile, another villain named Montana Mike pretends to be adventurer Crippled Jim and impersonates Mortlake so he can marry Grace. He takes her away to a gambling hall in Denver where Buffalo Bill and the real captain track them down. One of the villain's own men accidentally kills him with a bullet meant for Buffalo Bill. Captain Mortlake and Grace are united; virtue triumphs and vice perishes ignominiously. "The denouement ends happily to all concerned with the exception, of course, of those that had been murdered during the rendition of the play."[20]

A week after the combination assembled in Janesville, Wisconsin, a large audience jammed Myers Opera House for the performance, but there were problems. Even before the first act ended, the "tortured" spectators began to leave after watching Cody "laboring under a severe indisposition, superinduced by a too free indulgence of intoxicants." The drama suffered, and his supporting cast performed "necessarily at a great disadvantage." The reporter reminded Cody he has "a good company and a good orchestra, but he can't run a successful show unless he keeps sober."[21]

No one would call it a comedy, but two weeks later, Iowans roared with laughter, testifying how it contained "fun and lots of it." Quite probably, believed the critic, the janitor had to sweep up a barrel of buttons, "burst by the sudden gusts of laughter and cheers which overcame the audience." He praised the entire cast for their acting, but Jule Keen, one of the best stage comedians, scored the highest as a "button buster."[22]

One day while Cody was standing in front of the Barret house in Burlington, Iowa, a little girl approached and inquired if he was "Mr. Buffalo." Cody said no. "Are you Mr. Bill?" the child then asked. "You may call me that for short," said Cody. "You are a big handsome man; I was told you was," said the fair interviewer. Cody wanted to know from whom she had learned this. "Oh," she replied, "I heard the teachers at the central building this morning telling what a handsome man you were, and they were wondering among themselves why you did not marry. They thought you would make a splendid husband." Cody accepted the compliment, apparently not informing the child he was already married and a father as well.[23]

Music became an increasingly greater aspect of the production. In one act, Jule Keen and one of the actresses sang a song, and, between acts, Frank Thompson played the cornet. Although the interludes were entertaining, the gallery gods were eager for the show to resume. "There isn't a small boy in the city, no matter whether he goes to Sunday school or not, who is not crazy to set in the gallery and 'hi-hi' their demi-god," remarked Fort Wayne's *Weekly Sentinel*. After the show, "the timid housewife shuns the dark corners and by-ways of the household, where her young hopeful in the role of 'Sitting Bull' or 'Spotted Tail,' trips her unsuspecting feet, and scalps her with a convenient broomstick."[24]

Later in November 1882, Cody returned to Cleveland with his combination. The theatre was insufferably overcrowded and the loud, unruly throng committed numerous sins common to nineteenth-century audiences, including talking aloud, shuffling, arriving late, leaving early, noisily turning program pages, insisting on encores, sneaking snacks and spitting tobacco.[25] But they cheered Cody who "is becoming much more at home to the glare of the footlights than he was a few seasons ago, and his nervousness while shooting is wearing off. Last night he made but two misses in 20 fancy shots."[26] Each succeeding season showed his progressively improved acting talent, and "he has never appeared to such advantage as he did . . . in his new play." Though his Indians are a big attraction, "for circulating purposes among the people they are a nuisance of no inconsiderable dimension."[27]

A few weeks later, about dinnertime in Lewiston, Maine, a reporter found Cody standing in the DeWitt hotel corridor, dressed in "a stylish suit of bright mixed woolen goods, faultless in cut. . . . Magnificent diamonds blazed on his cuffs and fingers." The newsman watched one of the Indians saunter in, wrapped in his red blanket, then asked if Cody really enjoyed show business. He replied, "I like it as long as I can make $50,000 or $60,000 a year out of it," adding that he had gotten into it by accident when he went in with Ned Buntline. "He was such a poor manager I had to take hold of it myself." In answer to a question about his education, Cody said he had gone to school only about three weeks altogether—his mother taught him at home—but he was fond of reading, "No man with my advantages reads more than I." He particularly cared for "history, accounts of travel, etc. I am a great admirer of Shakespeare." The library at Cody's TE Ranch, which he acquired in 1895, substantiates his claim.

The journalist concluded his report. "Bill says Indians are easy to handle, if you know how to do it, but our Government don't [*sic*] know how." As for the combination Indians, they conducted themselves in a highly civilized manner. Their etiquette in the dining room was correct and dignified. "They ordered a plenty [*sic*] of side-dishes, and their digestive organs obviously were in good running order. The Indian maiden promenaded in with considerable style about her."[28]

Twelfth Annual Tour

BUFFALO BILL COMBINATION.

SEASON OF 1883-84

Hon. W. F. CODY, Proprietor and Manager.

Memoranda of Agreement made this _____ 5 _____ day of _____ Feb _____ 188 4

between _____ W W McKeon _____ Manager

of _____ Youngstown Ohio _____ of the first part, and W. F. Cody, (Buffalo Bill) of the second part, to wit:

The said _____ Mr McKeon _____ of the first part hereby agrees to furnish the house known as _____ Opera House _____ Feb 12 1884

well-lighted, warmed and cleaned; full orchestra, all stage hands, ushers, janitors, police, and door-keeper if wanted; ticket seller; all licenses and taxes, municipal and otherwise; set of fine furniture; calcium lights; dates for stands and bills, lithographs and window tickets. A band wagon with _____ horses, and _____ 6 _____ saddle horses for street parade; and to put the pieces on the stage according to models and scene plots given by the Agent, in every particular. The usual advertising in all daily, weekly and sunday newspapers published in this place _____ 5 _____ squares _____ 6 _____ days in advance; programmes for street and house, and _____ three-sheet posters; and to pay the expenses of all bill-posting and distributing; supers and ballet women, led fire and all perishable properties, etcæteras. For and in consideration of the faithful performance of the specifications hereinbefore named, the said _____ Mr McKeon _____ of the first part shall receive _____ 30 Ten _____ per cent. of the gross receipts accruing from each and every performance of the said BUFFALO BILL COMBINATION, as hereinafter specified. There are no passes to be given out except to the Press. No tickets to be _____.

The said W. F. CODY, (Buffalo Bill) of the _____ part hereby agrees to furnish the services of the organization known as the BUFFALO BILL COMBINATION, to _____ the entire entertainment, the usual amount of advance pictorial printing, lithographs and half sheets. For _____ in consideration of the faithful performance of which, the said W. F. CODY (or his authorized Agent,) shall receive _____ 70 Ten _____ per cent. of the gross receipts accruing from the said entertainments hereinafter specified Settlement to be made from ticket office statement and the ticket boxes during or at close of each and every performance. Said engagement to

commence on the _____ 12 _____ day of _____ Feb _____ 188 4

and continue _____ one _____ days/including matinee on _____ of each week.

Witness our signatures and seals this _____ 5 _____ day of _____ Feb _____ 188 4

_____ W W McKeon _____ [L. S.]

_____ [signature] _____ [L. S.]

Business Manager

For Hon. W. F. CODY, } Proprietor and Manager. (Buffalo Bill,)

A contract for the Buffalo Bill Combination's appearance in Youngstown, OH, February 12, 1884. Mahoning Valley Historical Society, Youngstown, OH.

Overall, spring 1883 was not an especially good season for Cody. His devotees and scoffers delivered plenty of disparate remarks. The *New York Mirror* stringer in Newport believed the drama was "[m]uch better than any of the former plays," but the Portland journalist decided "the company and play were the poorest he ever had." Agreeing was the Newburyport, Massachusetts, staffer who considered both "company and piece mediocre." Cody attested to his "poor luck" in a letter to his sister Julia, informing her "Money is awful scarse [*sic*]." The Cleveland lawsuit dragged on, increasing the legal fees. Besides those headaches, Cody had problems in Worcester when his Indians "got in too much fire-water after their performance and tried to clean out the hotel where they were. They drove the proprietor and Buffalo Bill into a corner and the police had to be called in."[29]

By this time, Cody's imitators had become well established in their own frontier dramas. Each year more companies added a wider range of theatre attractions indicative of the continued popularity of the American West. One dramatic critic observed the activity and believed the "possibilities of the western drama have about reached their limit."[30] What else could be left to say about the West?

Cody had plenty of ideas.

A year had passed since he first discussed the possibility of an outdoor arena exhibition with Nate Salsbury, and the idea never quit his mind for long. Taking the initiative, he telegraphed Salsbury asking if he were still interested. Meantime, Cody asked his friend Doc Carver about throwing in with him. Salsbury believed Cody had not waited for "our plan to go to Europe to ripen but no sooner had my ideas than he began to negotiate with Carver . . . and was kind enough, when they had laid all their plans, to let me in as a partner." With Carver on board, Cody offered Salsbury the opportunity to join the venture only if Carver did not object. This was a proviso Salsbury could not abide, and so he refused to join the venture. He had no use for Carver, considering him a "fakir in the show business."[31]

In March, John Burke told a reporter that "Bill and Carver are now at North Platte organizing and will start out before long with a reliable picture of Western life. There will be 200 men and as many animals employed in the exhibition. It will be a stupendous enterprise, and at least $20,000 will be spent before an exhibition is given." However, in March, Cody, who still had theatrical contracts to fulfill, was performing nightly in New Hampshire and Massachusetts. Instead, the other members of Cody's entourage were in Nebraska taking care of last-minute preparations.

The next month, the combination joined in a benefit being held in Buffalo for the New York Actors' Fund. Because many Americans regarded actors with scorn and condescension, they ranked near the bottom in social standing. Self-esteem within the profession rose when, by the late 1880s, performers began to centralize in New York to make and renew professional ties and keep abreast of new ideas. Some individual theatre companies introduced formal training, and the Actors' Fund was established in 1882 for those in need. To demonstrate his solidarity, Cody's company opened the show with the third act of their current drama.[32] Thirty years later, a group of outdoor showmen met in Chicago to found the Showmen's League of America. Much the same as the Actors' Fund, the Showmen's League promoted fellowship among the members and assisted its needy through its many programs. At the first meeting, members elected Cody president.

A few days after the benefit, the house was so packed in Syracuse it seemed "the wall paper had to be removed to make more room." The youngsters "cried themselves hoarse" when "one by one the poor painted-faced braves bit the dust. Occasionally Bill's gun failed to go off, but that didn't make the slightest difference, you know; they fell dead, just the same." The curtain fell to "tumultuous applause, red fire reigned supreme, and thus ended 'the greatest of all American plays.'"[33] Similarly, the rafters of Bradford, Pennsylvania's Wagner Opera House shook with applause when Cody "appeared just at the right time to frustrate the attempts of ruffians, and when he dug two bushels of sawdust out of a cliff and rescued the captain from a living tomb it actually seemed as though the roof would fall in." That night, Cody suffered from "an attack of giddiness and was extremely husky." He performed his marksmanship display but "in handling his rifle he assumed a variety of fancy positions, some of which were involuntary." However, near the close of the show, he seemed better and "rose superior to his fatigue and it is believed that he will have fully recovered by this morning."[34]

On April 14, Cody closed his season in Erie and headed to North Platte to conclude preparations for the first dates of the Wild West show, now less than a month away. His words indicate trepidation as well as eager anticipation:

> When the season of 1882–3 closed I found myself richer by several thousand dollars than I had ever been before, having done a splendid business at every place where my performance was given in that year. Immense success and comparative wealth, attained

in the profession of showman, stimulated me to greater exertion and largely increased my ambition for public favor. . . . I secured the services of nearly fifty cowboys and Mexicans skilled in lasso-throwing and famous as daring riders, but when these were engaged and several buffaloes, elk and mountain sheep were obtained, I found all the difficulties had not been overcome, for such exhibitions as I had prepared to give could only be shown in large open-air enclosures, and these were not always to be rented, while those that I found suitable were often inaccessible by such popular conveyances as street cars. The expenses of such a show as I had determined to give were so great that a very large crowd must be drawn to every exhibition or a financial failure would be certain; hence I soon found that my ambitious conception, instead of bringing fortune, was more likely to end in disaster. But having gone so far in the matter I determined to see the end whatever it might be.[35]

It is easiest to refer to Cody's exhibition as a "show" but he would not use the word in advertising, thinking it degrading and implying a circus. John Burke composed a "Salutatory" for the program introducing the Wild West, whose purpose was to illustrate life on the plains: Indian encampments; cowboys and vaqueros; herds of buffalo and elk; the lassoing of animals; the manner of robbing mail coaches; feats of agility, horsemanship, marksmanship, archery, and the kindred scenes and events characteristic of the border.[36]

The *Rocky Mountain and Prairie Exhibition* opened on May 19, 1883, in Omaha, then toured through the Midwest and several eastern states. During that summer, Josh Ogden, the combination's business manager for nine years, severed his connection with Cody. The *New York Mirror* gave no reason for his leaving, but Cody felt the loss of the talented man. Another, more personal, loss was just months away. While the show was in Chicago, Louisa summoned Cody home at the death of their eleven-year-old daughter Orra. Many times reporters observed how the wheels of Cody's carriage had scarcely stopped when dozens of boys converged on him. "Bovine William and the small boy's heart are inseparable."[37] Undeniably, Cody was a favorite with children. He had been unable to be present for the birth of his fourth child, Irma, in February and didn't see her until two months later. Now the distraught parents consoled each other over Orra's death, when only weeks before they had discussed divorce. Their marriage had not

John M. Burke, press agent for the Buffalo Bill Combination
and Wild West show. Courtesy Buffalo Bill Historical Center
(P.69.1405), Cody, WY.

been well matched, and Cody's constant absence added to Louisa's unhappiness, but the loss of another child brought them closer. However, once again, regardless of anyone's personal agenda, the show must go on, and shortly after the heartbroken parents laid Orra to rest beside her brother in Rochester's Mount Hope cemetery, William Frederick Cody squared his shoulders and resumed his role as Buffalo Bill.[38]

Reviews of the Wild West were as wildly enthusiastic as those for the combination. The *New York Mirror* called its realism "thrillingly effective," an accolade that no doubt warmed Cody's heart. However brilliant the show was in concept, Cody's and Carver's association did not bode well.[39] Carver accused Cody of being drunk all summer. Neither was expert at outdoor programming, and they made many miscalculations in management. Carver suggested continuing with a winter tour, but Cody had had enough. After the last performance, they agreed to split up and tossed a coin to divide the show's assets.

In late November 1883, Cody was still funding the Cleveland lawsuit even though his losses had been heavy. Because he needed money to continue the suit as well as for startup costs of his Wild West, he returned to the stage and opened the season late in Davenport, Iowa. From then until his return to the outdoor arena full-time, the press did not expend much ink discussing the virtues or failures of his dramas. Extensive post-show reviews or interviews are markedly absent. In some cases, the local press used remarks "from the exchange," that is, from newspapers in cities where he had previously appeared.

Nevertheless, "[t]he heart of the small boy will thrill to know Buffalo Bill has resumed the legitimate [theatre]," declared the *New York Daily Mirror* of December 3. Joining Cody in rifle shooting exhibits, Captain Bogardus shot at glass balls. "Neither missed a single shot," even though as actors they are not "what would be strictly called first class."[40]

Adam H. Bogardus had toured with Cody in the first few months of the Wild West and followed him back to the combination. From Albany County, New York, Bogardus won the title of Champion Wingshot of America in 1871. His abhorrence of pigeon slaughter led him to devise spring traps, which shot glass balls in simulation of bird flight. Successfully defeating the English champion in 1878, he became the World Champion Shot.[41]

Audiences and critics congratulated Cody for surrounding himself with such an excellent "Corps de Dramatique" as well as shooters of Bogardus's class. Well-known actors of considerable talent also rejoined him onstage:

Harry W. Mitchell, Jule Keen, George Beach, and C. H. Stanley. Lydia Denier returned to play the waif in *The Prairie Waif.* Frank Smith took over as leader of the uniformed band and performed solo cornets, while Chris Burger led the orchestra. This time around, a band of genuine Sioux as well as Lakota chief Red Cloud's niece and nephew would also tour with the combination.[42]

Cody's "managerical [*sic*] effort" was evident in his "care [and] attention to detail."[43] The press remarked how his combination's costumes and scenery were better than in some "more pretentious exponents of the drama."[44] Unfortunately, no reviewer took pains to describe them. The combination's publicist continued to extensively advertise upcoming shows. Having an appreciation for the results of advertising, Cody realized the need to spend money for bigger and bolder posters, banners, and programs.

In 1878, Cody's newspaper advertising had begun to incorporate a woodcut of his face. Other combinations splashed their ads with distinctive fonts. The use of a lot of white space or the repetition of the star's name were type techniques meant to catch the reader's eye. Another method was to crowd the ads with so many examples of what the performance would include that people believed they would really get their money's worth. Loyalty to a printing company was not a given. Searching for the best prices and service, circuses and other traveling companies often switched printers for their posters, sometimes every few seasons.[45]

Advance men posted notices for the combination's show on February 16 in Fort Wayne on buildings and fences. Blacksmith shops were also favored spots. The effort proved futile, however, as the house was only half filled; the *Journal Gazette* guessed Cody was "losing his grip." In former years when newspapers were more receptive and touted his show's arrival, Cody invariably played to crowded houses. "Times have changed since then and the long haired actor dont [*sic*] seem to paralyze so many people as formerly." As for his shooting, "Fort Wayne can produce a boy not yet of age who can do finer shooting than Buffalo Bill ever dreamt of." It may very well have been the same Fort Wayne critic who, two years earlier, gloated at what he took to be the improved discernment of the city's amusement patrons when Cody's show did rather poor business. Once more, he was "glad to notice that Fort Wayne people are beginning to evince some taste in the bestowal of their theatrical patronage."[46]

His penultimate appearance in Milwaukee also left him with less than enthusiastic reviews. The critic observed Cody had "smoothed down" much of his roughness, and "while he will never astonish the world as an actor, his magnificent figure and handsome face form a picture" which playgoers like. Lydia Denier looked "sweet" as the prairie waif, but was not particularly strong in the role. Even Jule Keen, whom newsmen usually singled out for special notice as the comic Dutchman, "should either give up attempting to sing or shut off the orchestra." The rest of the cast fared as badly; they were up to the situations, but called for "no special notice." Cody closed the season in Chicago on March 8, after alternating *Prairie Waif* and *Twenty Days* for the week's stay, then left to prepare for another Wild West season.

Two months later, he returned to Chicago with the outdoor show.

After splitting from Cody, Carver started his own western program. The following year, the two men's separate companies crisscrossed each other's routes. In early July 1885, Cody, now teamed up with Nate Salsbury, instigated a lawsuit in Willimantic, Connecticut, against his former partner over Carver's use of the title "Wild West." Cody claimed he had come up with it, preferring it to Carver's suggestion, "The Golden West." By attaching Carver's show for bond and having him jailed, Cody effectively disbanded his primary competition. Carver reacted by seeking a $25,000 attachment on Cody's show. Two weeks later, Cody was deposed. Carver's defense lawyers questioned him about his past and his stage career in attempts to gain some history to use against him. When the attorney asked if he were an actor or performer, Cody replied, "an actor or performer is the same; and I was both, although I might have been a d—d poor one."[47]

In *Life on the Border*, Cody didn't remember "whether it was in my business to rescue that girl, or for someone else to do it, but the girl got back all the same, and you can bet on that." Then the judge wanted to know about his role in *Knight of the Plains*. "What character common in western life, or uncommon, was known as a Knight?" Cody replied, "I presume the meaning of Knight is a man who did gallant acts and brave deeds as in olden times, and I don't see why the frontier cannot have Knights as well as any other country, or Knights as well as 'Evil Spirits,'" the latter a dig at Carver. He hadn't played *Buffalo Bill at Bay* long enough to remember any particular incident in it except that he had escaped trouble and would "get out of this as I did out of that scrape."[48]

The suit dragged on all summer 1885 and finally resulted in Cody's leaving Connecticut and not returning for eleven years. Salsbury ultimately offered to pay all court costs, which Carver interpreted as an admission that all he said about Cody was true. It was a fleeting victory, however. Late that summer, Carver sat in his attorney's office signing three thousand letters offering his services to any county fair for $300.

Carver was not the only bitter enemy Cody had; there was also Jack Crawford with whom he was obliged to contend. Although eight years had passed since Crawford's accident, the rift between the two men had not healed. In the midst of the Carver lawsuit, Cody heard reports of Crawford's also disparaging him. Jack declared his own works to be "the best, cleanest and most truthful plays of Frontier American life and history that have ever been written." Cody's dramas, he preached, were "gross exaggerations and untruthful fictions of frontier life and characters," prompting Cody to issue a challenge:[49]

> My Dear Jack, I see you are going back on the Stage. Now lets have a little friendly chat. and compare notes. For you don't leave a stone unturned to give me a dig when ever you can—in interviews with news papers you say . . . [t]hat I am a ten cent-novel scout &c. &c.—all of which you know is false. . . . I done all I could for you when you were hurt in Virginia City—I have never injured you or tried to by making slurring remarks about you—on the contrary have helped you when ever I could. . . . You say you are the only Scout with any Dramatic ability. Now if you wish to prove that you start your company—I will start me one and we will play the same towns this winter at the same time. and let the public decide that question—and this I will do if you dont stop your slurring me. But if you treat me as I have you I will not interfere with you in any way. but if you try to belittle me before the public I will be after you with a dramatic company and we will see who the public recognizes as the Actor Scout.[50]

The *Mirror* announced that Cody's combination would reopen in Philadelphia in mid-November, but Cody himself would not join it until January. What Cody would be doing until then was not questioned. The problem, Quincy's *Daily Whig* observed, is that "Buffalo Bill is at present traveling on his reputation, and as nearly everyone has seen him, his audiences will get smaller at every succeeding visit." In addition, his supporting troupe did not deserve large audiences because "[t]here is not a good actor in the entire outfit and the play is a disappointment to those who love to witness sensational dramas."[51]

He may have caught up with his combination intermittently because reviewers occasionally mentioned his shooting feats. For what was left of the 1885–86 theatre season he revived *The Prairie Waif* with Jule Keen and Lydia Denier starring in Buffalo Bill's Dutchman and Prairie Waif Combination. News reports do not mention Cody being in the play, nor was his name prominent in the advertising. The title change of the combination implies the Dutchman, longtime supporting cast member, was assuming a major role.

Matt Snyder opened the season playing Cody's role, and his impersonation seems to have fooled the press. He was "so handsome and gentlemanly a fellow that it is hard to believe that he passes so much time among the Indians." Besides resembling Cody, Snyder was also a proficient marksman, causing a critic to remark, "When he handles the rifle or revolver he does so with ease and abandon that are unapproachable, and his rifle shooting is perfection itself."[52]

Yet, four weeks into the season, Snyder's name was no longer featured in promotions; his replacement was Buck Taylor, "Western Scout and Daring Rider." Harkening back to the idea of chivalric brotherhood, Buck was touted as "King of the Cowboys." The tall, strong Texan, whose real name was William Levi Taylor, seemed built for a cowboy's life, and, in fact, he had worked on Cody and North's ranch. Besides Taylor, who led each morning's street parade in Cody's stead, the cast included four Pawnee Indians. In act 4 the warriors were given rein to perform their "wild and weird dances . . . under the control of Pawnee Bill, Interpreter and Boy Chief of the Pawnees."[53]

Pawnee Bill was Gordon Lillie who, as a young boy, watched in awe as Buffalo Bill, Texas Jack, and Wild Bill performed *Scouts of the Plains* in his hometown of Bloomington, Illinois. Inspired by the histrionics, he roamed the West and secured a job at the Pawnee agency. While living among the Indians, Lillie met Charles Burgess whom Cody had sent to procure Indians for the show. Lillie served as interpreter for them; then in 1883 he took over from Frank North. He, too, excelled in marksmanship and gave some "fine examples" of target shooting during the drama.[54]

In Allentown, Pennsylvania, the stringer for the *Mirror* reported in on December 5. *The Prairie Waif* drew a full house but, "the play is tame and the company with the exception of Jule Keene [*sic*] and the ladies is no better." Cody's absence bothered few critics. This seems remarkable in light of past seasons when he could have carried the whole show himself. In earlier years, the audience would have raved had he merely stood onstage

Allentown, PA, ad for the November 27, 1885, performance.

and recounted tall tales of his frontier exploits. Now he doesn't appear to
have been missed. Probably Cody did not miss the stage appearances either.
All of his energies were focused on the Wild West, which he intended to be
an authentic demonstration of life on the frontier. Histrionic dramas now
seemed restrictive and artificial.

He spent December in North Platte and may have accompanied Louisa
in her annual pilgrimage to their children's graves in Rochester. The combination performed without him until he joined it in Chicago early in 1886.[55]
By the time they reached Clinton, Iowa, the band of Indians, cowboys, and
actors were playing to a large audience, where "Mr. Cody exhibited some
of his old time favorite shots, and the troupe and play were highly pleasing
to the attendance."[56]

When they appeared in Columbus, Ohio, for a week, reviews indicate
Cody was again absent, but Keen kept the combination going. "[H]is inimi-
table songs fully sustained his reputation as one of the leading dialectic
comedians on the stage." Pawnee Bill, capable of many of the same stunts
as Cody, put on a marksmanship exhibit. The Indians also came in for their
share of notice, if only for being gentle and mild-mannered. Despite their
claim that palefaces' scalps filled their wigwams, a reporter discounted this
boast. It was his opinion that "any robust lady with a hoe handle could have
chased them all over town."[57]

The next time Cody gave a press interview, the reporter noticed that
his hair was "long and glossy and like his eyes, moustache and goatee, a
jetty black, although moustache and goatee are beginning to show traces
of gray." At a question about Wild Bill Hickok, Cody remembered, "I was
with him like a brother for twenty years. He was a man with a whole world
of nerve and one of the kindest, best-hearted fellows on earth. He seemed
to be unfortunate in getting into scrapes, but he always 'got' his man when
he went for him." After a gunfight with Hickok, "[t]he other fellow was
quietly buried, for none of Bill's subjects ever went away and got cured so
they could make him future trouble." Once Hickok had acquired a reputation, "murderous ruffians" began hunting him down to increase their own
notoriety. Cody was critical of Hickok's habit of shooting blank cartridges
close to the legs of supers during the short time he was with the combination, but he sighed his regrets over "[p]oor Bill" and his demise at the hand
of a "cowardly assassin."[58]

When the Burlington interviewer asked about the Winchester rifle he
used onstage, Cody said it was rapid enough that he could give a "more

fancy exhibition with it. . . . I have a fine rifle that I use in long distance shooting, made by Higby [*sic* Rigby], the famous Irish gunsmith. I consider it the most accurate shooting gun at long range that I ever saw." Cody explained he was better at shooting flying targets. "When shooting at a stationary object I wait too long. In shooting at an object in the air I pull just exactly at the instant my sights cover the mark. In fact I am so accustomed to that kind of work that I can go out with my Winchester and get twice as many prairie chickens in a day as any man can with a shotgun."

To conclude, Cody announced he was on his way to California with his combination. He hadn't planned on going out at all and had just recently rejoined the troupe. "I put this company out only because they were my people and could do nothing through the winter and I thought it would help them out." He explained he'd been at home on his ranch resting after being away all summer with the Wild West show.[59] He may also have returned at this particular time because Jule Keen broke his arm when his horse fell on him during the parade.[60]

After years of legal hassles, the verdict in Cleveland over ancestral land had finally come in against the Cody family. Nevertheless, he wrote confidently to his sister: "I think our poor days are over for I really believe the public now looks upon me as the one man in my business. And if they will only think so for a year or two I will make money enough for us all for our life time."[61]

The combination headed west and, after appearing in Cheyenne, it moved on to Salt Lake City where the *Herald* completely roasted the play and its actors with a critique in its Amusements column. Cody, it said, "has secured a coterie of artists whose merits might cause Salvini himself to blush—for his profession. Three real Pawnee Indians, whose unbridled grace recalls with a shudder all the youthful dread which used to seize us in reading Mr. Beadle's tales of the exploits of the renowned Ca-Ca, the Skunk." Buck Taylor reminded the journalist of "a heifer on skates," while the actor playing Yellow Hand strode about the stage reciting his lines in tragic tones. His histrionics "convulsed the down stairs portion of the house where it was intended they should be terror-struck." Lydia Denier, as the waif, uttered such "thrilling chestnuts as 'Unhand me, villain!' 'Your bride? Never, I'd rather be a corpse!' and 'Death rather than dishonor.'" The critic hoped never to have to sit through such a "grand spectacle" again. He even thought Cody "somewhat worse as an actor than he was ten years ago; he is a crack shot and that is all[.] . . . [H]e should shun the stage as he

William Levi "Buck" Taylor, "King of the Cowboys." Courtesy Buffalo Bill Historical Center (P.69.596), the Bradford-Decker Collection, Cody, WY.

would strong drink."[62] Small boys high in the gallery, not bothered by such critiques, still thrilled at the sight of him. Each lad yearned for a life on the plains where he could "kill an Indian before breakfast and half a dozen after dinner."[63]

In March, the combination once more delighted audiences in California: Sacramento, Woodland, Stockton, San Jose, Oakland, and San Francisco. Reviewers could find nothing new to say and, where they had once written three or four paragraphs of praise, or sometimes, denigration, their words in the Amusements column scarcely consisted of a paragraph. Editors used the "Short News of the Day" format to announce "One of the best shows on the road is the Buffalo Bill Combination" or "Buffalo Bill's troupe render a play well worthy the cost of admission," but they failed to send a critic.[64] When the actors arrived in Virginia City, Nevada, a circus-like atmosphere of several hundred people were on hand to greet them. One of those was Alfred Doten, a longtime newspaper editor, who attended the performance at the opera house. He succinctly noted in his journal that the show was "Pretty good—worth the money—$1 and 50 cts."[65]

Two weeks later, after the Denver performance on April 10, 1886, Buffalo Bill Cody disbanded his combination. Fourteen momentous years had come to an end. Cody was leaving the theatrical stage with which he was by now so familiar. We don't know whether his audience realized its significance, but the final bows almost certainly radiated excitement tinged with melancholy both for the principal character and for his loyal band of professional performers. Some of them had supported Cody for most of the troupe's existence; a few would join him in the Wild West. A new era was about to begin.

— CHAPTER TEN —

finale

◈

"Cody," I said to myself, "you have fetched 'em!"
—Cody, *Story of the Wild West*

CODY WAS FORTY YEARS OLD WHEN HE RETIRED FROM THE THEATRICAL
stage. He had only a moment to play Janus and look back on his accomplishments and forward to his biggest challenge. Experience had been a
commanding force in his education as an entertainer, and he was eager to
apply the lessons learned during the combination years.

No one had expected his frontier plays to make great contributions
to theatrical art, and they didn't. But, as journalists frequently observed,
they did give the plainsman and his scouting partners the opportunity to
show off frontier skills already proven, if only fictitiously, in hundreds of
dime novels. Later in his career, when he wrote stories, he apologized for
the "blood and thunder." "I am sorry to have to lie so outrageously in this
yarn. My hero has killed more Indians on one war-trail than I have killed
in all my life. . . . If you think the revolver and bowie-knife are used too
freely, you may cut out a fatal shot or stab wherever you deem it wise."[1]
Onstage, Cody's technique of underplaying his role reflected the emerging
realism style, while his status as bona fide frontiersman lent authenticity to

the performance. As the years went on and he became more respected as a performer, he grew more pragmatic than a dime-novel hero caricature. Referring in interviews to his land and cattle holdings, announcing in the theatrical papers his seasonal profits, and wearing ostentatious jewelry all reinforced the evolution.

The "savagery to civilization" theme, intrinsic to most border dramas, formed a backdrop to the action. The sights and sounds of wild and fierce Indians effortlessly exemplified the violence of the frontier, especially if their appearance and aggression corresponded to easterners' ideas of Indian hostility, until Cody allowed the Indians to act as themselves instead of formulaic savages. While the land and environs also tested a frontiersman's fortitude, the effect of acres of harsh landscape, unrelenting sun, or torrential rains was difficult to reproduce on a stage and relied for their portrayal on the playwright's talent and on skillfully painted scenery.

Cody had grown up on the plains, was more or less self-educated, and had spent years scouting and hunting buffalo. Expecting a man crude and uncivilized, easterners delighted in his and the other combination scouts' easy ability to deal with dangers, even those exaggerated for the stage. That the men possessed grace and charm surprised them. Instead of the anticipated hulking appearance, the scouts had "splendid manly forms which their wild lives on the plains have admirably developed." Newsmen were quick to report their bearing "is what might naturally be expected from men of undaunted bravery, self-conscious of their powers, fierce and powerful in struggles, but with the ease and gentleness of well bred men when unaffected by the excitement incident to their professions."[2] The *Wisconsin State Journal* observed Cody's "fine, intelligent, strong face" and concluded he was "a man ready to counsel or command or to cope with any adversary he may meet."[3] A buckskin suit worn alternately with evening clothes and diamond jewelry perfectly befitted the man billing himself as the link between savagery and civilization.

At the time the combination debuted in December 1872, Cody had acquired only a minute measure of business sense from several months following the Civil War spent managing the boardinghouse his mother had built in Salt Creek, Kansas. His sister, Helen Cody Wetmore, recalled that "Socially, he was an irreproachable landlord; financially, his shortcomings were deplorable."[4] New to acting, he left arrangements for the first season up to Ned Buntline who, from his many cross-country temperance tours, was familiar with trooping. Cody's decision to exclude Buntline the next season meant he and Texas Jack had to manage all aspects of the stage production. The experience taught him what an overwhelming task it was. After the first season, the *Omaha Daily Bee* informed its readers that the scouts had "each cleared $30,000 during the past eight months,"[5] yet Cody complained that he had only profited by $6,000. He blamed Buntline, thinking all those full houses should have translated into bigger takings. But suddenly, "[u]nheard extravagances became ours," Louisa recollected. "And Will, dear, generous soul that he was, believed that an inexhaustible supply of wealth had become his forever."[6] Once he began to balance the combination's income and expenses, Cody ceased criticizing Buntline for the lack of large end profits, which his and Texas Jack's expenditures as two of the nouveau riche had precluded. As late as 1880, Cody wrote to Jack Crawford, "I like Buntline. Always did. And expect to do something for him in his old age."[7]

During his scouting days with the army, Cody had seen too many officers who didn't seem to know much about army business. Resolving to do things differently, he hired people with expertise for his combination and put them in positions of trust and authority. John M. Burke handled publicity and bookings and occasionally filled in as actor. Josh Ogden joined the combination in 1874 as an already astute business manager. Jule Keen began as supporting actor and became the combination's general manager when Cody was preoccupied planning the Wild West. His star status secured, Cody hired professional theatrical companies, which included famous contemporary actors such as Constance Hamblin, Eliza Hudson, Robert Downing, Joseph Winter, Frank Mordaunt, and Fred Maeder as support.

During the mock battles, when he and Texas Jack clouded the stage with rifle smoke, the acrid odor and tremendous din pervaded the theatres. Soon enough, Cody realized he had underestimated how startlingly loud rifle reports sounded to anyone not familiar with them. Once aware of the fright, he underloaded the blank cartridges so audiences could enjoy the action without flinching. By the time he started his outdoor show, he ordered the gunfire of the first few performers muffled until the audience became accustomed to it.

Regardless of how boisterously the scouts behaved in the melodramas and no matter where their weapons were pointed, the Indians, having read the script, fell dead. At first, the combination's advertised "Indians" were whites in costume. It's a wonder how, in the flurry of "battle," an actor's black-haired wig didn't fall off or his red makeup smear to reveal white skin. Cody, appreciative of theatrical makeup and costuming, no doubt cringed at such fakery. In 1877, he negotiated with the U.S. Bureau of Indian Affairs to employ real American Indians to act alternately as friends or foes and to show off their bloodthirsty glares, torture at the stake, and bow-and-arrow shooting. Their burning the prairie or torching a settler's cabin appeared realistic through the use of "red fire," a powder that glowed a rich red when ignited, though its pungent odor was "enough to strangle white man or kill an Injun quicker than trader whiskey."[8]

Fed up with simulated action, particularly his misnamed "duel" with Yellow Hair, Cody envisioned an exact re-creation of the confrontation. He tested the idea with only one small gray donkey, but soon, he was reenacting the skirmish authentically on horseback. Such realism was only a frivolous improvement if theatre patrons didn't know the show was coming to town, so his advertising also grew more elaborate. In the beginning, combination ads were typical of others of the period. Announcements one column wide and four inches long hyped Cody's show as the "Original Border Combination with the Original Heroes." A few years later, new type would tease with information that the even more famous Cody was just back from an expedition to the Black Hills. By 1879, publicity extolled the other troupers' talents, particularly those of special interest like the Burgesses or Austin brothers' rifle shooting. When the parades Cody launched grew longer and more structured, announcements invited citizens to get a first look at the actors as they marched through the streets to the accompaniment of band music.

The combination ceased touring from March 1884 until November 1885 because, by then, Cody was becoming increasingly involved in his Wild West exhibition. Discontinuing the stage melodramas entirely a few months later was a decisive move that would have a profound effect on his future activities. Free at last to devote himself full time to touring with an outdoor show, he found there was much more he could incorporate into the production, little realizing it would bring him his greatest fame. He continued to rely on his innate sense of timing, honed during so many years of treading the boards, coupled with his grasp of melodramatic presentation. His knowledge of how to create a sense of anticipation that captivated audiences and, to some extent, his managerial capabilities, augured future success.

The transition from combination to Wild West show was inevitable. For years Cody had incorporated into the border dramas an increasingly factual depiction of life on the frontier as he knew it. Matters came to a head when, faced with the ever-growing inclusion of live animals, demonstrations of marksmanship, and the number of supporting actors that threatened to overrun the boundaries of any stage, Cody realized the only answer was an outdoor venue. His experiences with temperamental actors, late trains, dirty dressing rooms, hurried meals, unpredictable animals, and the occasional problems with disobedient Indians (who had largely replaced the original "supers"), together with audiences who raved over live action despite some disapproving critics, all contributed to his ability to handle the challenges ahead.

Cody was not the first to capitalize on the popularity of outdoor western shows. As early as 1860, James "Grizzly" Adams partnered with circus man P. T. Barnum to tour with his menagerie of bears. As soon as the Golden Spike was driven in 1869, traveling companies and circuses began touring the country by rail, and Cody surely attended such shows when he was scouting out of Fort McPherson.[9] In 1872, Sidney Barnett, a Niagara Falls museum owner, convinced Wild Bill Hickok to emcee a grand buffalo hunt. Thousands of spectators were disappointed when Indians and cowboys pursued only three buffalo around the arena; nonetheless, the display was one of Canada's first Wild West shows. By the time Cody started his show, more than fifty outdoor exhibitions and circuses were touring, among them James A. Bailey, Sells Brothers, and the Ringling Brothers. Some imitated Cody's program and also gave rip-roaring performances by cowboys. Because popularity of outdoor entertainment was at its height, Cody's Wild West performed all over the country and in several European cities, but like circuses, his biggest rival, it had limitations. Whereas the combination could move from city to city, sometimes overnight, the size and financial extravagance of the Wild West show as well the exorbitant cost of railroad equipment necessitated that it make extended stays in selected areas.[10]

Shortly after the Wild West's first performance in May 1883, several companies competed for that name, among them Fargo's Wild West, Hennessey's Wild West, and Adam Forepaugh's Wild West Combination. Cody objected to other companies using the term "Wild West," on the grounds that they were "encroaching upon his possessions, taking advantage of his discovery, and staking a claim on ground already claimed."[11] To protect his vision and to establish a legal claim to the entertainment narrative, Cody and Salsbury applied for copyright in December 1883. A year and a half later, John Burke announced that copyright had been granted. The full name of Cody's show was legally "The Wild West, or Life Among the Red Men and the Road Agents of the Plains and Prairies. An Equine

Dramatic Exposition on Grass or under Canvas of the Advantages of Frontiersmen and Cowboys," but it was more familiarly and simply known as "Buffalo Bill's Wild West."[12] While the copyright protected the show's narrative, Cody was essentially powerless to stop another showman from using the name.

For that reason, he found himself going head to head with a formidable competitor and former partner, Doc Carver. The problem began when Carver claimed he was the originator of the Wild West show genre while "Bill Cody was on the stage killing painted white men."[13] He told reporters that Cody, down to his last $17 after ten years with his combination, approached him on hearing that Carver was starting an outdoor show. He begged to be a part of it, even eagerly agreeing to Carver's stipulation that he stop drinking. Like many claims Carver made, nothing substantiates this account. Far from penniless, at the time of Carver's allegation, Cody was a nationally recognized performer. With receipts from *The Prairie Waif* netting him $40,000 to $50,000, he had amassed enough capital to acquire a ranch and livestock. Besides achieving financial success, he had also earned his company's loyalty. When he split the Wild West show's assets with Carver after their challenging first season, all the people, including John Burke and Jule Keen, chose to work with Cody rather than Carver.

When Cody's exhibit opened at the St. Louis Fairgrounds in late April 1884, Carver's show was finishing its run at the city's racetrack. According to one manager, both men had been spoiling to get at each other. By then, the mutual animosity was so great that, when Carver learned Cody was on the street, he approached him with gun drawn. Cody, nonplussed, drew his own pistol. Before either could fire a shot, friends intervened.[14]

When the two troupes crossed each other's route a year later in Connecticut, the showmen initiated lawsuits and countersuits against each other. The main issues stemmed from Cody's claim that his show's title was copyrighted, and that he was the sole owner of the words Carver used in his billing.[15] During their day in court, Carver's lawyer argued that he could prove the name "Wild West" originated with his client. Cody shook his head and said, "You can't do it."[16]

Another lawyer chimed in, "[b]oth Carver and Cody claim to have originated the Wild West idea, and I believe Salsbury claims to have been the first to suggest it too." Carver's attorney remarked sardonically, "[Bondsman] Henry Tuttle will claim it next." In his deposition, Cody testified that, when he and Carver were partners, the show was sometimes advertised as Buffalo Bill's Wild West because he was more well known than Carver. Carver had complained, but the publicity agents told the men they were working for the best interests of the show, and it would be more lucrative to advertise Cody's name prominently. Outside the judge's office, Carver's lawyer told reporters there was nothing whatever to Cody's claim of show copyright and, even if there was, Carver had the same interest in the show and therefore had as much right to it.[17]

The Carver-Cody imbroglio was not just a clash of egos but a clash of vision. Much like Cody's, Carver's show included cowboy ropers, Mexican vaqueros, wild broncos, and Sioux Indians. But despite the similarities between the two shows, Carver's experience as dentist-turned-shootist included no storytelling or dramatic background. The Wild West as a presenter of myth had been developed and established in the combination's stage plays, the fourteen years of melodrama serving as Cody's schooling in narrative structure. The Wild West did not begin as the extravagant program of frontier talents coalesced in a narrative into which it eventually developed, however. "It was an almost impromptu affair," Annie Oakley noticed when she joined the show in 1885, "—doing just what they were used to doing every day for a living[.] . . . [It was] no elaborate outfit[.] . . . [A]mong ourselves it was more like a clan than a show, or business performance."[18] More important than all the practical lessons Cody learned from the combination years was his burgeoning commitment to historical authenticity and education. His familiarity with the frontier legitimized his claim to being a link between it—its primitiveness and its ultimate evolution—and his Wild West's display of it, of the people and historical events therein.

Fortunately for Cody, Nate Salsbury was a competent businessman who kept the show up and running while Cody sat in court. Salsbury saw himself as the mastermind of the Wild West with Cody as frontrunner and showman. But no one man could manage all the performers, stock, and props required for the show. Burke retained title of publicist, ably assisted by press agent Dexter Fellows. John Y. Nelson and Frank North, both of whom had lived and worked with Indians, utilized their expertise as interpreters. We may never know the names of all the behind-the-scenes men who routinely set up bleachers, fed stock, or cooked meals, but they worked so efficiently that, during the time the show played in Germany, army officers came to take notes on their organization.

Besides experienced managers, Cody signed on top-billed performers. Buck Taylor, handsome "King of the Cowboys," awed audiences with his riding and roping tricks, as did Johnny Baker and his shooting as "the Cowboy Kid." Annie Oakley was already a champion shooter when she became the Wild West's number one act after Cody himself. Dexter Fellows remembered her as "a consummate actress, with a personality that made itself felt as soon as she entered the arena."[19] Skipping in and throwing kisses endeared her to audiences even before she thrilled them with a marksmanship equaling Cody's.

No matter the popularity or order of appearance of its other performers, when Cody rode into the arena on his snow-white steed and waved to the crowd, "Quick as a flash every kiddie is on his feet, hands waving at the hero of his imagination and of his love," *Denver Post* reporter Frances Wayne wrote.[20] A *Chicago Daily News* critic noticed that Cody had not lost the charisma he displayed since the beginning of his career. "No such engaging story-teller as Buffalo Bill figures in history or romance . . . and not a dozen men I know have his splendid magnetism, keen appreciation and happy originality. He sticks to the truth mainly and is more intensely beguiling than the veriest makers of fiction."[21]

By sticking to the truth mainly, Cody hoped to educate his audiences about the frontier he loved. By the 1890s, only vast areas of the West and the agriculture-oriented South remained untouched by urbanization. Americans anticipated reaping the fruits of the burgeoning industrial age while at the same time yearning after the halcyon myth of the agrarian frontier. Easterners extolled the West as a land of wide-open spaces and opportunities, a place where, according to Frederick Jackson Turner, "freedom of opportunity is opened, the cake of custom is broken, and new activities, new lines of growth, new institutions and new ideals, are brought into existence."[22] After a while, even the Indian seemed a fabrication who had never really existed. News of the last of the Indian wars coincided with Jackson's pronouncement of the closing of the frontier. For this reason, some, like Cody and the would-be cowboy, President Theodore Roosevelt, thought the western idealism needed to be preserved as "a sacred bulwark against profane industrialism."[23] Americans, with only faded memories of frontiersmen and faced with urban reality, coped by consuming dime novels about frontier heroes and attending Indian plays and Wild West shows.

From its inception with the "Old Glory Blowout," his Wild West was as authentic as Cody could make it. In order to frame the show's disorganized assortment of acts into a unifying narrative, Salsbury hired professional actor and playwright Steele Mackaye. The drama he designed brought many

William Frederick Cody, c. 1887. Courtesy Buffalo Bill Historical
Center (P.69.2088), Cody, WY.

aspects of American history into theatre for the first time and divided the program into four epochs: the Primeval Forest of America, the Prairie, the Cattle Ranch, and the Mining Camp. The extravaganza required a horse track–size arena, Matt Morgan's four semicircular panoramic drops, and Nelse Waldron's mechanical effects, including huge steam-powered fans to simulate a cyclone.[24] Nightly, the tremendous scope of the West was recreated under the same stars that glittered over the plains. The performance was acted "with great spirit and power by Buffalo Bill, several dozen cowboys, cowgirls, and genuine greasers, besides a hundred and fifty Indians of various tribes in full fig and feather."[25] To add to the count of performers, the production required up to five hundred horses, trivializing the donkey and two horses featured in the stage plays. Elk, buffalo, deer, mountain sheep, and longhorns also furthered the authentic effect.

The Wild West lineup evolved over the years, introducing new acts and improvements on the old ones, but popular features such as the Pony Express and the Indian Raid on a Settler's Cabin remained more or less unchanged. Buffalo Bill and his gun-blazing cowboys arrive to rescue the family in the nick of time. All the Indians who "die" during the subsequent fight rise to fight again, not unlike the resurrected Indians of his stage shows. Cody, more than anyone, rescued the cowboy from a reputation as a lawless ne'er-do-well, compelling the public instead to regard him as a chivalric knight of the plains, a reputation he still retains. Cody realized this colorful individual, who was a brilliant horseman as well, had a great appeal.[26]

John Burke's text for one season's posters read: "The Romantic West Brought East in Reality. Everything Genuine . . . Actual Scenes in the Nation's Progress to Delight, Please, Gratify, Chain and Interest the Visitor." To which Cody added, "A true rescript of life on the frontier as I know it to be, and which no fictitious pen can describe."[27] The *Montreal Gazette* valued the exhibition as "the picture of frontier life painted in intense realism, each scene standing forth in bold relief. . . . It is a place and a scene to visit . . . not for mere amusement's sake, but for the sake of studying in a school where all lessons are objective and for which have been gathered materials for observation and instruction which, in the nature of things, are perishable and soon destined to banish."[28]

In his zeal to demonstrate the theme of "Foes in '76, Friends in '85," Cody was finally able to persuade Sioux chief Sitting Bull to tour with him. The gesture not only educated audiences about the Indians but also parlayed Cody's status as friend to the American Indians and as link between the red man and the white to even greater credibility. In the Wild West, however, Indians were more than actors, as they had likewise been in the combination. Their daily lifestyle, at least as much as was feasible to demonstrate on the Wild West grounds, was on display. The innovation allowing visitors to wander around the show grounds fascinated Americans and Europeans.

Because advertising for the Wild West was more complex than for the combination, Cody's managers devised strategies months in advance in order to have time to design and execute new posters and programs. Cody's insistence on quality in his Wild West "quite naturally extended to the design and lithography of his 'paper.'" His celebrity brought him into contact with talented contemporary artists, including Matt Morgan, Frederic Remington, and Charles Russell. It is plausible he commissioned them to create elaborate, sophisticated posters to announce performances. The golden age of outdoor shows coincided fortuitously with the "golden age of the American poster," so Cody's advertisements were the best designed and crafted. As the principal method of advertising, "they had to be good."[29]

Photographs that once showed Cody grouped with his combination players now featured him in Wild West settings or front and center in group shots of hundreds. The woodcut running alongside the column of newsprint used during the later theatrical years seemed primitive compared to the multicolored Wild West bills that advance men plastered across building facades and fences. These kinds of playbills aggravated the dissension between Cody and Carver. As one company nailed up posters advertising its upcoming show, the other covered over them with admonitions to "Wait for the real thing!"

In the 1886 "Salutatory," John Burke identified Buffalo Bill as the one man "to whose sagacity, skill, energy, and courage . . . the settlers of the West owe so much for the reclamation of the prairie from the savage Indian and wild animals, who so long opposed the march of civilization."[30] Many posters for both the combination and Wild West illustrate Cody centered among vignettes of the mythical West and of his show. In others, the images of prominent generals or distinguished heads of state who had been guests at the Wild West encircle his profile, alluding to his role as both performer and historical figure.

Besides advertising, other aspects of the show were also complicated— some were so incredibly complex that its managers needed to plan a year in advance. One detail involved reserving acreage for the arena along a predetermined circuit with a nearby water source and railroad line. Whereas combination actors often carried their own scenery and costumes, Wild West managers had to lease over fifty railroad cars to transport all the trappings and riggings for one night's performance. Combination supporting actors came from the ranks of professional companies; Wild West performers needed to be auditioned, stock and props purchased and organized. When all else was ready, Salsbury insisted on frequent rehearsals, not only of the performance but also of the setting up and tearing down.[31]

Financing such an elaborate exhibition was similarly exhaustive. Extant ledgers show expenses for actors, animals, butchers, books, bill posting, ammunition, groceries, hotels, Indian goods, photos, livery, licenses, medicines, police, print jobs, rent, saddles, restaurants, and telegrams. Partners like Salsbury helped run the Wild West, overseeing the most monumental tasks and the most minute. Salsbury's ideas also influenced the development of the program. When it looked doubtful that the American Indians would receive continued government sanction to travel with the show, he designed "The Congress of Rough Riders of the World," featuring soldiers from America, England, France, Germany, and Russia. James Bailey, brought in when Salsbury's health began failing in 1894, helped with the routing and suggested Cody add sideshows and freak exhibits. However, when Bailey died in 1906, Cody reintroduced western acts more in keeping with the show's original purpose. It was a smart move. One newspaper reporter considered it "remarkable that the people of the east will pay good money year after year to see these sons of the plains do their cheap antics. But the show always draws big houses and pays large dividends."[32]

However, after a while, even large dividends could not compensate for the mounting shortfalls. Rising expenses, stiffer competition from rival companies, and some poor management decisions drove the Wild West dangerously close to shutting down. Upon Bailey's death, Gordon "Pawnee Bill" Lillie offered to buy out his interest and merge their two shows. The offer came at an opportune time, effectively rescuing Cody from bankruptcy. At first reluctant even though desperate for funding, Cody was nevertheless impressed with Lillie's business acumen. Fortunately, profits and attendance increased under his capable management.

For nearly thirty years, Cody's Wild West did more than any other medium to increase public awareness of the part-factual, part-mythical but rapidly disappearing West. His only regret was that for every day of the show's production, "I did not know the thrill of the trail, and feel a little sorry that my Western adventures would thereafter have to be lived in spectacles." Indeed, on Cody Day, celebrated in Omaha, Nebraska, in August 1898, Cody himself conceded the end of the frontier. "The whistle of the locomotive has drowned the howl of the coyote; the barbed-wire fence has narrowed the range of the cowpuncher[.] . . . [T]ime goes on and brings with it new duties and responsibilities, but we who are called old-timers cannot forget the trials and tribulations." That he never did was corroborated by many, including contemporary American author Mark Twain, who wrote to Cody, "I have now seen your Wild West show two days in succession, enjoyed it thoroughly. It brought back to me the breezy, wild life of the Rocky mountains, and stirred me like a war song. The show is genuine, cowboys, vaqueros, Indians, stage-coach, costumes, the same as I saw them in the frontier years ago."[33]

Despite careful planning and efforts to keep the acts current and compelling, the era of Wild West shows began to wane. Scarcely ten years after Cody oversaw North Platte's Fourth of July celebration, Francis Parkman, in the introduction to his 1892 book *The Oregon Trail*, wrote, "The wild west is tamed, and its savage charms have withered."[34] The next year, while Cody was celebrating one of his most lucrative years in show business outside the gates of the Chicago World's Fair, Frederick Jackson Turner was inside proposing that "the frontier has gone, and with its going has closed the first period of American history."[35] The bitter truth was that the same held for exhibitions glorifying that frontier.

America's entry into World War I signaled the beginning of the end of the public's nostalgic fascination with frontiersmen as well. Watching a cowboy shooting at glass balls was less exciting than watching team sports like baseball and football. Rodeos showcased "cowboy fun" more cheaply than could the Wild West. Cody and his stars were aging; even the Indians seemed resigned to settling down on reservations.

Furthermore, Thomas Edison, among others, was inventing a contraption that would make a series of photographs appear to move lifelike when rapidly flashed before a viewer's eyes. Within a short period, the resulting industry focused the nation's attention on a most innovative entertainment—the movies. From 1903 when *The Great Train Robbery* became the first "western" movie, interest in Cody's show steadily declined, and he went bankrupt in July 1913. Ironically, many plots of the first westerns were lifted straight out of Wild West show scenarios.

But perspicacity was Cody's strong suit. In the spirit of "if you can't beat 'em, join 'em," he persuaded Indian wars veterans, among them General

Nelson Miles, to work with him on a film reenacting the battles of Summit Springs, Warbonnet Creek, and Wounded Knee. Cody reprised his role with various Sioux and others from the Wild West playing battlefield opponents. When the five-reel film was released, some film critics echoed the earlier reviewers of his dramas and Wild West, proclaiming it educational and nearly uncanny in its realism. When asked to lecture with the film, Cody, almost seventy years old and suffering from various ailments, figuratively climbed back on his horse. "Lecturing is a new game for me," he wrote to his sister, "but I believe I can do it."[36] The old trouper recognized the importance of touring from the inception of his show business career when his combination visited nearly every American town with a music academy or opera house.

What began for Cody as competition for America's entertainment dollars in dramas written by others developed into his very personal interpretation of the West. The success of his combination years is chronicled in reports from Maine to California to Alabama. The frontier shaped Cody's life no matter whether he portrayed it in drama, a Wild West exhibition, or the movies. For him, its charms did not abate. At his death, Annie Oakley remembered, "His heart never left the great West. Whenever the day's work was done, he could always be found sitting alone watching the sinking sun, and at every opportunity he took the trail back to his old home."[37] Throughout forty years in show business, Buffalo Bill Cody creatively and lucratively merged realism and theatre. His legacy of education, romance, and history—beginning with quaint melodramas and achieving full expression in the Wild West show—still merits worldwide attention. Cody's skill and craw remain very much in evidence.

CHARACTER LISTS AND PROGRAM NOTES FOR BUFFALO BILL'S DRAMAS

Several names may be listed as having played the same character. While most roles were played by a single actor, occasionally he was replaced, or the same actor might play various roles.

1872 season

Scouts of the Prairie, and Red Deviltry As It Is by Ned Buntline
December 1872–June 1873

Buffalo Bill as himself
Texas Jack as himself
Cale Durg . . . . Ned Buntline
Dove Eye . . . . Mlle Morlacchi, Bessie Sudlow
Hazel Eye. . . . . Eloe Carfano
Mormon Ben . . . . Harry Wentworth
Phelim O'Laugherty . . . . . Harry Gilbert, George C. Davenport
Carl Pretzel. . . . . Walter Fletcher
Natolah . . . . Mrs. Beach
Wolf Slayer . . . . W. J. Fleming, W. J. Halpin, S. H. France
Little Bear . . . . .George Beach
Big Eagle . . . . W. H. Ferris, Joseph P. Winter
. . . . Mr. Walters

Grassy Chief} . . . . Pawnee . . . . {Ar-fi-a-ka
Prairie Dog} . . . . Indian . . . . {As-ge-tes
Water Chief} . . . . Chiefs . . . . {As-slu-ah-wa
Seven Stars} . . . . {Chuk-kak
Te-oo-Tig-pown
Kit-Kot-tons[1]

Act 1. Scene 1.   On the plains. Cale Durg, the trapper. Arrival of Buffalo
                  Bill and Texas Jack. Story of the hunt. A warning from
                  Dove Eye. Danger. "We'll wipe the red skins out." Off on
                  the trail. The war-whoop.

       Scene 2.   The Renegade's camp. Mormon Ben. Phelim O'Laugherty
                  and Pretzel. O'Laugherty's continued drouth [sic]. Danger
                  to Hazel Eye.

       Scene 3.   Hazel Eye's poetic tribute to Cale Durg. Hazel Eye sur-
                  prised. Cale Durg to the rescue. The Renegade foiled.
                  Wolf Slayer, the treacherous Ute. Cale Durg overpowered.
                  Search for the bottle. Cale Durg's temperance rhapsody.

       Scene 4.   Doomed to the torture post. Dove Eye's appeal to the
                  chief. "Death to the pale face." Then burn, ye cursed dogs,
                  burn. The blazing faggots. Dove Eye's knife. The severed
                  bonds. Cale Durg defiant. "We'll fight ye all." Timely
                  arrival. Buffalo Bill and Texas Jack. "Death to the Red
                  Skins." Rescue of Cale Durg.

Act 2. Scene 1.   Mormon Ben, Pretzel and Phelim O'Laugherty,
                  O'Laughterty declare[s] he is not a Mormon. The meet-
                  ing with the Indians. What Mormon Ben wanted. What
                  O'Laugherty wanted. Wolf Slayer's disdain of fire water.
                  "It's the curse of the Red Man as well as the White." The
                  departure of the Indian for the war-path. Dove Eye's
                  invocation to the Great Spirit.

       Scene 2.   Dove Eye and Hazel Eye, the two friends. Buffalo Bill
                  declares his love. It is reciprocated. Texas Jack arrives and
                  interrupts the meeting. "The Indians are coming." Buffalo
                  Bill and Jack retire to ambush. How Jack ropes them in.
                  "Buffalo Bill." "That's the kind of man I am!" How they
                  scalp 'em on the plains.

Scene 3. Phelim O'Laugherty and Montezuma, the Apache child of Cochise. Cale Durg to the Rescue. God's Beverage. Love Scene between Texas Jack and Hazel Eye.

Scene 4. The Search for Hazel Eye. "The Cage is here, but the Bird has flown." The Trail. The Search and Capture of the Forest Maidens. Dove Eye's contempt for the Renegades. Cale Durg arrives upon the Scene. "Fly, Fly, your enemies are too many!" Cale Durg never Runs. The Capture and Death of Cale Durg. The Dying Curse. The Trapper's Last Shot.

Act 3. Scene 1. Dove Eye and Hazel Eye. Grief for Cale Durg. Buffalo Bill and Texas Jack. Bill's Oath of Vengeance. "I'll not leave a Redskin to skim the Prairie." Dove Eye, Dejected. The White girl and Red Maiden's affections. "We'll be Sisters." Revenge for the Slain Trapper. Vengeance or Death.

Scene 2. The German Trader. The Loss of the Bottle. Carl Pretzel's Agony.

Scene 3. The Scalp Dance. Eagle and Wolf Slayer. "I Come to Kill you." The Knife Fight. Death of Wolf Slayer.

Scene 4. Phelim and Mormon Ben on their last legs. No prospect of the fiftieth wife, or a replenished bottle.

Scene 5. Dove Eye's faith in Manitou. The Indians. Buffalo Bill's red hot reception. "Give it to them, boys." One hundred Reds for one Cale Durg. The American Scout Triumphant. Great Heavens the PRAIRIE ON FIRE.[2]

1873 season
Buffalo Bill, King of the Border Men by Frederick G. Maeder
September 1873

Buffalo Bill as himself
Texas Jack . . . . Joseph P. Winter, Texas Jack Omohundro
The Old Vet, an 1812 Pounder . . . . Frederick G. Maeder,
Charles Foster
Snakeroot Sam, down on Snakes. . . . Walter Fletcher (Finlaison),
Richard W. Marston, Frederick G. Maeder

Col. Jake McKanlass . . . . Alfred Johnson, W. H. Gregston
Alf Coyle, a Renegade . . . . W. S. MacEvoy
Murty Mullins, the Sentinel . . . . R. Wheeler
Perkins, a Landlord . . . . E. N. Watson
Flipup . . . . W. G. Specke
Stockwell . . . . E. Cunningham
Fire Water Tom, a Drunken Red . . . . Joseph V. Arlington
Raven Feather, a Sioux Brave . . . . Jas. Johnson
Big Maple, a warrior . . . . }by the
Little Elk, the same . . . . }Tribe
White Arrow, the same . . . . }from the
Little Panther, same . . . . }Plains
Ma-no-tee, the Princess of the Ogallala Sioux . . . .
                              Esther Rubens, Emma Wheeler
Lillie Fielding, the Rose of the Plains . . . .
                              Lizzie Safford, Mrs. W. G. Jones
Lottie Fielding, the Wild Bud . . . . Eliza Hudson
Mrs. Fielding . . . . Jennie Fisher, Mrs. R. G. France
Kitty Muldoon, an Irish Girl . . . . Rena Maeder
Nellie Meeker . . . . Mrs. W. G. Jones
 . . . . John M. Burke[3]

Scouts of the Plains by Hiram Robbins
October 1873–June 1874

Buffalo Bill as himself
Wild Bill Hickok as himself
Texas Jack as himself
Pale Dove, a child of the forest . . . . Mlle Morlacchi
Jim Daws, a renegade and horse thief . . . .
                              Frank Mordaunt, Hiram Robbins
Nick Blunder, good-natured, would-be courageous Irishman . .
                              Walter Fletcher
Jebadiah Broadbrim, the Quaker . . . . Alfred Johnson
Uncle Henry Carter . . . . Joseph V. Arlington
Ebenezer Langlank, a Peace Commissioner . . . Alfred Johnson
Tom Doggett, rascally companion of Daws . . . .

Ella Carter . . . . Hollis
Lettie Carter . . . . Eliza Hudson
Mrs. Carter . . . .
Tall Oak, a friendly brave . . . . W. A. Reid
. . . . W. S. MacEvoy
Big Thunder, chief of the Comanches
Black Wolf, a brave
Bear Claw
Running Turkey[4]

Act 1. Scene 1. Cabin of Uncle Henry Carter, and High Mountain Pass.
Jim Daws disguised. The wolf at the door. "You have not
got a horse around here you'd like to SELL, have you."
Ella's message of love to poor sick Luke, the Trapper. "I
can shoot a gun, and load it, too." Ebenezer's mission of
civilization to the heathen. "By only speaking when thou
art spoken to, will save the wear and tear of thy lungs." A
Christian's home. A treat of purity and love. Buffalo Bill's
protection of Lettie. "It's my notion we'd better go after
them." Bill's acknowledgment of hospitality. "You protected me when I was wounded by the Indians, and your
kindness I can never forget." Bill pronounces Jim Daws
a renegade and horse thief. "I owe him one for stealing
my horse." Pale Dove appears. "Fly toward the setting
sun, and save thyself." The ruffians surrounded. Death
of Uncle Henry Carter. "Jim Daws did it; good bye, boys.
Maggie, wife, children, I come." Bill's resolve to never rest
until he has secured the stolen child, and killed Jim Daws.

Act 2. Scene 1. Ella's Vision. "Left without a brother, sister, home or
friend." "I would face a hundred Comanches for that girl."
The Barbecue of the Red Skins. Kansas whiskey used for
extinguishing fires.

Scene 2. Negotiations with the heathens for "peaceful intentions."
The treaty of peace accepted.

Scene 3. Big Thunder is happy; he has returned from the war trail
with many scalps, and the souls of his young warriors are
glad, for they have drank the blood of the pale faces.

Act 3. Scene 1. "I will avenge my father's blood." The Chief of the Kiowas is our friend. Kit Carson resolves to save Buffalo Bill.

Scene 2. "Big Thunder forgets his warriors killed the Pale Face settlers, burned their homes and scalped their women." "Sink your hatchets deep in the heads of the Pale Faces."

Scene 3. Ebenezer administers spiritual advice. The blood of the Chief in the empty lodge.

Scene 4. Buffalo Bill tied to a stake. "A fellow will imagine funny things sometimes." "No kind words have I ever known until you saved me from death.["] Buffalo Bill's dream.

Act 4. Scene 1. Micky Blunder becomes weary, but is assured by Ebenezer that "the governor pays the bills."

Scene 2. Ella in the hands of Daws. "There are those who will follow us, and make you pay the penalty you so richly deserve." "You'll have to watch her mightly [*sic*] close, for she's a tiger."

Scene 3. "Tall Oak is weak; he is like woman; the Snake stung him in the back, and stole from him the Pale Face squaws."

Scene 4. Buffalo Bill captures the Renegade, liberates Ella, and restores her to her friend. "I cannot say no to the brave scout who so bravely defended me and mine." The human wolf destroyed. "We have fully completed all we have sworn to do."[5]

1874 season

Scouts of the Plains; or, Red Deviltry As It Is
October 1874

Buffalo Bill as himself
Ebenezer, the missionary . . . . Kit Carson, Jr.
Antelope Ned . . . Joseph Winkler, L. Mortimer, John M. Burke
. . . . Henry Ryner
. . . . Mr. Horton
Dutchman . . . . Charles Bradshaw
. . . . Mary Young
Mickey Blunder . . . . Thomas Z. Graham
Villain . . . . Harry Hudson

Tom Doggett .... W. T. Dulaney
Quaker .... J. M. Charles
Pale Dove .... Mary L. Young[6]
Life on the Border by Hiram Robbins,
originally titled *Wild Bill; or, Life on the Border;*
arranged by Joseph V. Arlington
November 1874 alternated with *Scouts of the Plains*

Buffalo Bill .... Hon. Wm. F. Cody
Kit Carson, Jr. as himself
George Reed .... Arizona John Burke
Old Sloat, a trapper and one of the boys .. Joseph V. Arlington
Jebadiah Broadbrim, a Peace Commissioner ....
                                        Thomas Z. Graham
Grasshopper Jim .... Harry Irving
.... Hiram Robbins
.... May Marshall
.... Waite
.... Ward
.... Buell[7]

1875 season
Scouts of the Plains alternated with *Life on the Border*
September 1875–June 1876

Buffalo Bill as himself
Texas Jack as himself
Pale Dove .... Mlle Morlacchi
Old Sloat .... Joseph V. Arlington, Texas Jack Omohundro
Jebadiah Broadbrim .... Thomas Z. Graham
General Duncan .... Harry Moreland
Grasshopper Jim .... Harry Irving, J. R. Johnson
Betty Mullany, Irish girl .... Laura Fay
Mrs. Reynolds .... Lillian Waite
Emma Reynolds .... Ada Forrester
Capt. Huntley .... Charles B. Waite, Cody

Jim Reynolds .... J. M. Buell
Buffalo Bill .... John M. Burke (during Cody's absence)[8]

1876 season
Life on the Border alternated with *Scouts of the Plains*
October 1876–December 1876

Buffalo Bill, {A Western Judge, Jury and Executioner,
.... (by the Great Original)} Hon. W. F. Cody
Texas Jack .... Harry Duffield
Capt. Jack, can trail an Indian from the Missouri to the Pacific
John W. Crawford
George Reed, a victim of perjury, but a square man for all that
Geo. Denderon
Jebadiah Broadbrim, A Peace Commissioner ....
Thomas Z. Graham, Mr. Bradshaw
Capt. Huntley, of Regulators and Vigilance Committee ......
Charles B. Waite, Mr. Smith
Old Sloat, a trapper .... Joseph V. Arlington, A. D. Bradley
General Duncan of the U.S.A. .... Harry Moreland
Grasshopper Jim, Huntley's right bower .... Harry Irving
Toothpick Ben, Huntley's left bower .... W. S. MacEvoy
Jim Reynolds, a scout .... R. J. Evans
Lieut. Milford .... Fred Bennett
Wolfy Dick, who came West to grow up with the country ....
Harry Melmer
War Eagle, one of the noble red men of the far West ....
Charles Younger
Betty Mullany, a true hearted girl from Cork ....
Jessie Howard, Lizzie Hall, Gertie Granville
Mrs. Reynolds, wife of Jim Reynolds .... Julia Ly——
Emma Reynolds, betrothed to Buffalo Bill ....
Maria Wellesley, A. A. Adams
.... Pierce
.... Mrs. Hall
.... Mrs. Watson[9]

Red Right Hand; or, Buffalo Bill's First Scalp for Custer
by Prentiss Ingraham
December 1876–January 1877

Buffalo Bill, Chief of Scouts . . . . Hon. W. F. Cody

Capt. Jack, the Poet Scout of the Black Hills . . . .
Capt. Jack Crawford

Carter Bainbridge, Hermit of the Black Hills . . . .
Joseph V. Arlington, Mr. Bradley

Leo Randolph, alias Kansas King . . . . Charles B. Waite,
Mr. Mortimer

Dennis O'Gaff, a True Son of Erin . . . . Thomas Z. Graham,
Mr. Barrows

Vincent Vernon, The Red Right Hand . . . . Harry Moreland

White Slayer, an Indian Chief . . . . Harry Melmer,
W. S. MacEvoy, Mr. Allen

Lone Dick, an Indian Trapper . . . . W. S. MacEvoy

Lang-Wa-Hoo, a Chinaman . . . . Harry Irving, Mr. Simms

Yellow Hand, Chief of the Cheyennes . . . . . . Thomas R. Bruce

Bad Burke, an Outlaw Lieutenant . . . . Charles Armsbie

Capt. Ramsey, a Gold Hunte . . . . Al. R. Gray

Tom Stapleton, an Outlaw . . . . J. R. Younger

Wentworth, a Soldier . . . . Fred. Williams

Pearl, an Indian Princess . . . . Marie Wellesley,
Fannie Herring, Gertie Granville

Grace, the Spirit of the Haunted Valley . . . . Jessie Howard

Ruth Ramsey, a Frontier Maiden . . . . Ada Bemis

Trappers, Hunters, Scouts, Soldiers, &c., &c., &c.[10]

Act 1. Scene 1. The Haunted Valley in the Black Hills. Red Hand at the Grave of Boyd Bernard. "Hark!" Appearance of Grace, the Spirit of the Valley. "Oh, Horror! horror!" Pearl pursued by Indians. "Back! back! You red fiends!" Bill to the rescue. Red Hand meets Bill. "Hold on, pard!" "What! Bill Cody?" Hermit of the hills. "My rifle failed me, but this will not!" "Hello, Santa Claus!" "By heaven I will keep my vow!" Bill and Hermit. Struggle for Life. "Back! back! this must not

be!" "Red Hand, you are doomed!" Appearance of the
Spirit of the Valley. "Come! come! or we are lost!" Tableau.

Act 2. Scene 1. Indian Encampment. White Slayer and his warriors.
Appearance of the hermit. "White Slayer is false; you have
said it!" "White Slayer never breaks his word."

Scene 2. Dennis and Lang-Wa-Hoo. "We must be near the place
where the gould [sic] is." Christening of Lang by Dennis.
Lang called after a French Juke. Meeting of Lone Dick
with Bill and Red Hand.

Scene 3. Captain Ramsey and his party surprised by Indians. Bill
and Red Hand to the rescue.

Scene 4. Pearl on Bill's trail. "Yes, those are his foot prints." "I will
guard him from danger."

Scene 5. Bill's encounter with a bear. Terrible struggle. Pearl surprised. "Oh, heaven, is he dead?" "My heart will break."

Act 3. Scene 1. Bill and Red Hand on the trail. Lone Dick.

Scene 2. Dennis and Lang-Wa-Hoo. "Spare us! spare us!" "Me like
Melican man! No killie!"

Scene 3. Pearl. "They shall not be caught asleep." Kansas King. "I
mean you no harm." Hermit and White Slayer.

Scene 4. Bad Burke meets Pearl. "You are in my power." Bill to the
rescue. Burke surprised. "Who are you?" "A man always
ready to defend a helpless woman." Terrible knife fight.
Bill kills Bad Burke. Pearl's warning of danger. Dennis
and Lang pursued by Indians. "Oh, save us! save us!"
"Good'ee Ginjinee me lik'es [sic] all sam'es [sic] Melican
man!" Bill and Red Hand's encounter with the Indians.
Tableau.

Act 4. Scene 1. The Outlaw's plot. Dennis as a spy. Lone Dick on Bill's
trail. Bill surprises Dick. Outlaw's attempt to capture
Kansas King. A struggle. Retreat of Kansas King and the
outlaws.

Scene 2. Ruth Ramsey and Kansas King. "I will never be your wife!"
"You are in my power!" Pearl rescues Ruth. "I will kill you!"

Scene 3. The Haunted Valley. "I'll solve this mystery if I die in
the attempt." Grace attempts to kill Red Hand, Death of
Grace. "Grace, I forgive you." Tableau.

Act 5. Scene 1. Pearl and Lone Dick. Dennis' story of the Hermit and Kansas King.

Scene 2. Knife combat between Hermit and Kansas King. Hermit receives a death wound. Red Hand's story of his past life. "You are my son!" Kansas King's a prisoner. Death of the Hermit.

Scene 3. The scouts. Bill gets orders to start at once and guide the 5th Cavalry to Indian Creek. Dennis and Lang anxious for the war path.

Scene 4. Encampment of General Merritt's old 5th U.S. cavalry. The song "Tenting on the old camp ground to-night." Dennis and Lang sing. The Alarm. "The 'Old 5th' to the front!" Couriers pursued by Yellow Hand and his warriors. Bill kills Yellow Hand. The first scalp for Custer. Finale–Allegorical Tableau.[11]

Many of the supporting cast who had been with Cody from the beginning of the season did not accompany him to California in June 1877. The new cast list (for *Life on the Border*) reads as follows:

Buffalo Bill . . . . Hon. W. F. Cody
Captain Jack . . . . John W. Crawford
Emma Reynolds . . . . A. A. Adams
Betty Mullany . . . . Gertie Granville
Mrs. Reynolds . . . . Alice St. John
General Duncan . . . . A. D. Billings
Old Slote . . . . A. Bradley
Captain Huntley . . . . J. K. Mortimer
Jebadiah Broadbrim . . . . W. Simms
Grasshopper Jim . . . . J. B. Barrows
George Reed . . . . J. S. Lornton
Toothpick Ben . . . . George Galloway
Jim Reynolds . . . . E. Pembroke
Wolfy Dick . . . . Charles Allen
Lieut. Milford . . . . N. Sherwood
War Eagle . . . . Andrew Younger[12]

1877 season
Red Right Hand
September 1877 cast for New York City performance

Buffalo Bill as himself
Hermit of the Hills .... J. B. Ashton
Red Hand .... Harry Ellis
Tom Sunn, a scout .... Harry Bell
Lone Dick .... C. Wilson
Dennis O'Gaff .... George C. Charles
Lang-Wa-Hoo .... W. T. Johnson
Kansas King .... J. B. Browne
White Slayer .... W. Lansing
Bad Burk .... J. Burbeck
Pearl .... Constance Hamblin
Ruth Ramsay .... Fanny Prestige
Grace............................. Augusta Chambers[13]

May Cody; or, Lost and Won by Andrew S. Burt
September 1877–April 1878

Buffalo Bill as himself
John D. Lee ... Harry A. Ellis, Joseph P. Winter, Mr. Levaseur
Darby McCune ...... George C. Charles, Thomas Z. Graham
Black Dan .... C. Wilson
General Stoughton .... Harry Bell,
                     Joseph V. Arlington, R. L. Downing
Jim A. Bullwhacker .... Alfred Johnson
Brigham Young .... J. B. Ashton,
                     Harry Melmer, Charles Herbert
Capt. Chambers Officer of the Day .... Mr. Lansing
General Harney, U.S.A. .... Mr. Browne
Mormon No. 1 .... J. Curran
Mormon No. 2 .... J. Burbeck
May Cody .... Constance Hamblin,
                  Lydia Denier, Virginia Bray, Ada Forrester

Mrs. Stoughton . . . . Mrs. W. G. Jones, Kate Moffatt
Ann Eliza Young, wife of the prophet . . . . Fanny Prestige
Amalia Young . . . . Augusta Chambers
Anna Maria Young . . . . Agnes Wynne
Delia Young . . . . Susie Byron
Maria Jane Young . . . . Maude Mellen
. . . . E. Munroe
Emerson & Clarke, Sheehan & Jones; Harry Woodson,
George W. & W. J. Thompson; Laura Linden, Alf McDowell[14]

1878 season
May Cody
September 1878–October 1878

Buffalo Bill . . . . Hon. W. F. Cody
May Cody . . . . Lydia Denier,
Gussie DeForrest, Mrs. Huntington
Mrs. Stoughton . . . . Mrs. W. G. Jones,
Mrs. Courtaine, Mrs. Edmonds
John D. Lee . . . . Harry Mainhall, Mr. Bock, H. P. Kelly
Brigham Young . . . . H. J. Holmes,
Russell Bassett, Harry Melmer
George Stoughton . . . . Joseph V. Arlington, S. Philleo
Darby McCune . . . . W. F. Carroll, H. P. Kelly,
Felix Morris, Willie Simms
General Harnby . . . . M. J. Burton
Captain Chambers, Officer of the day . . . . Harry Melmer
Black Dan, hack driver . . . . J. L. Mathews
Bull Whacker . . . . J. H. Harvey
First Mormon . . . . Ed. Little
Second Mormon . . . . Frank Burrows
Ann Aliza Young} . . . . . . Prophet's . . . . Fanny Cary
Amelia Young} . . . . Wives . . . . Alice Lester[15]

Knight of the Plains; or, Buffalo Bill's Best Trail
by Prentiss Ingraham
November 1878–August 1879 (alternated with *May Cody*)

Buffalo Bill as himself
Rose Melton . . . . Lydia Denier, Lottie Cobb
Ralph Royston . . . . J. J. Loudon, Harry Mainhall
Wild Nellie . . . . Mrs. Huntington,
Lydia Denier; Mrs. W. G. Jones
Judge Chincapin Shyster . . . . Alf Beverly, John Ince,
D. Marbelle, Russell Bassett
Moses Moloch, the scheming Jew . . . . L. R. Willard,
W. F. Carroll, O. H. Tyler, George C. Stanley
Buttermilk, the Negro . . . . Harry Irving
Mushroom Melton . . . . Harry Melmer
Irishman . . . . Charles Wilson
Indians:
Little Warrior
Young-Grass-That-Sprouts-in-the-Spring
Eagle-That–Flies-High
Follow-the-Deer
Po-ga-has-ka (Captain Jack Nesbit)
Wah-ma-sou-ta (Alf. Chambers)[16]

Act 1. Sunset on the prairie. Red Eagle on the watch. Ralph
Royston lying in wait for his foe. "The white hunter must
die." Arrival of Buffalo Bill. The long shot. Friend or foe.
The Indian village. Wild Nellie's warning. The English
lord. The shooting match. The bow and arrow against
the rifle. "Nothing like it in all England, you know." The
accusation. Denounced. "Not a cartridge left." Judge
Lynch. Love stronger than revenge. Grand Tableau of the
Prairie on Fire.

Act 2. From the prairie to the parlor. Buttermilk and the Jew.
The three villains. The conspiracy. The terrible Jew. The
unknown Lover. Lord Edmondstone Howard. From
the grave. The shadow in the moonlight. The burglars.

Buffalo Bill's death shot. The recognition. The scout on hand. "Take that, sir." Grand Tableau in Mushroom Melton's parlor.

Act 3. The gambling hall in Cheyenne. The eagle bird by chance. Buffalo Bill as a detective. The only way to beat the game. The boy gambler. A match game for high stakes. The scout as a gambler. The pigeon or the eagle. The judge and the green gambler. Poker as an innocent game. Buttermilk and the Indian. "Four aces and another in the pack." The Jew curses the eagle bird. The judge robs the cattle king. The boy gambler draws a revolver. "Pay that bet." The duel. The aim in the mirror. "Is he dead, you know?" The Indian plays a game with the Jew. The warwhoop. Tableau.

Act 4. The pony express rider. The Knights of the Road. The stage horn. Buttermilk and his donkey. The attack on the stage coach. "Is there no one to save me?" The red mask torn off. Wild Nellie to the front. "The Red Eagle's tongue is not crooked." Rose Melton gives up father for lover. The knife encounter. The lost shot. "This is fate." Grand Tableau.[17]

1879 season

Knight of the Plains predominated
with an occasional performance of *May Cody*
September 1879–February 1880

Knight of the Plains cast list:

Buttermilk . . . . Harry Irving
Rose Melton . . . . Nellie Jones
Wild Nellie . . . . Lydia Denier
Ralph Royston . . . . J. J. Louden
Moses Moloch . . . . L.R. Willard
Shyster . . . . Alf Beverly
Mushroom Melton . . . . Harry Melmer
Noel Marmaduke . . . . Charles Wilson
Red Eagle . . . . Delancy Barclay

May Cody cast list:

May Cody . . . . Lydia Denier
Mrs. Stoughton . . . . Nellie Jones
Darby McCune . . . . Charles Wilson
John D. Lee . . . . Mr. Loudon
George Stoughton . . . . Lon Willard[18]

Buffalo Bill at Bay; or, the Pearl of the Prairie
by Prentiss Ingraham
March–May 1880

Buffalo Bill}
Denver Dick}
Capt. William Frederick} . . . . all of the above played by Cody
Guy Woodbridge . . . . Lon Willard
Corinne Kendall, a disappointed woman . . . . Nellie Jones
. . . . J. F. Louden
Irishman . . . . Charles Wilson
. . . . L. R. Millar
. . . . Alfred Beverly
African Servant . . . . Harry Irving
. . . . Henry Melmer
. . . . John Lendlow
. . . . Alfred Ward
Prairie Pearl . . . . Lydia Denier
. . . . Delancy Barclay
. . . . George Congrove
Indians:
White Eagle, Pawnee chief
Spotted Horse, Pawnee chief
Brave Hawk, Ponca chief
Sly Fox, Ponca chief[19]

> Act 1. Buffalo Bill's Home in the Rocky Mountains. The
> Burning Cabin[.]
> Act 2. Biting Wolf on the War path. Buffalo Bill at Bay.

Act 3. The Outlaw's Cave. Prairie Pearl a Captive. Crow and his Trained Donkey Jerry[.]

Act 4. The Secret Discovered. Tracked to Death.

1880 season

Prairie Waif, a Story of the Far West by John A. Stevens
September 1880–April 1881

Buffalo Bill as himself
Mark Stanley . . . . Richard C. White
Jack Hardie . . . . Harry Clifton, George T. James
Jim Hardie . . . . George T. James
Hans . . . . Jule Keen, Bonnie Runnels
Captain Russell . . . . C. Wilson Charles
General Brown . . . . Ralph Delmore, Robert Neil
R. Overton, a sutler . . . . Robert Neil,
                        Harvey M. Pike, William Wright
Lone Deer . . . . William Wright
Major Saunders . . . . Harry Irving
Cheyenne chief Yellow Hand . Charles Vedder, Harry Melmer
Lt. White . . . . E. Booth
Onita, the waif . . . . Lizzie Fletcher
Sadie . . . . Connie Thompson
Jerry, donkey . . . . Jack Cass
Cheyenne Indian chiefs[20]

1881 season

Prairie Waif
September 1881–April 1882

Buffalo Bill as himself
Onita, the waif . . . Jennie Gilbert, Lydia Denier, Lizzie Fletcher
Sadie . . . . Nellie Lingard, Connie Thompson
Hans . . . . Jule Keen
Capt. Russell . . . . Wilson Charles

Lone Deer . . . . Mr. Conklin
Mark Stanley . . . . . . Richard C. White, Mr. Bailey, Robert Neil
Jim Hardy . . . . Harry Clifton, T. J. Quinn
Jack Hardy . . . . Harry Melmer
General Brown . . . . Will McVey
E. Overton . . . . R. D. Dorsey
Lt. Saunders . . . . Harry Irving
Lt. White . . . . George Hancock
Flying Cloud
. . . . Dr. Frank Powell (White Beaver)
Winnebago Sioux Indians:
Sin-sa-retch-kaw
Ma-he-ut-un-kaw
De-co-ray
Hoo-wa-bet-fa
Wau-kon-chaw-nik-kaw
Sioux Indian Maiden . . . . He-nu-kaw (the First Born)[21]

1882 season

Twenty Days; or, Buffalo Bill's Pledge by Charles Foster
August 1882–May 1883

Buffalo Bill . . . . Hon. W. F. Cody
Abner Weldon . . . . Charles Foster, George Beach
  Montana Mike, a gambler}
  Crippled Jim, adventurer}
  Capt. Mortlake, assassin} . . . . all three played by W. J. Bailey
Real Captain Merton Mortlake . . . . W. C. Donaldson,
                                              Charles Krone
Jacob Broomblebeck, victimized
Dutchman from New Hampshire . . . . Jule Keen
Pete De Bassoon, an irrepressible coon . . . . . . George Sembler
Grace Weldon, heiress and belle of the plains . . . Mary Tucker
. . . . Tillie Shields
Pepper, conventional crusher
and deserted waif . . . . Sallie Adams, Loie Fuller

.... Charles Foster
.... William Flatt
.... John Wittich
.... J. Allstadt
.... W. J. Cogwell
Dan Miller, aka Lariat Dan .... Charles Krone
Tom Cranberry, swindler and outlaw .... Harry Melmer
Rev. Mr. Elliston, a clergyman .... Charles Thorne
Cornelia Cranberry, delicate flower
from New Hampshire .... Tillie Shields
Scouts, gamblers, bordermen, Indians, outlaws, etc.
Winnebago-Sioux and Pawnee chiefs: Chief Bear,
Ma-He-Ut-Un-Kaw, Rolling Thunder, He-nu-kaw (First Born),
Blue Hawk, Fire Lightning.[22]

1883 season

Twenty Days
December 1883

Prairie Waif
January, February 1884

Buffalo Bill as himself
Mark Stanley .... Harry W. Mitchell
Hans .... Jule Keen
.... George Beach
.... Flint Kennicott
.... H. C. Strong
.... C. H. Stanley
.... George Gardner
.... H. D. Scheedtz
.... Jake Alstadt
.... John Wittich
.... Charles E. Jones
Onita .... Lydia Denier
Sadie .... Lizzie Conway
.... Grace Addison

John Y. Nelson, Interpreter
Sioux Indians:
Ony-ne-lsony
L'a-pa-ng-en-e
Neer-cu-ba-na[23]

Twenty Days
March 1884

1885 season
Prairie Waif
November 1885–April 1886

Buffalo Bill . . . . Hon. W. F. Cody, Matt Snyder
Buffalo Bill's Dutchman . . . . Jule Keen
Buck Taylor as himself
Mark Stanley . . . . Okane Hills, Ed Clifford
Jim Hardy . . . . James Bradford, Charles Krone
Jack Hardy . . . . Harry Melmer
Hans . . . . Jule Keen, John Pendy
Capt. Russell . . . . John Pendy
Overton, the Sutler . . . . William Hoop
Lone Deer . . . . George Beach
Yellow Hand . . . . William Irving
Captain Saunders . . . . Gordon Lillie
General Brown . . . . C. Edward
Onita . . . . Lydia Denier
Sadie . . . . Jeffreys Warner Pendy
Kah-Kah-Kah-Lah-Hah . . . . }
Que-Lah-Lah-La-Sha . . . . } Sioux
O-Te-On-Te-On . . . . } Indians
Koo-Rooks-Tip-A-Hoo . . . . }
Indian Maiden . . . . He-nu-kaw
La-ta-le-sha . . . . Pawnee chief

Act 2. Home of Buffalo Bill—Specialties will be introduced by Jule Keen, John and Jeffreys Pendy, Capt. Russell, Sadie and Hans[.]

Act 4. The Band of Pawnee Indians in their wild and weird dances as follows: THE SCALP! HORSE! SQUAW! Under the control of PAWNEE BILLY, Interpreter and Boy chief of the Pawnees.[24]

BUFFALO BILL COMBINATION'S CITIES AND DATES

* indicates unverified dates

• 1872 •

DECEMBER
16–21 Chicago, IL
23–28 St. Louis, MO
30 Cincinnati, OH

• 1873 •

JANUARY
1–4 Cincinnati, OH
6–8 Louisville, KY
9–11 Indianapolis, IN
13 Toledo, OH
14–15 Cleveland, OH
16–18 Pittsburgh, PA
20 Franklin, PA
22 Oil City, PA
23–24 Titusville, PA
29–30 Syracuse, NY

31 Rochester, NY

FEBRUARY
1 Rochester, NY
3–4 Utica, NY
5–7 Albany, NY
11–15 Troy, NY
17 Pittsfield, MA
18–20 Providence, RI
24–25 Hartford, CT

MARCH
3–8 Boston, MA
13–14 Lowell, MA
17 Portsmouth, NH
18–19 Portland, ME
20 Lewiston, ME
21 Biddeford, ME*
24 Lawrence, MA
26 Taunton, MA
31 New York City

APRIL

1–13 New York City
14–15 Brooklyn, NY
19 Trenton, NJ
21–26 Philadelphia, PA
28–30 Baltimore, MD

MAY

1–3 Baltimore, MD
5–10 Washington, D.C.
12–15 Richmond, VA
16–17 Norfolk, VA
20 Wilmington, DE
21–24 Philadelphia, PA
26 Lancaster, PA
27 Harrisburg, PA
28 Reading, PA
29 Allentown, PA*
30–31 Pottsville, PA

JUNE

1 Harrisburg, PA*
2 Wilkes-Barre, PA
3–4 Scranton, PA
5 Binghamton, NY
6 Owego, NY*
7, 9 Elmira, NY
10 Hornell, NY*
11 Dunkirk, NY*
12–14 Buffalo, NY
16 Lockport, NY
17 Canandaigua, NY*
18 Auburn, NY
19 Oswego, NY
20 Watertown, NY
21 Rome, NY*
23 Albany, NY
25 New York City*
28 Port Jervis, NY*

AUGUST

25–30 New York City

SEPTEMBER

1–6 New York City
8 New Brunswick, NJ
9 West Chester, PA
11–13 New York City
15–17 Columbus, OH
22–27 Cincinnati, OH
29–30 Lexington, KY

OCTOBER

2–4 Louisville, KY
6 Hamilton, OH
7 Dayton, OH
8 Richmond, IN
9–11 Terre Haute, IN
13–14 Indianapolis, IN
15 Lafayette, IN
17–18 Fort Wayne, IN
22–23 Toledo, OH
24 Fremont, OH
25 Sandusky, OH
27–28 Cleveland, OH
29–30 Akron, OH

NOVEMBER

1 New Castle, PA
4 Meadville, PA
6 Titusville, PA
8 Jamestown, NY
10–13 Buffalo, NY
14–15 Erie, PA
17–22 Pittsburgh, PA
24 Johnston, PA
26–27 Williamsport, PA
28 Wilkes-Barre, PA
29 Scranton, PA

DECEMBER

2 Port Jervis, NY
3 Poughkeepsie, NY
10 Newark, NJ
11 Trenton, NJ
13 Bethlehem, PA
15 Easton, PA
16 Pottsville, PA
17 Reading, PA
18 Lancaster, PA
19 Harrisburg, PA
22–23 Baltimore, MD
29–31 Philadelphia, PA

• 1874 •

JANUARY

1–3 Philadelphia, PA
6–7 Bridgeport, CT
8 New Haven, CT
10 Waterbury, CT
12 Middletown, CT
13–14 Hartford, CT
16–17 Providence, RI
20 Taunton, MA
21 New Bedford, MA
22–27 Cambridge, MA*
29–30 Portland, ME*
31 Bath, ME*

FEBRUARY

2 Augusta, ME
3 Gardiner, ME (canceled)
4–5 Bangor, ME
6 Lewiston, ME
7 Portland, ME
9 Dover, NH

10 Concord, NH
12 Manchester, NH
13 Haverhill, MA
14 Lawrence, MA
16 Lowell, MA
17–18 Worcester, MA
20 Springfield, MA*
21 Pittsfield, MA
23 North Adams, MA
24–25 Troy, NY
26–28 Albany, NY

MARCH

2 Schenectady, NY
3–4 Utica, NY
5 Oswego, NY
6–7 Syracuse, NY
10–11 Rochester, NY
12 Lockport, NY*
13 Buffalo, NY*
13 Dunkirk, NY*
14 Erie, PA
16 Union City, PA*
17 Kent, OH*
18 Mansfield, OH
19 Sandusky, OH
23–24 Detroit, MI
26 Ann Arbor, MI
27 Jackson, MI*
27–28 Toledo, OH*
29 Rockford, IL*
30 Marshall, MI
31 Battle Creek, MI

APRIL

1 Kalamazoo, MI
2 Niles, OH*
3 South Bend, IN

4 Joliet, IL
7–8 Bloomington, IL
9–11 Springfield, IL
13 Jacksonville, IL
15–16 Quincy, IL
17–18 Keokuk, IA
20–21 Burlington, IA
22–23 Davenport, IA
24–25 Peoria, IL
27 Rock Island, IL
28 Clinton, IA
29 Freeport, IL
30 Rockford, IL*

MAY

1 Freeport, IL*
2, 4 Madison, WI
5–8 Milwaukee, WI
9 Racine, WI
11–16 Chicago, IL
20–21 Saginaw, MI
22 Bay City, MI
25–26 London, ON
27–28 Hamilton, ON
29–30 Toronto, ON

JUNE

2–4 Montreal, QC
10 Lowell, MA
11 Lawrence, MA
12 Salem, MA*
13 Lynn, MA
15–20 Boston, MA
29–30 New York City

NOVEMBER

1–4 New York City
13 Utica, NY
14 Rome, NY

16 Williamsport, PA
17 Elmira, NY
18 Hornell, NY
19 Lockport, NY
20 Seneca Falls, NY*
21 Syracuse, NY
23 Auburn, NY
24 Oneida, NY
26 Binghamton, NY
27 Scranton, PA
28 Pittsburgh, PA*
30 Wilkes-Barre, PA

DECEMBER

1 Mauch Chunk, PA*
2 Harrisburg, PA
3–4 Wilmington, DE
5 Chester, PA*
7 West Chester, PA
14 Harlem, NY*
15 Stamford, CT*
17 Danbury, CT
18 New Britain, CT*
19 Waterbury, CT
21 Meriden, CT
22 New Haven, CT
23–24 Hartford, CT
25–26 Providence, RI*
25, 28 Norwich, CT*
29 Taunton, MA
30 Pawtucket, RI*
31 Woonsocket, RI

• 1875 •

JANUARY

1 Chelsea, MA*
2 Salem, MA*

4 Lynn, MA
5 Portsmouth, NH
6 Portland, ME
8 Bath, ME
9, 11 Lewiston, ME
12 Biddeford, ME*
13 Dover, NH
14 Concord, NH
15–16 Manchester, NH
19 Lawrence, MA
20 Lowell, MA
21 Worcester, MA
23 Springfield, MA
25 Pittsfield, MA
26 North Adams, MA
27 Cohoes, NY*
27–28 Albany, NY*
29–30 Troy, NY

FEBRUARY
1 Cohoes, NY*
2 Schenectady, NY
3 Little Falls, NY
4 Amsterdam, NY*
5 Utica, NY*
6 Syracuse, NY
8 Geneva, NY
9–13 Rochester, NY
15 Batavia, NY
16 Albion, NY
17 Lockport, NY
18–19 Erie, PA
20 Meadville, PA
22–24 Pittsburgh, PA
25 Steubenville, OH
26 Wheeling, WV
27 Zanesville, OH

MARCH
1 Newark, OH*
2–3 Columbus, OH
4 Springfield, OH
5–6 Dayton, OH
8–13 Cincinnati, OH
14–15 Louisville, KY
19–25 Washington, D.C.*
30–31 Boston, MA

APRIL
1–4 Boston, MA
5–10 Philadelphia, PA*
12–14 Baltimore, MD
19–24 Washington, D.C.

MAY
1–15 New York City*
17–22 Brooklyn, NY
31 New York City

JUNE
1–5 New York City
21–26 New York City*

SEPTEMBER
2–4 Albany, NY
6–8 Troy, NY
20 Syracuse, NY
27–29 Rochester, NY
30 Batavia, NY

OCTOBER
8 Scranton, PA*
10 Wilkes-Barre, PA*
11 Pittston, PA*
12 Easton, PA
14 Trenton, NJ
15 Burlington, NJ*
16 Wilmington, DE

18–20 Richmond, VA
25–26 Wilmington, NC
29–30 Augusta, GA

NOVEMBER
1–3 Charleston, SC
4–6 Savannah, GA
8 Macon, GA*
9 Memphis, TN
10 Griffin, GA*
11–12 Atlanta, GA
13 Columbus, GA
15 Selma, AL*
16–17 Montgomery, AL
18–20 Mobile, AL
22–25 Galveston, TX
27 San Antonio, TX
29–30 Houston, TX

DECEMBER
1–2 Houston, TX
5–17 New Orleans, LA
20–25 Memphis, TN
27–30 Nashville, TN
31 Evansville, IN

• 1876 •

JANUARY
1 Evansville, IN
3–7 St. Louis, MO
13 Quincy, IL
14 Keokuk, IA
20 Peoria, IL
21 Pekin, IL*
24–29 Cincinnati, OH
31 Indianapolis, IN

FEBRUARY
1–2 Indianapolis, IN
3 Lafayette, IN
4 Springfield, IL
8 Terre Haute, IN
10–11 Louisville, KY
14 Hamilton, OH
15 Richmond, IN
19 Columbus, OH
21 Newark, OH*
25 Wheeling, WV
28–29 Pittsburgh, PA

MARCH
1–4 Pittsburgh, PA
6 New Castle, PA
7 Youngstown, OH
8 Alliance, OH
17–18 Toledo, OH
19–20 Springfield, OH*
20–22 Detroit, MI*
23 Chatham, ON
24–25 London, ON
27 Toronto, ON
28–29 Hamilton, ON

APRIL
4–5 Buffalo, NY
8 Syracuse, NY
10–12 Rochester, NY
19–20 Springfield, MA
22 Worcester, MA
25 Salem, MA

MAY
1 Lowell, MA
5–6 Portland, ME
12 Taunton, MA
13 Hartford, CT

15 Norwich, CT*
16 New London, CT
17 Newport, RI
18 New Bedford, MA
22–24 Providence, RI
25 New Haven, CT
27 Newark, NJ
29 Paterson, NJ

June
3 Wilmington, DE

October
2–7 Rochester, NY
18 Elmira, NY
19 Williamsport, PA
20 Pittston, PA*
21 Wilkes-Barre, PA
24–26 Rochester, NY*
28 Syracuse, NY*
30–31 New York City

November
1–19 New York City
20–26 Philadelphia, PA*
25 Ilion, NY*
26 Utica, NY*
27 Oswego, NY*
28 Syracuse, NY*

December
11 Trenton, NJ
12 Newark, NJ
13 Bridgeport, CT
14 Hartford, CT
15 Meriden, CT
19 Newport, RI
20 Fall River, MA
21 Providence, RI*

22 Taunton, MA*
23 New Bedford, MA
25 Haverhill, MA
26 Lynn, MA
28 Lawrence, MA
30 Lowell, MA

• 1877 •

January
1 Concord, NH
2 Manchester, NH
3 Newburyport, MA*
4 Biddeford, ME*
5–6 Portland, ME
8–13 Boston, MA
15 Woonsocket, RI
16 Worcester, MA
17–18 Springfield, MA
19 Pittsfield, MA
20 North Adams, MA*
26–27 Albany, NY
29–30 Troy, NY

February
5 Auburn, NY
6–7 Rochester, NY
10 Lockport, NY*
14–15 Buffalo, NY
16–17 Erie, PA
19–22 Cleveland, OH
23 Youngstown, OH
24 Sharon, PA*
26 Meadville, PA
27 Oil City, PA
28 Edenburg, PA

MARCH
1 St. Petersburg, PA
2 Petrolia, PA
5 Parker City, PA
6–7 Pittsburgh, PA
9–10 Wheeling, WV
12 Zanesville, OH
14 Columbus, OH
15 Springfield, OH
16 Piqua, OH
17 Dayton, OH
19–24 Cincinnati, OH
26 Richmond, IN
27–29 Indianapolis, IN
30–31 Terre Haute, IN

APRIL
2–7 St. Louis, MO
11–12 Kansas City, MO
13–14 Leavenworth, KS
17 St. Joseph, MO
18 Nebraska City, NE
20–21 Omaha, NE

MAY
14–31 San Francisco, CA

JUNE
1–8 San Francisco, CA
13 Oakland, CA
14–16 San Jose, CA
18–19 Stockton, CA
20–23 Sacramento, CA
25–29 Virginia City, NV
30 Carson City, NV

SEPTEMBER
3–15 New York City
17–22 Baltimore, MD
24–29 Washington, D.C.

OCTOBER
3–13 Philadelphia, PA
15–21 New York City
22–24 Providence, RI
25 Newport, RI
26 New Bedford, MA
27 Lynn, MA
29 Salem, MA
30 Gloucester, MA
31 Lawrence, MA

NOVEMBER
1 Concord, NH
2–3 Manchester, NH
5–6 Portland, ME
7 Bath, ME
8 Rockland, ME
9–10 Bangor, ME
12 Waterville, ME
13 Lewiston, ME
14 Augusta, ME
15 Portland, ME
16 Dover, NH
17 Haverhill, MA
19 Lowell, MA
20–21 Worcester, MA
22 Springfield, MA
23 Hartford, CT
24 New Haven, CT
26 Bridgeport, CT
27 Pittsfield, MA
28 North Adams, MA*
29 Cohoes, NY*
30 Albany, NY

DECEMBER
1 Albany, NY
3 Troy, NY

5 Gloversville, NY*
6 Ilion, NY*
7 Utica, NY
8 Syracuse, NY
10 Auburn, NY
11 Medina, NY
12 Lockport, NY
13–15 Rochester, NY
17–19 Buffalo, NY
20–22 Cleveland, OH
24–25 Toledo, OH
28 Grand Rapids, MI
29 Niles, OH*
30–31 Milwaukee, WI

• 1878 •

JANUARY
1–3 Milwaukee, WI
4 Madison, WI
5 Janesville, WI
7–12 Chicago, IL
14 Joliet, IL
15 Ottawa, IL
16 Rock Island, IL
17 Davenport, IA
18 Iowa City, IA
19 Cedar Rapids, IA
23 Keokuk, IA
24 Burlington, IA
29 Peoria, IL
30 Bloomington, IL
31 Springfield, IL

FEBRUARY
1 Decatur, IL
2 Terre Haute, IN
4 Evansville, IN
5–6 Nashville, TN
7 Bowling Green, KY*
8–9 Louisville, KY
11–12 Indianapolis, IN
13 Lafayette, IN
14 Logansport, IN
15 Ft. Wayne, IN
16 Dayton, OH
18–20 Cincinnati, OH
21 Springfield, OH
22 Columbus, OH
25 Mansfield, OH
26 Akron, OH
27 Youngstown, OH
28 Wheeling, WV

MARCH
2–3 Pittsburgh, PA
11 Oil City, PA
12 Titusville, PA
13 Erie, PA
14 Jamestown, NY
15 Bradford, PA
16 Olean, NY*
18 Hornellville, NY*
19 Elmira, NY
20 Towanda, PA
21 Binghamton, NY
22 Scranton, PA*
25 Pittston, PA*
26 Wilkes-Barre, PA
27 Easton, PA
28 Allentown, PA
29 Reading, PA
30 Pottsville, PA

APRIL
1 Tamaqua, PA
2 Danville, PA
3 Williamsport, PA
4 Harrisburg, PA
5 Columbia, PA
6 Lancaster, PA
8 Coatesville, PA*
9 Wilmington, DE
11 Trenton, NJ
12 Newark, NJ
13 Paterson, NJ
15–20 Brooklyn, NY

MAY
1–4 New York City*
6–11 Philadelphia, PA

SEPTEMBER
9–14 Baltimore, MD
16–21 Washington, D.C.
22 Petersburg, VA
23–24 Norfolk, VA
26–28 Richmond, VA
30 Lynchburg, VA

OCTOBER
1 Danville, VA*
2–3 Charlotte, NC
4–5 Wilmington, NC
7 Columbia, SC
8–9 Augusta, GA
10–12 Charleston, SC
14–16 Savannah, GA
21 Wilmington, DE
22 Trenton, NJ
30 Danbury, CT
31 Norwalk, CT

NOVEMBER
1 Stamford, CT
2 New Haven, CT
4 Bridgeport, CT
5 Waterbury, CT
6 Winsted, CT*
7 Hartford, CT
8 Willimantic, CT
9 Norwich, CT*
22–23 Portland, ME
28 Lewiston, ME

DECEMBER
2 Milford, RI*
9 Woonsocket, RI
10 Milford, MA
11–12 Providence, RI
13 Springfield, MA
16–21 Chicago, IL
27–28 Detroit, MI
30 Toledo, OH*

• 1879 •

JANUARY
1 Erie, PA
3–4 Buffalo, NY
6 Lockport, NY
7 Medina, NY
8 Brockport, NY*
9–11 Rochester, NY
13 Oswego, NY
14 Ilion, NY*
15 Syracuse, NY
17–18 Albany, NY
21 Scranton, PA
24 Wilkes-Barre, PA
26 Bradford, PA*

29 Corry, PA*
30 Titusville, PA
31 Oil City, PA

FEBRUARY
1 Meadville, PA
4–6 Cleveland, OH
7–8 Pittsburgh, PA*
11 Petrolia, PA*
13 Parker, PA*
14 New Castle, PA
15 Youngstown, OH
17 Akron, OH
18 Masillon, OH*
19 Canton, OH
20 Alliance, OH
21 Steubenville, OH
22 Wheeling, WV
24 Zanesville, OH
25 Chillicothe, OH
26 Columbus, OH
27 Springfield, OH
28 Dayton, OH

MARCH
1 Terre Haute, IN
3–8 Cincinnati, OH
24–31 San Francisco, CA

APRIL
1–12 San Francisco, CA
17–19 Sacramento, CA
21–22 Carson City, NV
23–26 Virginia City NV

MAY
2–3 Salt Lake City, UT

JULY
21–23 Denver, CO
24 Colorado Springs, CO

25–26 Pueblo, CO
29 Georgetown, CO
30 Central City, CO
31 Laramie, WY*

AUGUST
1–2 Cheyenne, WY

SEPTEMBER
1–2 Davenport, IA
3 Rock Island, IL
4 Clinton, IA
5 Dubuque, IA
6–7 Cedar Rapids, IA*
8 Iowa City, IA
9 Des Moines, IA*
10 Keokuk, IA
11 Burlington, IA
12 Galesburg, IL*
13 Peoria, IL
15 Bloomington, IL
16 Danville, IL
17 Decatur, IL
18 Jacksonville, IL
19 Springfield, IL
20 Quincy, IL
22–27 St. Louis, MO
29–30 Cincinnati, OH

OCTOBER
1–4 Cincinnati, OH
6–8 Indianapolis, IN
10 Evansville, IN
11 Terre Haute, IN
14 Lafayette, IN
16 Richmond, IN*
17 Muncie, IN
18 Ft. Wayne, IN
22 Sandusky, OH

23–25 Cleveland, OH
28 Akron, OH

NOVEMBER
1 Youngstown, OH
3 Greenville, PA
4 Sharon, PA
5–6 Pittsburgh, PA
7 Steubenville, OH
8 Wheeling, WV
10 Zanesville, OH
11 Newark, OH
12 Chillicothe, OH
13 Columbus, OH
14 Springfield, OH
15 Dayton, OH
18 Lexington, KY
20–22 Louisville, KY
24–25 Nashville, TN
26 Jackson, TN*
28–30 Memphis, TN

DECEMBER
1–2 Little Rock, AK
3 Shreveport, LA*
4 Ft. Worth, TX
5 El Paso, TX*
6 Dallas, TX*
8 Corsicana, TX*
9–10 Austin, TX
11 Brenham, TX
12 Houston, TX*
15–16 San Antonio, TX
17–19 Galveston, TX
21–27 New Orleans, LA
29–30 Mobile, AL
31 Montgomery, AL

• 1880 •

JANUARY
1 Montgomery, AL
2 Selma, AL
3 Eufala, AL*
5 Albany, GA*
6 Columbus, GA*
7 Opelika, AL
8–10 Atlanta, GA
13 Macon, GA
14 Augusta, GA*
15–17 Savannah, GA
19–20 Charleston, SC
21 Columbia, SC
22 Wilmington, NC
23 Raleigh, NC
24 Petersburg, VA*
26–27 Richmond, VA
28 Alexandria, VA
29–30 Washington, D.C.*
31 West Chester, PA

FEBRUARY
1 West Chester, PA
2–8 Philadelphia, PA
10–15 Baltimore, MD
16 Wilmington, DE
23–29 Brooklyn, NY*

MARCH
1–13 New York City
15 New Haven, CT
16–17 Providence, RI
18 Hartford, CT
19 Taunton, MA
20 Lynn, MA
22–28 Boston, MA
29 Newport, RI

30 Fall River, MA
31 New Bedford, MA

APRIL

1 Salem, MA
2 Lawrence, MA
3 Manchester, NH
5 Lewiston, ME
6–7 Portland, ME
8 Haverhill, MA
9 Lowell, MA
10 Worcester, MA
12 Springfield, MA
13 Holyoke, MA*
14 Westfield, MA
15 Troy, NY
16–17 Albany, NY*
17–18 Portland, ME*
19 Utica, NY
20 Watertown, NY
21 Oswego, NY
22–24 Rochester, NY
26 Auburn, NY
27 Ithaca, NY*
27 Syracuse, NY*
28 Binghamton, NY
29 Scranton, PA*
30 Wilkes-Barre, PA*

MAY

1 Danville, PA
3 Williamsport, PA
4 Elmira, NY
5 Hornellville, NY*
6 Olean, NY*
7 Bradford, PA
8 Erie, PA
10–12 Buffalo, NY
13–14 St. Catherines, ON*

AUGUST

23–28 New York City
31 Milwaukee, WI

SEPTEMBER

1 Milwaukee, WI
2 St. Paul, MN*
3–4 Minneapolis, MN
6 Red Wing, MN
7 Winona, MN*
8 Lacrosse, WI
9 Portage, MN*
10 Watertown, WI
11 Racine, WI*
13–19 Chicago, IL
21 Clinton, IA
22 Rock Island, IL
23 Davenport, IA
24 Burlington, IA
25 Springfield, IL
28 Decatur, IL
29 Bloomington, IL

OCTOBER

1 Keokuk, IA
2 Quincy, IL
4–9 St. Louis, MO
11–16 Cincinnati, OH
19 Toledo, OH
20–21 Detroit, MI
22–23 Toronto, ON
25 Hamilton, ON
26 Port Hope, ON
27 Peterborough, ON
30 Brockville, ON*

NOVEMBER

1–3 Ottawa, ON
4–6 Montreal, QC

8 Burlington, VT

9 Rutland, VT*

10 North Adams, MA*

11 Fitchburg, MA

12 Concord, NH

13 Manchester, NH

15 Portsmouth, NH

16 Dover, DE*

17–18 Portland, ME

19 Bath, ME*

22–23 Bangor, ME

24 Augusta, ME

25 Lewiston, ME

26 Biddeford, ME*

27 Haverhill, MA

29 Lowell, MA

30 Lawrence, MA

DECEMBER

1 Newburyport, MA

2 Gloucester, MA

3 Salem, MA

4 Lynn, MA

6–11 Boston, MA

13 Brockton, MA

14 New Bedford, MA

15 Fall River, MA

24 Woonsocket, RI

25 Worcester, MA

27 Westfield, MA

28 Northampton, MA*

29 Holyoke, MA*

30 Springfield, MA

31 Hartford, CT

• 1881 •

JANUARY

1 New Haven, CT

12 New Brunswick, NJ

13 Easton, PA

14 Norristown, PA

15 Jersey City, NJ*

17–29 New York City

31 Brooklyn, NY

FEBRUARY

1–6 Brooklyn, NY

8 Albany, NY

9 Troy, NY

11 Utica, NY

12 Syracuse, NY

15–16 Rochester, NY

17 Albion, NY*

17 Brockport, NY*

18 Borodine, NY*

19 Lockport, NY*

21–22 Buffalo, NY

23 Erie, PA

24–26 Cleveland, OH

28 Sandusky, OH

MARCH

1 Tiffin, OH

3 Logansport, IN

4 Lafayette, IN

7–8 Indianapolis, IN

9 Vincennes, IN

10 Evansville, IN

11–12 Nashville, TN

14–15 Louisville, KY

16 Dayton, OH

17 Springfield, OH

18 Delaware, OH

19 Columbus, OH
21 Zanesville, OH
22 Wheeling, WV
23 Steubenville, OH
24–26 Pittsburgh, PA
28 Youngstown, OH*
29 Akron, OH
30 Meadville, PA
31 Bradford, PA

APRIL
1 Elmira, NY
2 Binghamton, NY
4 Scranton, PA
5 Pittston, PA
6 Wilkes-Barre, PA
7 Danville, PA
8 Williamsport, PA
9 Harrisburg, PA
11–16 Philadelphia, PA
18–23 Baltimore, MD
25 Wilmington, DE
26 Columbia, PA
27 Lancaster, PA
28 Reading, PA
29 Trenton, NJ
30 Newark, NJ

SEPTEMBER
1 Davenport, IA
2 Rock Island, IL
3 Clinton, IA
5–10 Chicago, IL
12 Ottawa, IL
15 Freeport, IL
16 Janesville, WI
17 Madison, WI
18–20 Milwaukee, WI

22 Lacrosse, WI
23–24 St. Paul, MN
26 Stillwater, MN
27 Minneapolis, MN

OCTOBER
1 Des Moines, IA
3 Council Bluffs, IA
4 Omaha, NE
5 Lincoln, NE
6 Nebraska City, NE
7 St. Joseph, MO
8 Leavenworth, KS
10 Atchison, KS
11 Topeka, KS
12 Lawrence, KS
13–14 Kansas City, MO
15 Jefferson, MO*
16–22 St. Louis, MO
24–26 Louisville, KY
27 New Albany, IN
28–29 Nashville, TN
30 Evansville, IN

NOVEMBER
1 Vincennes, IN
2 Terre Haute, IN
3 Springfield, IL
7 Quincy, IL
10 Keokuk, IA
11 Peoria, IL
12 Bloomington, IL
14–19 Cincinnati, OH
21 Richmond, IN
22 Muncie, IN
23–24 Indianapolis, IN
25 Frankfort, KY*
26 Lafayette, IN

28 Kokomo, IN
29 Logansport, IN
30 Ft. Wayne, IN

DECEMBER
1 Toledo, OH
2 Sandusky, OH
3 Mansfield, OH
5 Galion, OH
6 Delaware, OH*
7 Bellefontaine, OH
8 Springfield, OH
9 Xenia, OH
10 Dayton, OH
12 Columbus, OH
13 Zanesville, OH
15 Steubenville, OH
16 Johnstown, PA
17 Altoona, PA
19–24 Philadelphia, PA
26 Harrisburg, PA
27 Lancaster, PA
28 Columbia, PA .

• 1882 •

JANUARY
9–14 Brooklyn, NY
16–21 New York City
23 Easton, PA
24 Reading, PA
25 Bradford, PA*
27 Williamsport, PA
28 Danville, PA
30 Wilkes-Barre, PA
31 Pittston, PA

FEBRUARY
1 Scranton, PA
9 Oil City, PA
13–15 Cleveland, OH
17 Erie, PA
18 Dunkirk, NY
23 Batavia, NY*
24–25 Rochester, NY
27 Auburn, NY
28 Rome, NY*

MARCH
1 Utica, NY
2 Ilion, NY
4 Glens Falls, NY
6 Saratoga, NY
7 Whitehall, NY*
8 Rutland, VT
9–10 Albany, NY
11 Poughkeepsie, NY
13 Troy, NY
14 North Adams, MA
15 Greenfield, MA
16 Fitchburg, MA
17 Concord, NH
18 Manchester, NH
20 Portsmouth, NH
21 Biddeford, ME
23 Lewiston, ME
24–25 Portland, ME
31 Gloucester, MA

APRIL
1 Lynn, MA
3 Lowell, MA
4 Waltham, MA
7 Newport, RI
8 Fall River, MA

10–15 Boston, MA
17–18 Providence, RI
19 Woonsocket, RI
20 Worcester, MA
21 Springfield, MA
22 Holyoke, MA*
24 Hartford, CT
25 Meriden, CT
26 Waterbury, CT
27 Stamford, CT
28 Bridgeport, CT
29 New Haven, CT

AUGUST
31 Janesville, WI

SEPTEMBER
1–3 Milwaukee, WI
4–9 Chicago, IL
11 Rockford, IL*
12 Clinton, IA
13 Aurora, IL
14 Ottawa, IL
15 Joliet, IL
16 Streaton, IL*
18 Peoria, IL
19 Galesburg, IL*
20 Monmouth, IL*
21 Rock Island, IL
23 Davenport, IA
25 Iowa City, IA
26 Des Moines, IA
27 Ottumwa, IA
28 Burlington, IA
29 Keokuk, IA
30 Quincy, IL

OCTOBER
2–7 St. Louis, MO
9–14 Cincinnati, OH

16 Marysville, KY*
17 Lexington, KY
18 New Albany, IN
19 Bowling Green, KY*
20–21 Nashville, TN
23 Cairo, IL
24 Evansville, IN
25 Vincennes, IN
26–28 Louisville, KY
30 Terre Haute, IN
31 Decatur, IL

NOVEMBER
1 Springfield, IL
2 Jacksonville, IL
3–4 Indianapolis, IN
6 Kokomo, IN
7 Lafayette, IN
8 Logansport, IN*
9 Ft. Wayne, IN
10 Richmond, IN
11 Dayton, OH
12 Piqua, OH*
14 Bellefontaine, OH
15 Urbana, OH*
16 Springfield, OH
17 Xenia, OH
18 Columbus, OH
20–22 Cleveland, OH
23 Akron, OH
24 Canton, OH
25 Youngstown, OH*
27–30 Pittsburgh, PA

DECEMBER
1–2 Pittsburgh, PA
4 Johnstown, PA
5 Altoona, PA*

6 Williamsport, PA

7 Danville, PA*

8 Wilkes-Barre, PA

9 Scranton, PA

11–16 Philadelphia, PA

18–23 Baltimore, MD

25 Reading, PA

26 Harrisburg, PA

27 Pottsville, PA*

28 Columbia, PA

29 Lancaster, PA

30 Wilmington, DE

• 1883 •

JANUARY

1 Burlington, NJ*

2 Trenton, NJ

3 Easton, PA

4 New Brunswick, NJ

5 Paterson, NJ

6 Newark, NJ

8–13 Brooklyn, NY

15–20 New York City

22–27 Brooklyn, NY

29–30 Jersey City, NJ

31 Newburg, NJ*

FEBRUARY

1 Poughkeepsie, NY

2 Norwalk, CT

4 New Haven, CT

5 Waterbury, CT

6 New Britain, CT*

7 Hartford, CT

8 Willimantic, CT

9 Norwich, CT*

10 Taunton, MA

12 New Bedford, MA

13 Fall River, MA

14 Newport, RI

15 Brockton, MA

16–17 Providence, RI

19 Clinton, MA

20 Nashua, NH

21 Concord, NH

22 Lowell, MA

23 Lawrence, MA

24 Manchester, NH

26 Dover, DE*

27 Biddeford, ME*

28 Gardiner, ME*

MARCH

1 Augusta, ME

2–3 Bangor, ME

5 Belfast, ME

6 Rockland, ME

7 Bath, ME

8 Lewiston, ME

9–10 Portland, ME

12 Portsmouth, NH*

13 Newburyport, MA

13 Gloucester, MA*

14 Haverhill, MA

15 Salem, MA

16 Marble Head, MA*

17 Gloucester, MA

19 Woonsocket, RI

20 Springfield, MA*

21 New Amsterdam, MA*

22 Holyoke, MA

23 Worcester, MA

24 Lynn, MA

26–31 Boston, MA

APRIL

2 Albany, NY
3 Troy, NY
4 Amsterdam, NY
5 Utica, NY
6 Oneida, NY*
7 Syracuse, NY*
9–10 Rochester, NY
11 Batavia, NY
12 Buffalo, NY
13 Bradford, PA
14 Erie, PA
16–17 Buffalo, NY*
19 St. Catherines, ON*
20–21 Toronto, ON*
24 Lockport, NY*
25 Auburn, NY*
26 Syracuse, NY*
27 Rochester, NY*

DECEMBER

1 Davenport, IA
3 Rock Island, IL
4 Galesburg, IL*
5 Peoria, IL
7 Jacksonville, IL
8 Springfield, IL
13 Xenia, OH
14–15 Springfield, OH
17 Urbana, OH
18 Bellefontaine, OH
19 Galion, OH
20 Mt. Vernon, OH*
21–22 Columbus, OH
24 Meadville, PA
28 Williamsport, PA
29 Scranton, PA*
30 Philadelphia, PA

• 1884 •

JANUARY

1–5 Philadelphia, PA
7 Trenton, NJ
8 Newark, NJ
9 Waterbury, CT
10 New Haven, CT
11 Hartford, CT
12 Providence, RI
14 Brockton, MA
15 Waverly, MA*
15 Haverhill, MA*
17 Manchester, NH
18 Suncook, NH
19 Lowell, MA
21 Lawrence, MA
22 Salem, MA
23 Lynn, MA
24 Springfield, MA
25 Norwalk, CT
26 Stamford, CT
28–31 New York City

FEBRUARY

1–2 New York City
4 Poughkeepsie, NY
5 Troy, NY
7 Syracuse, NY
8–9 Rochester, NY
11 Sharon, PA
12 Youngstown, OH
14 Akron, OH
15 Mansfield, OH
16 Ft. Wayne, IN
18–24 Chicago, IL
29 Milwaukee, WI

MARCH
1–2 Milwaukee, WI
3–9 Chicago, IL

• 1885 •

NOVEMBER
16–21 Philadelphia, PA
23 Mount Holly, NJ*
24 Salem, NJ
25 Wilmington, DE
26 Reading, PA
27 Allentown, PA
28 Hazleton, PA
30 Newark, NJ

DECEMBER
1–5 Newark, NJ
7 Wilkes-Barre, PA
8 Pittston, PA*
9 Shamokin, PA
10 Lewisburg, PA*
11 Danville, PA
12 Lock Haven, PA
14 Altoona, PA*
15 Greensburg, PA
16 New Castle, PA
17 Beaver Falls, PA*
18 Steubenville, OH
19 Wheeling, WV
21 Massillon, OH*
22 Wooster, OH*
23 Canton, OH
24 Alliance, OH
25 Youngstown, OH*
26 Sharon, PA
27–31 Cleveland, OH*

• 1886 •

JANUARY
1–2 Cleveland, OH*
4–10 Chicago, IL
11–16 Columbus, OH
18–24 Chicago, IL
25 Clinton, IA
26 Rock Island, IL
27 Monmouth, IL
28 Burlington, IA
29 Keokuk, IA
30 Quincy, IL

FEBRUARY
1–3 Kansas City, MO
4 Leavenworth, KS
5–6 St. Joseph, MO
8 Topeka, KS
9 Atchison, KS
10 Lincoln, NE
11–12 Omaha, NE*
13 Council Bluffs, IA
14 Kansas City, MO*
15 Fremont, NE
16 Columbus, NE
17 Grand Island, NE
18 Hastings, NE
19 Kearney, NE
20 North Platte, NE*
22 Cheyenne, WY
23 Laramie, WY
24 Rawlins, WY*
25 Evanston, UT
26 Ogden, UT
27 Salt Lake City, UT

MARCH
2–3 Sacramento, CA
4 Woodland, CA*

5 Stockton, CA
6 San Jose, CA
8–21 San Francisco, CA
22–23 Oakland, CA
25 Virginia City, NV
26 Carson City, NV
27 Reno, NV
29 Park City, UT*
31 Cheyenne, WY

APRIL
1 Boulder, CO
2 Central City, CO
3 Georgetown, CO
5–10 Denver, CO

NEWSPAPER SOURCES

Akron (OH) Beacon Journal, Feb. 17, Oct. 27, 1879; Mar. 29, 30, 1881

Akron (OH) Daily Beacon, Oct. 25, 30, 31, 1873

Akron (OH) Summit County Beacon, Nov. 23, 1882

Albany (NY) Argus, Feb. 6, 7, June 21, 1873; Aug. 27, Sept. 4, 1875; Jan. 27, Dec. 1, 1877; Jan. 18, 1879; Feb. 7, 1881; Mar. 9, 1882; Apr. 2, 1883

Albany (NY) Evening News, Feb. 26, 27, 28, 1874

Albion (NY) Orleans American, Feb. 11, 1875

Alexandria (VA) Gazette, Jan. 27, 1880

Allentown (PA) Chronicle & News, Nov. 27, 28, 1885

Allentown (PA) Lehigh Register & Patriot, Mar. 27, 1878

Alliance (OH) Review, Dec. 23, 1885; Mar. 4, 1876; Feb. 15, 1879

Amsterdam (NY) Daily Democrat, Apr. 4, 1883

Atchison (KS) Daily Champion, Apr. 10, 14, 15, 17, 1877; Oct. 11, 1881

Atchison (KS) Globe, Oct. 10, 1881; Feb. 8, 1886

Atlanta (GA) Daily Constitution, Nov. 11, 1875; Oct. 12, 1878; Jan. 8, 1880

Auburn (NY) Daily Advertiser, June 17, 1873; Nov. 21, 24, 1874; Dec. 10, 1877; Feb. 26, 27, 1882

Auburn (NY) Daily Bulletin, Feb. 1, 1877

Auburn (NY) Evening Auburnian, Apr. 24, 1880

Augusta (GA) Chronicle, Oct. 22, 30, 1875

Augusta (GA) Chronicle & Constitutionalist, Oct. 9, 1878

Augusta (ME) Daily Kennebec Journal, Feb. 2, 1874

Augusta (ME) Kennebec Journal, Nov. 14, 1877; Nov. 24, 1880; Mar. 1, 1883

Aurora (IL) Beacon, Sept. 9, 1882

Austin (TX) Daily Democratic Statesman, Dec. 9, 10, 11, 1879; Jun. 15, 1881

Baltimore (MD) American & Commercial Advertiser, Apr. 28, 29, 1873; Sept. 17, 18, 1877; Sept. 10, 11, 14, 1878; Feb. 7, 10, 1880; Apr. 15, 1881; Dec. 18, 20, 1882

Baltimore (MD) Sun, Dec. 19, 20, 22, 1873

Bangor (ME) Daily Commercial, Nov. 16, 1880; Mar. 1, 3, 1883

Bangor (ME) Daily Whig & Courier, Jan. 31, 1874

Batavia (NY) Republican Advocate, Feb. 11, Sept. 28, 1875

Batavia (NY) Spirit of the Times, Apr. 7, 1883

Bath (ME) Daily Times, Jan. 4, 1875; Nov. 7, 1877; Mar. 5, 1883

Battle Creek (MI) Daily Journal, Mar. 30, 1874

Belfast (ME) Republican, Mar. 1, 1883

Bellefontaine (OH) Examiner, Dec. 14, 21, 1883

Bellefontaine (OH) Weekly Examiner, Dec. 2, 9, 1881; Nov. 10, 17, 1882

Bethlehem (PA) Daily Times, Dec. 10, 1873

Binghamton (NY) Daily Republican, June 5, 1873; Nov. 25, 1874; Apr. 27, 29, 1880

Binghamton (NY) Democrat, Nov. 24, 27, 1874; Apr. 2, 3, 1881

Binghamton (NY) Republican & Times, Mar. 21, 22, 1878

Bloomington (IL) Daily Pantagraph, Apr. 7, 1874; Jan. 30, 31, 1878; Sept. 13, 15, 16, 1879; Sept. 29, 30, 1880; Nov. 11, 1881

Boston Daily Advertiser, Mar. 4, 1873

Boston Daily Globe, Mar. 5, 1873; Mar. 25, 27, 30, 1883

Boston Evening Transcript, Mar. 3, 4, 7, 1873; June 15, 16, 1874; Mar. 30, Apr. 2, 1875; Jan. 8, 9, 12, 1877; Mar. 22, 23, Dec. 6, 7, 1880; Apr. 10, 12, 1882

Boston Herald, Oct. 2, 1927

Boston Ray, Mar. 5, 1873

Boston Telegraph, June 16, 1874

Boulder (CO) Weekly Herald, Mar. 31, 1886

Bradford (PA) Era, Mar. 15, 1878; May 6, 8, 1880; Apr. 1, 1881; Apr. 12, 14, 1883

Brenham (TX) Daily Banner, Dec. 7, 12, 1879

Bridgeport (CT) Daily Standard, Jan. 6, 7, 1874; Dec. 14, 1876; Nov. 26, 1877; Nov. 4, 1878; Apr. 26, 28, 1882

Brockton (MA) Daily Enterprise, Dec. 9, 1880; Feb. 13, 1883; Jan. 11, 1884

Brooklyn (NY) Daily Eagle, Apr. 14, 15, 1873; Apr. 15, 16, 1878; Jan. 31, Feb. 1, 1881; Jan. 9, 10, 1882; Jan. 8, 9, 10, 11, 12, 1883

Brooklyn (NY) Daily Graphic, Jan. 31, 1880(?)

Buffalo (NY) Courier, Feb. 21, 1881; Apr. 12, 13, 1883

Buffalo (NY) Daily Courier, June 12, 1873; Apr. 4, 5, 1876; Feb. 14, 15, Dec. 17, 1877; Jan. 3, 1879; May 10, 11, 1880

Buffalo (NY) Evening Post, Nov. 10, 11, 12, 13, 1873

Burlington (IA) Daily Hawk-Eye, Jan. 25, 1878; Sept. 9, 12, 1879; Sept. 25, 1880; Sept. 28, 29, 1882; Jan. 27, 29, 1886

Burlington (IA) Hawk-Eye, Apr. 18, 21, 1874; Jan. 24, 25, 1878

Burlington (VT) Daily Free Press & Times, Nov. 6, 8, 9, 1880

Canton (OH) Daily Repository, Feb. 19, 20, 1879; Nov. 24, 25, 1882; Dec. 21, 1885

Carson City (NV) Morning Appeal, June 30, 1877; Apr. 21, 22, 23, 1879; Mar. 25, 1886

Central City (CO) Daily Register Call, July 28, 29, 30, 31, 1879

Central City (CO) Weekly Register, Call, Apr. 9, 1886

Charleston (SC) Courier, Oct. 27, Nov. 3, 1875; Jan. 18, 21, 1880

Charleston (SC) News & Courier, Oct. 8, 12, 1878

Charlotte (NC) Daily Observer, Oct. 1, 3, 4, 1878

Chatham (ON) Tri-weekly Planet, Mar. 22, 24, 1876

Cheyenne (WY) Daily Leader, July 29, 31, Aug. 3, 1879; Feb. 23, 1886

Cheyenne (WY) Daily Sun, July 30, 31, Aug. 2, 3, 5, 1879

Cheyenne (WY) Democratic Leader, Mar. 30, 31, 1886

Chicago Daily Tribune, Dec. 17, 18, 19, 1872

Chicago Evening Journal, Dec. 19, 1872

Chicago Inter-Ocean, Dec. 17, 1872

Chicago Times, Dec. 15, 16, 17, 18, 19, 20, 21, 1872; May 14, 1874; Dec. 17, 20, 1878; Sept. 4, 5, 1882; Feb. 19, Mar. 3, 1884; Jan. 4, 18, 1886

Chicago Tribune, Jan. 6, 7, 9, 1878; Sept. 14, 17, 1880; Sept. 5, 1881; Feb. 18, 19, 21, 1884; May 26, 1885

Chillicothe (OH) Scioto Gazette, Feb. 19, 25, 26, Nov. 12, 1879

Cincinnati (OH) Commercial, Dec. 28, 1872; Mar. 18, 1877

Cincinnati (OH) Daily Enquirer, Sept. 29, 30, Oct. 2, 4, 1879

Cincinnati (OH) Daily Gazette, Dec. 27, 30, 31, 1872; Sept. 19, 23, 24, 1873;
    Jan. 25, 1876; Feb. 19, 1878

Cincinnati (OH) Enquirer, Jan. 15, 1873; Mar. 8, 1875; Jan. 24, 25, 26, 27, 28, 29,
    1876; Mar. 3, 1879; Oct. 11, 1880; Nov. 14, 15, 1881; Dec. 1, 1882

Cincinnati (OH) Post, Oct. 9, 1882

Cleveland (OH) Herald, Feb. 19, 20, 21, 22, 23, Dec. 21, 1877; Feb. 7, 1879;
    Oct. 23, 24, 1879; Feb. 13, 14, 15, Nov. 20, 21, 1882

Cleveland (OH) Leader, Jan. 14, Oct. 27, 28, 1873; Dec. 20, 1877; Feb. 25, 1881;
    Mar. 24, 1905

Cleveland (OH) Penny Press, Feb. 4, 1879; Nov. 21, 1882

Cleveland (OH) Plain Dealer, Dec. 20, 21, 1877; Feb. 24, 25, 1881; Dec. 27, 1885;
    Jan. 2, 1886

Clinton (IA) Age, Sept. 15, 1882

Clinton (IA) Daily Herald, Apr. 28, 29, 1874; Sept. 4, 5, 1879; Sept. 20, 21, 22,
    1880; Sept. 3, 5, 1881; Sept. 12, 13, 1882; Jan. 23, 26, 1886

Clinton (MA) Courant, Feb. 19, 1883

Colorado Springs (CO) Daily Gazette, July 24, 1879

Columbus (GA) Sunday Enquirer, Nov. 7, 14, 1875

Columbus (OH) Daily Dispatch, Sept. 12, 16, 1873; Mar. 3, 4, 1875; Feb. 16, 17,
    18, 19, 1876; Feb. 22, 1878

Columbus (OH) Dispatch, Feb. 25, 26, 27, 1879; Nov. 17, 18, 20, 1882;
    Jan. 11, 1886

Columbus (OH) Ohio State Journal, Mar. 1, 2, 3, 4, 1875; Feb. 16, 18, 1876;
    Mar. 14, 15, 1877; Feb. 21, 22, 1878; Feb. 25, 26, 27, Nov. 12, 13, 14, 1879;
    Mar. 17, 18, 19, 21, Dec. 10, 12, 13, 1881; Nov. 18, 20, 1882; Dec. 20, 21,
    22, 1883; Jan. 9, 11, 12, 13, 14, 1886

Columbus (NE) Columbus Democrat, Feb. 12, 1886

Columbia (PA) Lancaster Intelligencer, Apr. 6, 1878

Columbia (SC) Register, Oct. 5, 1878; Jan. 20, 1880

Concord (NH) Daily Monitor, Feb. 5, 10, 11, 1874; Jan. 14, 1875; Jan. 1,
    Nov. 1, 1877; Nov. 11, 1880; Mar. 14, 1882; Feb. 19, 1883

Council Bluffs (IA) Nonpareil, Sept. 29, Oct. 4, 5, 1881; Feb. 10, 14, 1886

Danbury (CT) News, Dec. 16, 23, 1874; Oct. 30, 1878

Danville (IL) Daily Commercial, Sept. 11, 17, 1879

Danville (PA) Intelligencer, Mar. 29, 1878; Apr. 30, 1880

Danville (PA) Montour American, Apr. 7, 1881; Jan. 26, 1882

Danville (PA) Sun, Dec. 8, 10, 1885

Davenport (IA) Democrat, Apr. 23, 24, 1874; Jan. 15, 17, 18, 1878; Aug. 19, 30, Sept. 1, 2, 1879; Sept. 23, 24, 1880; Sept. 1, 1881

Davenport (IA) Sunday Democrat, Sept. 24, 1882

Dayton (OH) Evening Herald, Oct. 4, 1873

Dayton (OH) Daily Journal, Mar. 4, 5, 6, 1875; Mar. 16, 17, 1877; Feb. 15, 16, 1878; Feb. 27, Mar. 1, 1879; Nov. 14, 15, 17, 1879; Mar. 15, 16, 17, Dec. 8, 9, 1881; Nov. 10, 11, 13, 1882

Decatur (IL) Daily Republican, Jan. 29, 1878; Sept. 12, 1879; Oct. 30, 1882

Denver (CO) Daily Times, July 21, 1879

Denver (CO) Rocky Mountain News, Apr. 4, 5, 6, 1886

Denver (CO) Tribune, June 1, 1882

Des Moines (IA) Iowa State Register, Oct. 1, 2, 1881; Sept. 26, 27, 1882

Detroit (MI) Free Press, Mar. 24, 25, 26, 1874; Dec. 27, 28, 1878

Detroit (MI) News, Oct. 21, 22, 1880

Dover (NH) Enquirer, Jan. 14, 1875

Dover (NH) Foster's Daily Democrat, Feb. 9, 1874

Dubuque (IA) Herald, Sept. 4, 6, 1879

Dunkirk (NY) Weekly Journal, Feb. 15, 22, 1882

Easton (PA) Daily Express, Dec. 6, 15, 16, 1873; Jan. 13, 14, 1881; Jan. 23, 1882

Easton (PA) Express, Mar. 27, 1878; Jan. 3, 4, 1883

Easton (PA) Free Press, Oct. 20, 1875

Elmira (NY) Daily Advertiser, June 6, 7, 9, 10, 1873; Nov. 12, 14, 16, 17, 18, 1874; Oct. 17, 18, 19, 1876; Mar. 16, 19, 20, 1878; May 1, 3, 5, 1880; Apr. 1, 2, 1881

Erie (PA) Daily Dispatch, Feb. 18, 1875; Feb. 16, 17, 1877; Mar. 13, 14, 1878

Erie (PA) Morning Dispatch, Nov. 7, 14, 15, 1873; Mar. 9, 15, 16, 1874; Jan. 1, 3, 1879; May 7, 1880; Feb. 22, 1881; Feb. 17, 18, 1882; Apr. 14, 1883

Evansville (IN) Courier, Mar. 10, 11, 1881

Evansville (IN) Daily Courier, Dec. 30, 31, 1875; Jan. 1, 2, 1876; Feb. 4, 1878; Oct. 10, 11, 1879; Oct. 30, 1881; Oct. 24, 25, 1882

Fall River (MA) Daily Evening News, Dec. 15, 1876; Feb. 13, 1883

Fall River (MA) Daily Herald, Mar. 27, 30, Dec. 11, 1880

Fall River (MA) Evening News, Apr. 5, 1882; Mar. 28, 1910

Fitchburg (MA) Daily Sentinel, Nov. 11, 12, 1880; Mar. 14, 17, 1882

Fort Wayne (IN) Daily News, Feb. 9, 12, 15, 16, 1878; Oct. 15, 16, 17, 19, 20, 1879;
     Nov. 29, 30, Dec. 1, 1881; Nov. 9, 15, 1882

Fort Wayne (IN) Gazette, Oct. 15, 18, 1873

Fort Wayne (IN) Journal Gazette, Feb. 14, 15, 17, 1884

Fort Wayne (IN) Morning Gazette, Feb. 9, 12, 16, 1878

Fort Wayne (IN) Sentinel, Oct. 16, 1879

Fort Wayne (IN) Weekly Sentinel, Nov. 8, 15, 1882

Fort Worth (TX) Democrat, Dec. 4, 1879

Freeport (IL) Daily Bulletin, Apr. 23, 30, 1874, Sept. 14, 15, 1881

Fremont (OH) Weekly Journal, Oct. 24, 1873

Galion (OH) Inquirer, Dec. 8, 1881; Dec. 14, 1883

Galveston (TX) News, Nov. 21, 25, 1875; Dec. 17, 18, 19, 1879

Gardiner (ME) Home Journal, Feb. 28, 1883

Gardiner (ME) Kennebec Reporter, Jan. 31, Feb. 7, 1874

Geneva (NY) Courier, Feb. 3, 1875

Georgetown (CO) Colorado Miner, July 26, Aug. 2, 1879

Georgetown (CO) Courier, Apr. 1, 1886

Glens Falls (NY) Messenger, Mar. 3, 1882

Gloucester (MA) Cape Ann Bulletin, Dec. 1, 8, 1880; Mar. 29, Apr. 5, 1882

Gloucester (MA) Cape Ann Weekly Advertiser, Oct. 26, 1877; Mar. 16, 23, 1883

Gold Hill (NV) News, June 27, 28, 29, 30, 1877

Grand Island (NE) Independent, Feb. 17, 18, 1886

Grand Rapids (MI) Daily Eagle, Dec. 28, 1877

Greenfield (MA) Gazette & Courier, Mar. 13, 1882

Greensburg (PA) Evening Press, Dec. 14, 1885

Hamilton (OH) Telegraph, Oct. 2, 1873; Feb. 17, 1876

Hamilton (ON) Spectator, May 26, 27, 28, 29, 1874; Mar. 25, 28, 1876;
     Oct. 25, 26, 1880

Harrisburg (PA) Daily Patriot, May 27, Dec. 13, 20, 1873; Dec. 2, 3, 1874;
     Apr. 4, 5, 1878; Apr. 9, 1881; Dec. 25, 1882

Hartford (CT) Courant, Feb. 22, 24, 26, 1873; Jan. 9, 12, 13, 14, Dec. 22, 24, 1874;
     May 12, 13, Dec. 13, 1876; Nov. 22, 24, 1877; Nov. 7, 8, 1878; Mar. 17, 18,
     Dec. 30, 31, 1880; Apr. 24, 25, 1882; Feb. 6, 7, 8, 1883; Jan. 11, 12, 1884

Hastings (NE) Daily Gazette Journal, Feb. 18, 1886

Haverhill (MA) Daily Bulletin, Feb. 14, 1874; Dec. 23, 1876; Apr. 5, Nov. 23,
 1880; Mar. 14, 1883

Holyoke (MA) Daily Transcript, Mar. 21, 22, 23, 1883

Hornell (NY) Weekly Tribune, Nov. 20, 1874

Houston (TX) Daily Telegraph, Nov. 30, 1875

Ilion (NY) Citizen, Feb. 24, Mar. 3, 1882

Indianapolis (IN) Journal, Aug. 27, Oct. 1, 6, 7, 13, 14, 1873

Indianapolis (IN) News, Jan. 31, Feb. 2, 1876; Mar. 27, 29, 1877; Feb. 12, 1878;
 Oct. 4, 6, 7, 1879; Mar. 7, 8, Nov. 21, 1881; Nov. 3, 4, 1882

Iowa City (IA) Daily Republican, Jan. 17, 1878; Sept. 2, 13, 1879;
 Sept. 25, 26, 1882

Jacksonville (IL) Daily Journal, Apr. 13, 14, 1874; Sept. 17, 19, 1879;
 Nov. 2, 3, 1882; Dec. 7, 8, 1883

Jamestown (NY) Daily Journal, Nov. 1, 7, 1873; Mar. 11, 15, 1878

Janesville (WI) Daily Gazette, Sept. 16, 17, 1881; Aug. 29, Sept. 1, 1882

Janesville (WI) Gazette, Jan. 2, 7, 1878

Janesville (WI) Times, Aug. 31, Sept. 7, 1882

Jersey City (NJ) Journal, Jan. 27, 1883

Johnstown (PA) Tribune, Nov. 20, 1873; Dec. 13, 17, 1881; Dec. 1, 1882

Joliet (IL) Daily News, Sept. 15, 17, 1882

Joliet (IL) Morning News, Jan. 14, 15, 19, 1878

Joliet (IL) Signal, Mar. 31, 1874

Kalamazoo (MI) Daily Telegraph, Mar. 28, 1874

Kansas City (KS) Times, Apr. 10, 1877

Kansas City (MO) Journal, Oct. 11, 12, 14, 1881; Feb. 2, 1886

Kansas City (MO) Journal of Commerce, Apr. 8, Aug. 3, 1876; Apr. 10, 13, 1877

Kearney (NE) New Era, Feb. 13, 1886

Keokuk (IA) Constitution, Sept. 10, 1879; Oct. 1, 1880; Nov. 7, 9, 10, 11, 1881

Keokuk (IA) Daily Constitution, Sept. 29, 1882; Jan. 26, 27, 28, 29, 1886

Keokuk (IA) Daily Gate City, Apr. 12, 18, 1874; Jan. 14, 1876; Jan. 20, 23,
 24, 1878; Sept. 10, 11, 1879

Kokomo (IN) Dispatch, Nov. 24, Dec. 1, 3, 1881; Nov. 2, 9, 11, 1882

Kokomo (IN) Saturday Tribune, Dec. 3, 1881

La Crosse (WI) Chronicle, Sept. 8, 9, 1880; Sept. 22, 23, 1881; June 13, 1948;
 Jan. 9, 1976

La Crosse (WI) Tribune, June 13, 1948

Lafayette (IN) Daily Courier, Feb. 13, 14, 1878; Oct. 11, 15, 1879; Mar. 3, 4, 1881; Nov. 25, 26, 1881; Nov. 7, 1882

Lafayette (IN) Daily Journal, Oct. 13, 16, 1873; Feb. 3, 1876

Lancaster (PA) Daily Examiner, May 24, 27, Dec. 18, 1873; Apr. 25, 28, Dec. 24, 27, 28, 1881

Lancaster (PA) Daily Examiner & Express, Apr. 5, 8, 1878

Lancaster (PA) Daily Intelligencer, Apr. 27, 1881; Dec. 28, 29, 30, 1882

Laramie (WY) Daily Sentinel, July 9, 1877; Feb. 20, 27, 1886

Lawrence (KS) Daily Journal, Oct. 12, 13, 1881

Lawrence (MA) Daily American, Feb. 11, June 11, 12, 1874; Jan. 18, 20, 1875; Dec. 28, 29, 1876; Jan. 19, 21, 22, 1884

Lawrence (MA) Daily Eagle, Mar. 24, 1873; Oct. 27, 1877; Nov. 29, Apr. 1, Dec. 1, 1880; Feb. 22, 24, 1883

Leadville (CO) Herald-Democrat, Sept. 6, 1908

Leavenworth (KS) Daily Times, Apr. 11, 1877

Leavenworth (KS) Times, Oct. 2, 8, 9, 1881; Feb. 5, 1886

Lewiston (ME) Evening Journal, Mar. 20, 21, 1873; Feb. 3, 1874; Jan. 9, 11, 12, 1875; Nov. 13, 1877; Nov. 28, 29, 1878; Mar. 3, Nov. 24, 26, 1880; Mar. 22, 24, 1882; Mar. 7, 8, 9, 1883

Lexington (KY) Daily Transcript, Nov. 18, 19, 1879; Oct. 17, 18, 1882

Lexington (KY) Kentucky Daily Lexington Press, Sept. 27, 30, Oct. 1, 1873

Lincoln (NE) Daily Nebraska State Journal, Oct. 5, 6, 1881; Feb. 10, 11, 1886

Little Falls (NY) Journal & Courier, Feb. 2, 1875

Little Rock (AK) Arkansas Gazette, Nov. 29, Dec. 2, 3, 1879

Lock Haven (PA) Daily Democrat, Dec. 8, 9, 10, 11, 12, 14, 1885

Lockport (NY) Daily Sun, June 13, 1873; Nov. 19, 1874; Feb. 11, 1875; Dec. 5, 1877; Jan. 2, 1879

Logansport (IN) Daily Journal, Feb. 13, 1878; Mar. 1, 3, 5, Nov. 27, 29, 30, 1881; Nov. 7, 1882

London (ON) Daily Free Press, May 23, 1874; Mar. 25, 1876

Louisville (KY) Courier-Journal, Jan. 2, 7, 8, Oct. 3, 4, 5, 1873; Feb. 11, 1876; Feb. 8, 9, 1878; Nov. 16, 20, 21, 22, 1879; Mar. 14, 15, Oct. 24, 25, 1881; Oct. 26, 27, 1882

Lowell (MA) Daily Citizen, Nov. 29, 1880

Lowell (MA) Daily Courier, Mar. 11, 1873; Feb. 14, 16, 17, June 10, 1874; Jan. 18, 20, 1875; May 1, Dec. 28, 29, 1876; Nov. 19, 20, 1877; Apr. 9, 1880; Apr. 1, 3, 4, 1882; Feb. 21, 23, 1883; Jan. 18, 19, 1884

Lynchburg (VA) News, Sept. 30, Oct. 1, 1878

Lynn (MA) Daily Evening Item, Dec. 3, 1880; Apr. 1, 1882; Mar. 23, 1883; Jan. 23, 1884

Lynn (MA) Record, Jan. 2, 1875

Lynn (MA) Reporter, June 13, 1874; Dec. 23, 1876; Oct. 27, 1877; Mar. 20, 1880

Macon (GA) Telegraph & Messenger, Jan. 8, 14, 1880

Madison (WI) State Journal, May 1, 5, 1874; Jan. 3, 1878; Sept. 16, 1881

Manchester (NH) Daily Mirror & American, Jan. 3, 1877; Mar. 14, 20, 1882

Manchester (NH) Daily Union, Feb. 9, 1874; Jan. 14, 15, 16, 1875; Jan. 2, 3, Nov. 2, 5, 1877; Apr. 2, Nov. 12, 13, 1880

Manchester (NH) Mirror & American, Nov. 2, 5, 1877; Nov. 13, 15, 1880

Manchester (NH) Mirror & American Express, Jan. 17, 18, 1884

Manchester (NH) Union Express, Feb. 22, 26, 1883

Mansfield (OH) Herald, Mar. 12, 1874

Mansfield (OH) Richland Shield & Banner, Feb. 23, 1878; Dec. 3, 1881; Feb. 9, 1884

Marshall (MI) Statesman, Mar. 30, 1874

Meadville (PA) Crawford Journal, Dec. 21, 1883

Meadville (PA) Daily Republican, Mar. 24, 1881

Meadville (PA) Evening Republic, Oct. 29, Nov. 4, 1873; Feb. 20, 1875; Feb. 26, 1877; Jan. 29, 1879

Medina (NY) Tribune, Dec. 6, 1877; Jan. 2, 1879

Memphis (TN) Call, Nov. 10, 1875; Nov. 28, 1954, Sept. 21, 1957

Memphis (TN) Daily Memphis Avalanche, Dec. 19, 21, 1875

Meriden (CT) Daily Republican, Jan. 8, Dec. 19, 22, 1874; Dec. 14, 15, 1876; Apr. 22, 1882

Middletown (CT) Daily Constitution, Jan. 8, 1874

Milford (MA) Journal, Dec. 4, 11, 1878

Milwaukee (WI) Daily Republican Sentinel, Sept. 2, 3, 1882

Milwaukee (WI) Sentinel, May 1, 4, 5, 6, 7, 8, 1874; Dec. 28, 31, 1877; Jan. 1, 3, 1878; Aug. 30, Sept. 1, 1880; Feb. 28, Mar. 1, 2, 1884

Minneapolis (MN) Tribune, Sept. 1, 1880

Mobile (AL) Daily, Nov. 20, 1875; Dec. 29, 1879

Monmouth (IL) Review, Jan. 29. 1886

Montgomery (AL) Daily Advertiser, Nov. 14, 1875; Jan. 1, 1880

Montreal (QC) Gazette, June 1, 1874; Nov. 1, 5, 1880

Muncie (IN) Daily News, Oct. 16, 1879; Nov. 22, 1881

Nashua (NH) Telegraph, Feb. 19, 1883

Nashville (TN) Banner, Oct. 28, 1881; Oct. 21, 1882

Nashville (TN) Daily American, Dec. 26, 28, 1875; Feb. 5, 6, 1878; Nov. 25, 1879; Mar. 11, 12, 1881

Nebraska City (NE) News, Apr. 14, 18, 19, 25, 1877; Aug. 7, Oct. 5, 6, 7, 1881

New Albany (IN) Ledger, Oct. 24, 26, 27, 1881; Oct. 16, 18, 1882

New Bedford (MA) Daily Mercury, May 18, 1876; Oct. 26, 1877

New Bedford (MA) Evening Standard, Dec. 23, 1876; Feb. 12, 1883

New Bedford (MA) Intelligence, Jan. 21, 1874

New Bedford (MA) Morning Mercury, Mar. 26, Dec. 14, 1880

New Brunswick (NJ) Daily Times, Sept. 9, 1873; Jan. 10, 13, 1881; Jan. 3, 5, 1883

New Brunswick (NJ) Sunday Times, Apr. 1, 1929

New Castle (PA) Courant, Mar. 10, 1876; Feb. 14, 1879

New Castle (PA) Courant Guardian, Oct. 31, 1873

New Castle (PA) Lawrence Guardian, Dec. 11, 1885

New Haven (CT) Evening Register, Dec. 21, 22, 23, 1874; May 24, 25, 1876; Nov. 23, 24, 1877; Nov. 2, 4, 1878; Apr. 29, 1882; Jan. 9, 11, 1884; May 17, 1897

New Haven (CT) Journal & Courier, July 16, 17, 1885

New Haven (CT) Register, Mar. 15, 1880

New London (CT) Telegram, May 16, 1876

New Orleans (LA) Bee, Dec. 12, 1875; Dec. 21, 1879

New Orleans (LA) Picayune, Dec. 20, 21, 23, 1879

New York Clipper, Apr. 1873–March 1879

New York Dramatic Mirror, Jan. 1879–Dec. 1879

New York Herald, Feb. 16, 1872, Apr. 1, Aug. 25, 30, Sept. 1, 1873; Jan. 13, June 29, 30, 1874; May 31, June 1, 1875; Oct. 3, Nov. 7, 1876; Sept. 3, 8, 9, 15, 1877; Apr. 22, 1878; Mar. 1, 2, 10, Aug. 23, 24, 1880; Jan. 18, 1881; Jan. 16, 1882; Jan. 16, 22, 1883

New York Mirror, Jan. 1880–May 1886

New York Times, June 26, Nov. 13, 1872; Apr. 1, 8, 12, 18, 1873; June 29, Nov. 2, 3, 1874; Oct. 27, Dec. 18, 1880; Apr. 13, 1917

New York Tribune, Apr. 1, 1873; Nov. 7, 1876; Aug. 27, 1880; Jan. 28, 29, 1884

Newark (NJ) Daily Advertiser, Dec. 5, 1873; May 27, Dec. 12, 1876; Apr. 11, 13, 1878; Apr. 29, 1881; Jan. 5, 1883; Jan. 7, 1884; Nov. 30, 1885

Newark (NJ) Sunday Call, Dec. 7, 1873

Newark (OH) Advocate, Nov. 14, 1879

Newburyport (MA) Herald, Nov. 27, Dec. 2, 1880; Mar. 12, 13, 1883

Newport (RI) Daily News, Dec. 15, 20, 1876; Oct. 24, 26, 1877; Mar. 25, 1880; Apr. 4, 1882

Newport (RI) News, Feb. 14, 1883

Norfolk (VA) Virginian, May 15, 16, 17, 1873; Sept. 22, 25, 1878

Norristown (PA) Register, Jan. 11, 15, 1881

North Adams (MA) Adams Transcript, Feb. 19, 1874

North Adams (MA) Hoosac Valley News, Jan. 21, 1875

North Adams (MA) Transcript, Mar. 9, 1882

North Platte (NE) Enterprise, July 19, 1873

Norwalk (CT) Gazette, Oct. 29, 1878; Jan. 30, 1883; Jan. 22, 1884

Oakland (CA) Daily Evening Tribune, Mar. 20, 23, 1886

Oakland (CA) Transcript, June 12, 14, 1877

Oil City (PA) Derrick, Jan. 22, 23, 1873; Feb. 27, 28, Mar. 3, 6, 7, 1877; Mar. 7, 11, 1878; Jan. 30, Feb. 1, 3, 1879; Feb. 6, 8, 10, 1882

Omaha (NE) Daily Bee, July 17, 28, 1873; July 7, 1882

Omaha (NE) Daily Herald, July 17, 1873

Omaha (NE) Republican, Aug. 8, 1873; Apr. 21, 1877; Oct. 4, 5, 1881

Omaha (NE) Weekly Herald, Jan. 1, Dec. 21, 1873

Omaha (NE) Weekly Tribune & Republican, Dec. 21, 1872

Oneida (NY) Dispatch, Nov. 19, 20, 1874

Opelika (AL) Leader, Jan. 8, 1880

Opelika (AL) Observer, Jan. 9, 1880

Oswego (NY) Daily Palladium, June 18, 20, 1873; Mar. 5, 6, 1874

Oswego (NY) Daily Times, Jan. 10, 1879; Apr. 21, 1880

Ottawa (IL) Free Trader, Jan. 12, 19, 1878; Sept. 3, 10, 17, 1881; Sept. 9, 12, 14, 16, 1882

Ottawa (ON) Citizen, Oct. 28, 29, Nov. 1, 1880

Ottumwa (IA) Daily Democrat, Sept. 27, 1882

Paterson (NJ) Daily Guardian, Apr. 10, 11, 13, 1878, Jan. 3, 5, 6, 1883

Peoria (IL) Daily Transcript, Apr. 24, 25, 1874; Jan. 29, 30, 1878; Sept. 15, 19, 1882; Dec. 3, 1883

Peoria (IL) Journal, Sept. 11, 1879

Peoria (IL) Journal Transcript, Jan. 18, 1876

Peoria (IL) Transcript, Nov. 8, 12, 1881

Peterborough (ON) Daily Evening Review, Oct. 27, 28, 1880

Philadelphia Inquirer, Apr. 21, Dec. 27, 29, 1873; Jan. 2, 1874; Feb. 2, 3, 1880; Apr. 11, Dec. 19, 20, 1881; Dec. 11, 12, 1882; Jan. 1, 4, 1884

Philadelphia Times, Oct. 5, 8, 1877; May 10, 1878; Nov. 16, 19, 1885

Piqua (OH) Miami Democrat, Mar. 10, 1877

Pittsburgh (PA) Commercial Gazette, Mar. 6, 1877; Mar. 1, 1878; Nov. 5, 1879; Mar. 23, 1881; Nov. 27, 1882

Pittsburgh (PA) Post Gazette, Jan. 16, Nov. 14, 17, 18, 1873; Mar. 1, 1876

Pittsfield (MA) Berkshire County Eagle, Feb. 19, 1874; Jan. 21, 28, 1875

Pittsfield, (MA) Sun, Feb. 12, 1873; Jan. 17, Nov. 21, 1877

Port Hope (ON) Daily Guide, Oct. 26, 28, 1880

Port Jervis (NY) Evening Gazette, Dec. 2, 1873

Portland (ME) Daily Advertiser, Mar. 19, 1873; Feb. 6, 1874; Jan. 6, 1875; May 6, 1876; Jan. 5, 6, Nov. 6, 15, 1877; Nov. 22, 1878; Apr. 7, Nov. 17, 1880; Mar. 25, 1882; Mar. 9, 1883

Portland (ME) Daily Eastern Argus, Mar. 21, 1882

Portsmouth (NH) Chronicle, Mar. 17, 18, 19, 1873; Nov. 10, 1880

Portsmouth (NH) Daily Chronicle, Mar. 16, 1882

Portsmouth (NH) Daily Evening Times, Mar. 18, 1873; Jan. 5, 1875

Pottsville (PA) Daily Miners' Journal, May 30, Dec. 12, 1873; Mar. 30, 1878

Poughkeepsie (PA) Daily Eagle, Dec. 3, 4, 1873; Mar. 1, 1882; Jan. 31, Feb. 1, 1883

Poughkeepsie (NY) Sunday Courier, Feb. 3, 4, 1884

Providence (RI) Journal, Feb. 17, 19, 1873; Jan. 16, 1874; May 22, 23, 25, 1876; Oct. 22, 23, 1877; Dec. 10, 12, 1878; Mar. 15, 17, 1880; Apr. 15, 1882; Feb. 15, 17, 1883; Jan. 12, 13, 1884

Pueblo (CO) Chieftain, July 25, 27, 1879

Quincy (IL) Daily Herald, Jan. 13, 14, 1876; Sept. 19, 21, 1879; Nov. 5, 6, 1881; Sept. 28, 30, Oct. 1, 1882

Quincy (IL) Daily Journal, Jan. 29, Feb. 1, 1886

Quincy (IL) Daily Whig, Oct. 1, 2, 1880; Jan. 29, 31, 1886

Quincy (IL) Whig, Apr. 11, 15, 16, 17, 1874

Racine (WI) County Argus, May 7, 1874

Raleigh (NC) Observer, Jan. 22, 24, 1880

Reading (PA) Daily Eagle, May 28, 1873; Mar. 29, 1878; Apr. 28, 1881; Jan. 24, Dec. 25, 1882

Reading (PA) Eagle, Nov. 26, 1885

Reading (PA) Times, Dec. 13, 1873

Red Wing (MN) Advance, Sept. 1, 8, 1880

Reno (NV) Evening Gazette, July 2, 1877; Mar. 24, 27, 1886

Richmond (IN) Daily Independent, Feb. 13, 15, 1876; Mar. 22, 25, 1877

Richmond (IN) Evening Item, Nov. 17, 22, 1881; Nov. 10, 11, 1882

Richmond (IN) Times, Oct. 4, 1873

Richmond (VA) Dispatch, May 12, 13, 1873; Oct. 18, 20, 1875; Sept. 26, 1878; Jan. 27, 1880

Richmond (VA) State, Sept. 27, 28, 1878

Rochester (NY) Democrat & Chronicle, Jan. 31, Feb. 1, Sept. 1, 1873; Mar. 10, 11, 13, 1874; Sept. 27, 28, 1875; Sept. 18, Oct. 2, 3, 1876; Feb. 6, 7, 1877; Jan. 9, 1879; Apr. 22, 23, 1880; Feb, 15, 16, 1881; Feb. 24, 1882; Apr. 9, 1883; Feb. 9, 1884

Rochester (NY) Union & Advertiser, Apr. 10, 1872; Feb. 3, 8, 10, 1875; Apr. 10, 1876; Dec. 13, 1877

Rock Island (IL) Argus, Jan. 12, 1878; Sept. 3, 1879; Sept. 22, 1880; Sept. 2, 1881; Dec. 3, 1883

Rockland (ME) Courier-Gazette, Mar. 6, 1883

Rockland (ME) Gazette, Nov. 1, 1877

Rome (NY) Daily Sentinel, Nov. 10, 1874

Rutland (VT) Daily Herald & Globe, Mar. 6, 9, 1882

Sacramento (CA) Daily Bee, June 20, 21, 22, 23, 1877; Apr. 12, 18, 1879; Mar. 2, 1886

Saginaw (MI) Daily Courier, May 16, 17, 21, 22, 1874

Salem (MA) Evening News, Mar. 12, 16, 1883; Jan. 19, 23, 1884

Salem (MA) Gazette, Apr. 21, 1876; Oct. 26, 1877; Mar. 23, Nov. 30, 1880

Salem (NJ) National Standard, Nov. 18, 1885

Salem (NJ) South Jerseyman, Nov. 18, 24, 1885

Salt Lake City (UT) Deseret News, May 3, 1879; Feb. 27, 1886

Salt Lake City (UT) Herald, Feb. 28, 1886

Salt Lake City (UT) Tribune, May 1, 2, 3, 1879

San Antonio (TX) Daily Express, Dec. 13, 16, 17, 1879

San Francisco Chronicle, May 13, 15, 20, 24, 25, 27, 28, June 2, 9, 1877;
 Mar. 21, 25, 30, Apr. 9, 1879; Mar. 13, 1886; Aug. 13, 1916

San Francisco Daily Alta, Mar. 30, 1879

San Francisco Daily Bee, Apr. 8, 1879

San Jose (CA) Daily Mercury, June 14, 15, 16, 17, 1877; Mar. 5, 7, 1886

Sandusky (OH) Daily Register, Oct. 22, 25, 27, 1873; Mar. 19, 1874;
 Oct. 22, 1879; Feb. 28, Dec. 2, 1881

Saratoga (NY) Sentinel, Mar. 2, 1882

Savannah (GA) Morning News, Nov. 4, 5, 6, 7, 1875; Oct. 12, 15, 17, 1878;
 Jan. 16, 17, 1880

Schenectady (NY) Daily Union, Feb. 28, Mar. 2, 3, 1874, Feb. 1, 3, 1875

Schenectady (NY) Evening Star, Feb. 26, Mar. 3, 1874

Scranton (PA) Morning Republican, June 2, Nov. 27, Dec. 1, 1873;
 Nov. 26, 28, 30, 1874

Scranton (PA) Republican, Jan. 20, 22, 1879; Apr. 4, 5, 6, 1881, Jan. 29, 30, 31,
 Feb. 1, Dec. 8, 11, 1882

Selma (AL) Morning Times, Jan. 1, 1880

Shamokin (PA) Herald, Dec. 5, 1885

Sharon (PA) Herald, Oct. 31, Nov. 7, 1879; Feb. 8, 1884; Dec. 25, 1885

South Bend (IN) Tribune, Apr. 3, 4, 1974

Spirit of the Times, Feb. 1874–Aug. 1879

Springfield (IL) Illinois State Journal, Apr. 10, 14, 1874; Feb. 5, 1876; Jan. 31,
 Feb. 1, 1878; Sept. 19, 1879; Nov. 2, 3, 1881; Nov. 1, 2, 1882; Dec. 8, 1883

Springfield (MA) Daily Republican, Jan. 22, 1875; Apr. 19, 20, 1876

Springfield (MA) Daily Union, Jan. 15, Nov. 21, 1877; Dec. 11, 1878; Apr. 10,
 Dec. 29, 1880; Apr. 18, 1882; Jan. 22, 1884

Springfield (OH) Daily Republic, Mar. 4, 1875; Mar. 15, 1877; Feb. 21, 22, 1878;
 Feb. 27, 1879; Mar. 17, 18, Dec. 9, 1881; Nov. 16, 1882; Dec. 13, 14, 1883

St. Joseph (MO) Daily News, Feb. 3, 6, 1886

St. Joseph (MO) Daily Gazette, Feb. 2, 3, 6, 1886

St. Joseph (MO) Evening News, Oct. 6, 1881

St. Joseph (MO) Gazette, Apr. 14, 15, 17, 1877; Oct. 1, 2, 4, 6, 8, 1881

St. Louis (MO) Daily Democrat, Mar. 15, 23, May 4, 5, 1873

St. Louis (MO) Daily Globe-Democrat, Apr. 1, 2, 3, 4, 6, 1877; Oct. 4, 9, 10,
 1880; Oct. 16, 1881

St. Louis (MO) Dispatch, Jan. 4, 7, 1876

St. Louis (MO) Globe-Democrat, Apr. 26, 1884

St. Louis (MO) Post Dispatch, Sept. 21, 22, 23, 24, 25, 1879; Oct. 3, 8, 1882

St. Louis (MO) Times, June 18, 1876

St. Paul (MN) Dispatch, Sept. 13, 1876

St. Paul (MN) Pioneer Press, Sept. 2, 1880; Sept. 23, 24, 25, 1881

Stamford (CT) Advocate Weekly, Nov. 1, 1878; Apr. 21, 1882; Jan. 25, 1884

Stamford (CT) Mirror, Dec. 14, 1875

Steubenville (OH) Daily Herald, Feb. 25, 26, 1875; Feb. 21, Nov. 7, 8, 1879;
    Mar. 23, 24, Dec. 5, 16, 1881; Dec. 16, 17, 18, 19, 1885

Stillwater (MN) Daily Sun, Sept. 20, 28, 1881

Stockton (CA) Daily Independent, June 13, 19, 21, 1877; Mar. 5, 6, 1886

Suncook (NH) Journal, Jan. 12, 1884

Syracuse (NY) Journal, Mar. 3, 7, 1874

Syracuse (NY) Standard, Jan. 28, 1873; Nov. 19, 23, 1874; Feb. 5, 6, 8, 1875;
    Sept. 18, 1875; Apr. 7, 1876; Dec. 7, 10, 1877; Jan. 14, 1879; Feb. 11, 14, 1881;
    Feb. 6, 1884

Tamaqua (PA) Courier, Mar. 30, 1878

Taunton (MA) Daily Gazette, Mar. 26, 27, 1873; Jan. 20, 21, Dec. 29, 30, 1874;
    May 12, 13, 1876; Mar. 18, 19, 1880; Feb. 10, 1883

Terre Haute (IN) Daily Express, Oct. 10, 11, 1873; Mar. 30, 1877; Feb. 1, 3, 1878;
    Mar. 1, Oct. 11, 1879; Oct. 28, 31, 1882

Terre Haute (IN) Evening Gazette, Oct. 8, 10, 1873; Feb. 8, 1876; Mar. 1, 1879;
    Nov. 2, 3, 1881

Tiffin (OH) Tribune, Feb. 24, Mar. 3, 1881

Titusville (PA) Herald, Jan. 23, 24, 25, Oct. 31, Nov. 6, 7, 1873; Mar. 8, 1878

Titusville (PA) Morning Herald, Jan. 29, 31, 1879

Toledo (OH) Blade, Jan. 13, Oct. 17, 23, 24, 1873; Mar. 17, 1876; Dec. 24, 26, 1877;
    Oct. 19, 20, 1880; Dec. 1, 1881

Topeka (KS) Daily Capital, Oct. 11, 1881; Feb. 6, 7, 9, 1886

Toronto (ON) Evening Telegram, Oct. 22, 23, 1880

Toronto (ON) Globe & Mail, May 30, 1874; Mar. 27, 1876

Towanda (PA) Bradford Argus, Mar. 14, 1878

Trenton (NJ) Daily State Gazette, Apr. 21, Dec. 8, 1873; Oct. 12, 15, 1875;
    Dec. 12, 1876; Apr. 9, 12, Oct. 18, 23, 1878; Apr. 26, 30, 1881; Jan. 1, 3, 1883

Trenton (NJ) Daily True American, Apr. 19, 21, 1873; Oct. 14, 1875; Dec. 8, 12, 1876; Apr. 12, Oct. 23, 1878; Apr. 30, 1881; Jan. 2, 1883; Jan. 5, 8, 1884

Trenton (NJ) Times, Jan. 4, 1884

Troy (NY) Daily Times, Jan. 28, 30, 1875; Jan. 29, Dec. 3, 1877; Feb. 9, 1881; Mar. 13, 1882; Apr. 3, 8, 1883; Feb. 5, 1884

Troy (NY) Press, Feb. 11, 12, 13, 17, 1873

Troy (NY) Times, Feb. 24, 25, 26, 1874; Sept. 8, 1875

Urbana (OH) Citizen-Gazette, Dec. 13, 1883

Utica (NY) Daily Observer, Mar. 1, 3, 4, 5, Nov. 12, 14, 1874; Dec. 6, 7, 1877; Feb. 10, 1881; Feb. 28, Mar. 1, 2, 1882

Utica (NY) Morning Herald, Feb. 4, 1873; Apr. 16, 20, 1880; Apr. 5, 1883

Vincennes (IN) Daily Sun, Mar. 8, 10, Oct. 31, Nov. 1, 2, 1881; Oct. 24, 25, 26, 1882

Virginia City (NV) Territorial Enterprise, June 24, 26, 27, 28, 29, 30, July 4, 1877; Apr. 22, 1879

Waltham (MA) Weekly Record, Mar. 31, Apr. 7, 1882

Washington Daily Morning Chronicle, May 5, 6, 7, 8, 9, 1873

Washington Evening Star, May 5, 1873; Apr. 19, 1875; Sept. 22, 1877

Washington Post, Sept. 16, 17, 18, 19, 20, 1878

Waterbury (CT) American, Feb 5, 1883; Jan. 8, 1884

Waterbury (CT) Daily American, Jan. 7, 10, 12, Dec. 19, 1874; Nov. 4, 1878; Apr. 25, 26, 1882

Watertown (NY) Daily Times, June 20, 1873; Jan. 14, 16, 17, 1879; Apr. 20, 21, 1880

Watertown (WI) Republican, Sept. 8, 9, 1880

Waterville (ME) Mail, Nov. 9, 1877

West Chester (PA) American Republic, May 27, 1873

West Chester (PA) Daily Local News, May 22, 31, July 12, 23, Aug. 4, 8, 9, 11, Sept. 11, 16, Dec. 29, 31, 1873; Feb. 26, 28, Mar. 3, 4, Aug. 21, Dec. 3, 4, 1874; Feb. 23, 1875; May 5, Sept. 10, 1878; Feb. 3, Aug. 14, 1880

Western Nebraskian, Aug. 24, 1878; Nov. 15, 1879

Westfield (MA) Times & Newsletter, Apr. 7, Dec. 22, 1880

Wheeling (WV) Daily Register, Feb. 26, 1875; Feb. 24, 1876; Mar. 9, 1877; Feb. 28, 1878

Wheeling (WV) Register, Feb. 22, Nov. 8, 1879; Mar. 22, 1881, Nov. 29, 1930

Wilkes-Barre (PA) Daily Record of the Times, Nov. 27, 29, 1873;
　　Mar. 23, 27, 1878; Jan. 25, 1879

Wilkes-Barre (PA) Daily Union, Jan. 28, Dec. 4, 1882

Wilkes-Barre (PA) Daily Union-Leader, Apr. 6, 1881

Wilkes-Barre (PA) Luzerne Union, May 28, 1873

Wilkes-Barre (PA) Record of the Times, Mar. 27, 1878; Dec. 7, 8, 1885

Williamsport (PA) Gazette & Bulletin, Nov. 6, 19, 22, 25, 26, 1873;
　　Nov. 16, 17, 1874; Oct. 18, 1876; Apr. 3, 4, 1878; May 3, 1880; Apr. 6, 8, 9,
　　1881; Jan. 27, 28, Dec. 6, 1882; Dec. 28, 29, 1883

Willimantic (CT) Enterprise, Nov. 5, 12, 1878; Feb. 7, 1883

Wilmington (DE) Daily Gazette, Oct. 16, 18, 1875

Wilmington (DE) Evening Journal, Nov. 24, 25, 26, 1885

Wilmington (DE) Every Evening, May 20, 1873; Dec. 2, 3, 4, 1874; June 2, 1876;
　　Apr. 9, 10, 1878; Feb. 16, 1880

Wilmington (DE) Morning News, Apr. 25, 26, 1881; Dec. 30, 31, 1882

Wilmington (NC) Daily Journal, Oct. 20, 23, 26, 27, 1875

Wilmington (NC) Morning Star, Oct. 23, 1875; Sept. 29, Oct. 2, 4, 5, 6, 1878;
　　Jan. 18, 22, 23, 1880; Oct. 12, 1968

Woonsocket (RI) Daily Reporter, Dec. 30, 1874; Jan. 1, 1875

Woonsocket (RI) Evening Reporter, Jan. 15, 17, 1877; Dec. 9, 10, 1878; Dec. 23,
　　27, 1880; Apr. 19, 20, 1882; Mar. 19, 20, 1883

Worcester (MA) Daily Press, Jan. 22, 1875; Apr. 22, 24, 1876

Worcester (MA) Daily Spy, Apr. 24, 1876; Jan. 15, 17, Nov. 20, 21, 22, 1877;
　　Apr. 10, Dec. 24, 26, 1880

Worcester (MA) Evening Gazette, Feb. 14, 16, 17, 18, 19, 1874; Jan. 22, 1875;
　　Apr. 20, 22, 24, 1876; Jan. 17, Nov. 20, 21, 22, 1877; Apr. 19, 20, 21, 1882;
　　Mar. 22, 23, 24, 1883

Xenia (OH) Daily Gazette, Dec. 9, 1881; Nov. 16, 1882; Dec. 13, 1883

Youngstown (OH) Daily Register & Tribune, Mar. 7, 8, 1876; Feb. 23, 24, 1877;
　　Feb. 15, 17, 1879; Sept. 3, 1885

Youngstown (OH) Vindicator, Feb. 22, 1878; Oct. 31, 1879

Zanesville (OH) Courier, Nov. 10, 1879; Mar. 21, Dec. 13, 1881

Zanesville (OH) Signal, Feb. 25, 1875

Zanesville (OH) Times Recorder, Mar. 9, 1877; Feb. 22, 1879

NOTES

ACKNOWLEDGMENTS

1. Pete Dexter noted the "ripples" effect in *Deadwood* (New York: Random House, 1986; repr., New York: Viking Penguin, 1987), 153.

INTRODUCTION

1. A 1974 MCA-Universal, Public Arts production starring Matt Clark as Cody, Ben Murphy as Hickok, and Kim Darby as Calamity Jane.

2. Annie Oakley, eulogy published in the *Cody (WY) Enterprise* after his death in January 1917, n.d.

3. William F. Cody, *Story of the Wild West and Camp-fire Chats* (Philadelphia: Historical Publishing Co., 1888; repr., Freeport, NY: Books for Libraries Press, 1970), 403.

4. *New York Mirror*, Oct. 30, 1880.

5. Don Russell, *The Lives and Legends of Buffalo Bill* (Norman: University of Oklahoma Press, 1960), 179.

6. William F. Cody, *The Life of Hon. William F. Cody, Known as Buffalo Bill, the Famous Hunter, Scout and Guide: An Autobiography* (Hartford, CT: Frank E. Bliss, 1879), 282.

7. Joseph G. Rosa and Robin May, *Buffalo Bill and His Wild West* (Lawrence: University Press of Kansas, 1989), 34.

8. Craig F. Nieuwenhuyse, "Six-Guns on the Stage: Buffalo Bill Cody's First Celebration of the Conquest of the American Frontier" (Ph.D. diss., University of California, Berkeley, 1981); William S. E. Coleman, "Buffalo Bill on Stage," *Players* 47, no. 2 (1972); James Monaghan, "The Stage Career of Buffalo Bill," *Journal of the Illinois State Historical Society* 31, no. 4 (1938).

9. "The only known extant copy of any of Cody's melodramas is a hand-written copy of *Life on the Border,* owned by Mrs. Buford Richardson of Socorro, New Mexico, a direct descendant of Capt. Jack Crawford," wrote Paul T. Nolan in a foreword to the play's edition published by the Pioneer Drama Service, Cody, WY.

10. Richard Slotkin, *Regeneration through Violence: The Mythology of the American Frontier, 1600–1860* (Middletown, CT: Wesleyan University Press, 1973), 564–65.

11. *St. Joseph (MO) Daily Gazette,* Feb. 6, 1886.

12. Jay Monaghan, *Custer: The Life of General George Armstrong Custer* (Lincoln: University of Nebraska Press, 1959), 358.

13. *Providence (RI) Sunday Telegram,* clipping, n.d., MS 6, William F. Cody collection, Buffalo Bill Historical Center, Cody, WY, hereafter BBHC.

CHAPTER ONE

1. Frederick Jackson Turner, "The Significance of the Frontier in American History," in the American Studies hypertext collection, University of Virginia, http://xroads.virginia.edu/~Hyper/TURNER (accessed Apr. 16, 2007); *Terre Haute (IN) Daily Express,* Oct. 10, 1873.

2. George C. D. Odell, *Annals of the New York Stage,* 15 vols. (New York: Columbia University Press, 1927–49), 2:292.

3. Garff B. Wilson, *Three Hundred Years of American Drama and Theatre* (Englewood Cliffs, NJ: Prentice-Hall, 1973), 145–46; *New York Times,* Dec. 18, 1880.

4. *New York Mirror,* May 1, 1880; Barnard Hewitt, *Theatre U.S.A., 1665 to 1957* (New York: McGraw Hill, 1959), 278; Lawrence W. Levine, *Highbrow/Lowbrow: The Emergence of Cultural Hierarchy in America* (Cambridge, MA: Harvard University Press, 1988), 78.

5. Philip C. Lewis, *Trouping: How the Show Came to Town* (New York: Harper Row, 1973), 115.

6. Lewis, *Trouping,* 83; Deborah Ford Dickinson, *On With The Show! Theatrical Touring Companies in the 19th Century American West* (Bismarck: State Historical Society of North Dakota, sponsored by the North Dakota Humanities Council, 2004), 3.

7. Don B. Wilmeth and Christopher Bigsby, eds., *The Cambridge History of American Theatre, Vol. 2, 1870–1945* (Cambridge, UK: Cambridge University Press, 1999), 150; Lewis, *Trouping,* 83.

8. *Cheyenne (WY) Daily Leader,* Aug. 3, 1879.

9. Wilson, *Three Hundred Years of American Drama*, 127.

10. *Quincy (IL) Daily Herald*, Jan. 13, 1876.

11. Nellie Snyder Yost, *Buffalo Bill: His Family, Friends, Fame, Failures and Fortunes* (Chicago: Sage Books, 1979), 41; Peter Alexis and Henry Kucharzyk, *Texas Jack and the Peerless Morlacchi* (Lowell, MA: Patrick J. Mogan Cultural Center, 1994).

12. *New Haven (CT) Evening Register*, May 17, 1897.

13. Ibid., 713.

14. L. O. Leonard, "Buffalo Bill's First Wild West Rehearsal," *The Union Pacific Magazine* 1, no. 8 (Aug. 1922).

15. From a display in the Buffalo Bill Museum, Golden, CO, Sept. 2001.

16. Cody, *Autobiography*, 17.

17. Cody, *Autobiography*, 327.

18. Philadelphia interview quoted in *St. Louis (MO) Daily Democrat*, May 4, 1873.

19. Cody, *Autobiography*, 360.

20. James L. Smith, *Melodrama* (London: Methuen, 1973), 17.

21. Thomas J. Schlereth, *Victorian America: Transformations in Everyday Life, 1876–1915* (New York: HarperCollins, 1991), xiv.

22. Levin, *Highbrow/Lowbrow*, 24.

23. *Boston Daily Globe*, Mar. 5, 1873; *Boston Daily Advertiser*, Mar. 4, 1873.

24. *Lexington (KY) Gazette*, Oct. 1, 1873.

25. Robert G. Athearn, *The Mythic West in Twentieth-Century America* (Lawrence: University Press of Kansas, 1986), 274.

CHAPTER TWO

1. Cody, *Autobiography*, 260.

2. Louisa Frederici Cody and Courtney Riley Cooper, *Memories of Buffalo Bill* (New York: D. Appleton, 1919), 160.

3. Richard M. Ketchum, "Faces from the Past," pt. 20, *American Heritage* 17, no. 3 (1966): 65.

4. This version is untrue because North was in Omaha at the time; see Russell, *Lives and Legends of Buffalo Bill*, 155.

5. *New York Herald*, Feb. 16, 1872.

6. Cody, *Autobiography*, 310.

7. Henry Llewellyn Williams, *Buffalo Bill (The Hon. William F. Cody): Rifle and Revolver Shot, Pony Express Rider, Teamster, Buffalo Hunter, Guide and Scout* (London: George Routledge and Sons, 1887) in the Western American Frontier History, 1550–1900, microfilm collection, reel 604, no. 6226, 168; Cody, *Autobiography*, 311.

8. Cody, *Autobiography*, 320.

9. Cody, *Autobiography*, 321.

10. Cody and Cooper, *Memories of Buffalo Bill*, 233.

11. Rosa and May, *Buffalo Bill and His Wild West*, 45; Russell, *Lives and Legends of Buffalo Bill*, 192.

12. Cody, *Autobiography*, 322.

13. Jay Monaghan, *The Great Rascal: The Life and Adventures of Ned Buntline* (Boston: Little, Brown, 1951), 250.

14. Cody, *Autobiography*, 324.

15. Ledger, n.d. n.p., quoted in Nieuwenhuyse, who notes that the Troop C Ledger, William F. Cody collection, MS 6, BBHC, contains many clippings cut up in order that as many as possible could be pasted on a single scrapbook page. Titles, sources, and dates are missing (Nieuwenhuyse, "Six-Guns on the Stage," 65). Today we call "supernumeraries," or "supers," "extras."

16. *Chicago Evening Journal*, Dec. 19, 1872.

17. Ibid.

18. Nieuwenhuyse, "Six-Guns on the Stage," 110.

19. Alexis and Kucharzyk, *Texas Jack and the Peerless Morlacchi*.

20. Cody, *Autobiography*, 325.

21. *Chicago Times*, Dec. 15, 1872.

22. Ledger, n.p., n.d., quoted in Nieuwenhuyse, "Six-Guns on the Stage," 53.

23. Ibid.

24. Cody, *Autobiography*, 326–27.

25. Coleman, "Buffalo Bill on Stage," 84–85.

26. *Louisville (KY) Courier-Journal*, Oct. 4, 1873.

27. Cody and Cooper, *Memories of Buffalo Bill*, 245–46.

28. Clipping, n.d., William F. Cody collection, MS 6, BBHC.

29. Monaghan, *The Great Rascal*.

30. *New York Herald*, Apr. 1, 1873.

31. *Troy (NY) Times*, Feb. 13, 1873.

32. *Scouts of the Prairie* program, William F. Cody collection, MS 6, BBHC.

33. Ledger, quoted in Nieuwenhuyse, "Six-Guns on the Stage," 73.

34. *Scouts of the Prairie* program, William F. Cody collection, MS 6, BBHC.

35. Ledger, quoted in Nieuwenhuyse, 72.

36. Nieuwenhuyse, "Six-Guns on the Stage," 72 n. 178, 67–73; *Chicago Inter-Ocean*, Dec. 17, 1872; clipping, n.d., William F. Cody collection, MS 6, BBHC.

37. Cody, *Autobiography*, 327.

38. *Chicago Times*, Dec. 18, 1872.

39. *Chicago Tribune*, Dec. 19, 1872.

40. Cody, *Autobiography*, 327.

41. *Chicago Times*, Dec. 18, 1872.

42. Roger A. Hall, *Performing the American Frontier, 1870–1906* (Cambridge, UK: Cambridge University Press, 2001), 13.

43. Ibid.

44. *Chicago Daily Tribune*, Dec. 19, 1872; *Chicago Times*, Dec. 18, 1872.

45. *Omaha (NE) Weekly Tribune & Republican*, Dec. 21, 1872.

46. Cody, letter to editor, dated Dec. 22, 1872, *Omaha (NE) Weekly Herald*, Jan. 1, 1873.

47. Cody, letter to editor, *Omaha (NE) Weekly Herald*, Dec. 21, 1873.

48. Cody and Cooper, *Memories of Buffalo Bill*, 249–50.

49. *Cincinnati (OH) Daily Gazette*, Dec. 31, 1872; Louis S. Warren, *Buffalo Bill's America: William Cody and the Wild West Show* (New York: Alfred A. Knopf, 2005), 191; Charles Phillips, *Encyclopedia of the American West* (New York: Simon and Schuster, 1996), 3:1026–27. Montezuma became one of the first American Indian physicians.

50. Nieuwenhuyse, "Six-Guns on the Stage," 44.

51. *Cincinnati (OH) Enquirer*, Jan. 15, 1873.

52. *Titusville (PA) Herald*, Jan. 24–25, 1873; the phrase is an allusion to a line in Alexander Pope's "Essay on Man": "Lo! The poor Indian, whose untutored mind sees God in clouds, or hears him in the wind."

53. *Providence (RI) Journal*, Feb. 19, 1873.

54. *Troy (NY) Times*, Feb. 12, 1873.

55. *Chicago Daily Tribune*, Dec. 17, 1872.

56. *Chicago Daily Tribune*, Dec. 19, 1872; clipping, n.d., William F. Cody collection, MS 6, BBHC.

57. Wilmeth and Bigsby, eds., *Cambridge History of American Theatre*, 2:203.

58. *Pittsfield (MA) Sun*, Feb. 12, 1873.

59. Quoted in *St. Louis (MO) Daily Democrat*, Mar. 15, 1873.

60. *Boston Evening Transcript*, Mar. 4, 7, 1873.

61. Clipping, n.d., William F. Cody collection, MS 6, BBHC.

62. *New York Herald*, Apr. 1, 1873.

63. *Boston Ray*, Mar. 5, 1873.

64. *Portsmouth (NH) Daily Evening Times*, Mar. 18, 1873.

65. *Portsmouth (NH) Chronicle*, Mar. 19, 1873.

66. *Lewiston (ME) Evening Journal*, Mar. 21, 1873.

67. *Lewiston (ME) Evening Journal*, Mar. 20, 1873.

68. *New York Herald*, Jan. 8, 1873; Nieuwenhuyse, "Six-Guns on the Stage," 156; *St. Louis (MO) Daily Democrat*, Mar. 23, 1873.

69. *New York Herald*, Apr. 1, 1873.

70. Hall, *Performing the American Frontier*, 53.

71. *New York Herald*, Apr. 1, 1873.

72. Clipping, n.d., William F. Cody collection, MS 6, BBHC.

73. *New York Times*, Apr. 1, 1873.

74. *New York Tribune*, Apr. 1, 1873.

75. *Brooklyn (NY) Daily Eagle*, Apr. 15, 1873.

76. Ibid.

77. *New York Clipper*, Apr. 12, 1873.

78. Clipping, n.d., William F. Cody collection, MS 6, BBHC.

79. Philadelphia interview quoted in *St. Louis (MO) Democrat*, May 4, 1873.

80. Eventually, the army drove out the Modocs and hanged Captain Jack. Cody had no part in the affair.

81. Dee Brown, *Wondrous Times on the Frontier* (Little Rock: August House Publisher, 1991), 86–95.

82. Clipping, n.d., William F. Cody collection, MS 6, BBHC.

83. *Baltimore (MD) American & Commercial Advertiser*, Apr. 29, 1873.

84. Clipping, n.d., William F. Cody collection, MS 6, BBHC.

85. *Lancaster (PA) Daily Examiner*, May 27, 1873.

86. *West Chester (PA) Daily Local News*, May 22, 31, 1873.

87. *West Chester (PA) Daily Local News*, May 22, 1873.

88. *New York Clipper*, Apr. 12, 1873.

89. Cody, *Autobiography*, 328.

90. *New York Clipper*, Aug. 16, 1873.

91. *Stamford (CT) Mirror*, Dec. 14, 1875.

92. R. L. Wilson with Greg Martin, *Buffalo Bill's Wild West: An American Legend* (New York: Random House, 1998), 23.

93. *West Chester (PA) Daily Local News*, July 12, 1873; *Omaha (NE) Daily Herald*, July 17, 1873.

94. Rosa and May, *Buffalo Bill and His Wild West*, 49; *Omaha (NE) Daily Herald*, July 17, 1873.

95. When friends put his name on the ballot in 1872, forty-four voters elected Cody to the Nebraska legislature. The win was contested; Cody never assumed his seat, but he did claim the title "Honorable" and used it in show promotions.

96. *Omaha (NE) Daily Herald*, July 17, 1873.

97. *West Chester (PA) Daily Local News*, Aug. 11, 1873.

CHAPTER THREE

1. *New York Herald*, Aug. 25, 1873.

2. Walter J. Meserve, "The American West of the 1870s and 1880s as Viewed from the Stage," *Journal of American Drama and Theatre* 3, no. 1 (1991): 56.

3. *Rochester (NY) Democrat & Chronicle*, Sept. 1, 1873.

4. Gerald Bordman, ed., *Oxford Companion to American Theatre: A Chronicle of Comedy and Drama, 1869–1914* (New York: Oxford University Press, 1984), 454.

5. *New York Herald*, Aug. 30, 1873.

6. Phil Hart, "Buffalo Bill's Days on the Stage Recalled by Fellow Actor," *Boston Herald*, Oct. 2, 1927. The actor is misidentified as A. C. Irving.

7. Russell, *Lives and Legends of Buffalo Bill*, 202–3.

8. Nate Salsbury, "The Origin of the Wild West Show," *The Colorado Magazine* 32, no. 3 (1955): 208.

9. Burke, *The Noblest Whiteskin* (New York: G. P. Putnam's Sons, 1973), 104.

10. Cody, *Autobiography*, 329.

11. *New York Times*, June 26, 1872.

12. Cody, *Story of the Wild West*, 653.

13. *West Chester (PA)* Daily *Local News*, Aug. 11, 1873.

14. *New York Clipper*, Sept. 13, 1873.

15. *New Brunswick (NJ) Daily Times*, Sept. 9, 1873; *New Brunswick (NJ) Sunday Times*, Apr. 1, 1929; *Cincinnati (OH) Daily Gazette*, Sept. 23, 24, 1873.

16. Joseph G. Rosa, *They Called Him Wild Bill: The Life and Adventures of James Butler Hickok* (Norman: University of Oklahoma Press, 1974), 253.

17. Hiram Robbins, "Wild Bill's Humors," *Arkansaw Traveler*, n.d.

18. Cody, *Autobiography*, 329.

19. Burke, *The Noblest Whiteskin*, 107.

20. *New York Clipper*, Sept. 27, 1873.

21. *Lexington (KY) Kentucky Gazette*, Oct. 1, 1873.

22. *Louisville (KY) Courier-Journal*, Oct. 3, 4, 1873.

23. *Terre Haute (IN) Daily Express*, Oct. 10, 1873.

24. Ibid.

25. *Indianapolis (IN) Journal*, Oct. 6, 1873.

26. *Indianapolis (IN) Journal*, Oct. 13, 1873.

27. The article about Hickok by George Ward Nichols appeared in *Harper's New Monthly Magazine* in February 1867.

28. *Indianapolis (IN) Journal*, Oct. 14, 1873.

29. *Lafayette (IN) Daily Journal*, Oct. 16, 1873.

30. *Toledo (OH) Blade*, Oct. 23, 24, 1873.

31. *Sandusky (OH) Daily Register*, Oct. 25, 27, 1873.

32. Cody, *Autobiography*, 329–30.

33. Cody, *Autobiography*, 330–31.

34. *Buffalo (NY) Evening Post*, Nov. 13, 1873.

35. *Erie (PA) Morning Dispatch*, Nov. 15, 1873; *Haverhill (MA) Daily Bulletin*, Feb. 14, 1874; *Quincy (IL) Whig*, Apr. 15, 1874.

36. *Jamestown (NY) Daily Journal*, Nov. 7, 1873; *Erie (PA) Morning Dispatch*, Nov. 14, 15, 1873; *Williamsport (PA) Gazette & Bulletin*, Nov. 26, 1873.

37. *Easton (PA) Daily Express*, Dec. 16, 1873.

38. Robbins, "Wild Bill's Humors."

39. *Bridgeport (CT) Daily Standard*, Jan. 7, 1874.

40. *Waterbury (CT) Daily American*, Jan. 10, 1874; *New York Clipper*, Jan. 17, 1874.

41. Rosa, *They Called Him Wild Bill*, 255.

42. Hart, "Buffalo Bill's Days on the Stage."

43. *Worcester (MA) Evening Gazette*, Feb. 19, 1874.

44. *Utica (NY) Daily Observer*, Mar. 5, 1874.

45. *Troy (NY) Times*, Feb. 25, 1874.

46. *Albany (NY) Evening News*, Feb. 27, 1874.

47. *Schenectady (NY) Evening Star*, Mar. 3, 1874.

48. *Utica (NY) Daily Observer*, Mar. 4, 5, 1874.

49. Robbins, "Wild Bill's Humors."

50. *Rochester (NY) Democrat & Chronicle*, Mar. 11, 1874.

51. Cody, *Autobiography*, 333.

52. Cody, *Autobiography*, 332–33.

53. *Rochester (NY) Democrat & Chronicle*, Mar. 13, 1874.

54. Robbins, "Wild Bill's Humors."

55. *Pittsfield (MA) Berkshire County Eagle*, Jan. 28, 1875.

56. Rosa, *They Called Him Wild Bill*, 353.

CHAPTER FOUR

1. *Davenport (IA) Democrat*, Apr. 24, 1874.

2. *Keokuk (IA) Daily Gate City*, Apr. 18, 1874.

3. *Erie (PA) Morning Dispatch*, Mar. 16, 1874; *Jacksonville (IL) Daily Journal*, Apr. 13, 14, 1874.

4. *Davenport (IA) Democrat*, Apr. 24, 1874.

5. Richard Butsch, *The Making of American Audiences: From Stage to Television, 1750–1990* (Cambridge, UK: Cambridge University Press, 2000), 7; Kathy Peiss, *Cheap Amusements* (Philadelphia: Temple University Press, 1986), 22, 140–44.

6. *Quincy (IL) Whig*, Apr. 11, 1874; Richard Slotkin, *The Fatal Environment: The Myth of the Frontier in the Age of Industrialization, 1800–1890* (New York: Atheneum, 1985; repr., Norman: University of Oklahoma Press, 1998), 318.

7. Robert V. Hine, *The American West* (Boston: Little, Brown, 1984), 40; Patricia Nelson Limerick, *The Legacy of Conquest* (New York: W. W. Norton, 1987), 199; *New York Tribune*, July 21, 1969.

8. *Peoria (IL) Daily Transcript*, Apr. 25, 1874.

9. *Hamilton (ON) Spectator*, May 28, 29, 1874. A strong abolitionist, physician James G. Blunt volunteered for Civil War service and became the first major general from Kansas. Cody may have served under him during his orderly days; "General Blunt's Account of His Civil War Experiences," *Kansas Historical Quarterlies* 1, no. 3 (1932), http://www.kancoll.org/khq/1932/32_3_blunt.htm (accessed Apr. 15, 2004).

10. *Madison (WI) State Journal*, May 5, 1874.

11. *Binghamton (NY) Democrat*, Nov. 27, 1874.

12. *Madison (WI) State Journal*, May 5, 1874.

13. Cody, *Autobiography*, 336.

14. *Chicago Times*, May 14, 1874.

15. Hall, *Performing the American Frontier*, 14.

16. *Atlantic Monthly* 40 (Nov. 1877): 624–25; quoted in Levine, *Highbrow/Lowbrow*, 218.

17. *Hamilton (ON) Spectator*, May 28, 29, 1874.

18. *Lawrence (MA) Daily American*, June 12, 1874.

19. *Boston Evening Transcript*, June 15, 16, 1874.

20. Russell, *Lives and Legends of Buffalo Bill*, 208.

21. *New York Herald*, June 30, 1874.

22. Cody, *Autobiography*, 337.

23. Cody, *Autobiography*, 338.

24. *West Chester (PA) Daily Local News*, Aug. 21, 1874; Russell, *Lives and Legends of Buffalo Bill*, 209–12; Yost, *Buffalo Bill*, 75.

25. Mike Flanagan, *The Old West: Day by Day* (New York: Facts on File, 1995), 259.

26. *West Chester (PA) Daily Local News*, Aug. 21, 1874.

27. Warren, *Buffalo Bill's America*, 117.

28. Russell, *Lives and Legends of Buffalo Bill*, 211–12.

29. *Utica (NY) Daily Observer*, Nov. 12, 1874.

30. *Williamsport (PA) Gazette & Bulletin*, Nov. 16, 1874.

31. *Williamsport (PA) Gazette & Bulletin*, Nov. 17. 1874.

32. *Elmira (NY) Daily Advertiser*, Nov. 17, 18, 1874.

33. "Dion Boucicault: Sensation and Melodrama," http://www.btinternet.com/~torichard/victorianplays/Boucicault1.htm (accessed Apr. 4, 2004).

34. *Elmira (NY) Daily Advertiser*, Nov. 18, 1874.

35. *Auburn (NY) Daily Advertiser*, Nov. 24, 1874.

36. John M. Burke, *Buffalo Bill from Prairie to Palace* (Chicago: Rand, McNally, 1893), 192.

37. *Danbury (CT) News*, Dec. 16, 1874; Monaghan, "The Stage Career of Buffalo Bill," 419–20.

38. *Worcester (MA) Evening Gazette*, Feb. 18, 1874.

39. *Wheeling (WV) Register*, Nov. 29, 1930.

40. *Spirit of the Times*, Dec. 26, 1874; Jan. 2, 1875.

41. Schlereth, *Victorian America*, 49–52, 78, 84.

42. Hiram Robbins, *Wild Bill; or, Life on the Border, a Sensational Drama in 5 Acts* (Cincinnati, OH: n.p., 1873).

43. *Worcester (MA) Evening Gazette*, Jan. 22, 1875.

44. *Life on the Border*, Pioneer Drama Service, Cody, WY.

45. *Lewiston (ME) Evening Journal*, Jan. 12, 1875.

46. *Troy (NY) Daily Times*, Jan. 28, 1875.

47. *Rochester (NY) Union & Advertiser*, Feb. 10, 1875.

48. *Columbus (OH) Daily Dispatch*, Mar. 3, 4, 1875.

49. Wilmeth and Bigsby, eds., *Cambridge History of American Theatre*, 2:497.

50. Harlowe R. Hoyt, *Town Hall Tonight: Intimate Memories of the Grassroots of the American Theatre* (Englewood Cliffs, NJ: Prentice-Hall, 1955), 50.

51. *Cincinnati (OH) Enquirer*, Dec. 1, 1882.

52. "19th Century American Theater," University of Washington Libraries, http://content.lib.washington.edu/19thcenturyactorsweb/essay.html (accessed Apr. 13, 2004).

CHAPTER FIVE

1. *Easton (PA) Free Press*, Oct. 20, 1875.

2. Joseph G. Rosa, *The Gunfighter: Man or Myth* (Norman: University of Oklahoma Press, 1969), vii; Joseph G. Rosa, *Age of the Gunfighter* (London: Salamander Books, 1993), 10, 14.

3. *West Chester (PA) Daily Local News*, Aug. 4, 8, 9, 1873.

4. Bordman, ed., *American Theatre*, 3.

5. *Savannah (GA) Morning News*, Nov. 4, 5, 6, 1875.

6. Rosa, *The Gunfighter*, vii.

7. *Mobile (AL) Daily*, Nov. 20, 1875.

8. Joseph Gallegly, *Footlights on the Border: The Galveston and Houston Stage before 1900* (The Hague: Mouton, 1962), 96–97.

9. *Nashville (TN) Daily American*, Dec. 28, 1875.

10. Hoyt, *Town Hall Tonight*, 79, 80.

11. *Dramatic Compositions Copyrighted in the United States, 1870–1916*, vol. 2 (Washington, D.C.: GPO, 1918), listing no. 50951.

12. *Quincy (IL) Daily Herald*, Jan. 14, 1876.

13. *Cincinnati (OH) Daily Gazette*, Jan. 25, 1876.

14. *Springfield (IL) Illinois State Journal*, Feb. 5, 1876.

15. *Rochester (NY) Union & Advertiser*, Apr. 10, 1876.

16. Cody, *Autobiography*, 339.

17. *Worcester (MA) Evening Gazette*, Apr. 24, 1876; *Worcester (MA) Daily Spy*, Apr. 24, 1876.

18. Helen Cody Wetmore and Zane Grey, *Last of the Great Scouts (Buffalo Bill)* (New York: Grosset and Dunlap, 1918), 213.

19. *Wilmington (DE) Every Evening*, June 2, 1876; Cody, *Autobiography*, 340.

20. *Kansas City (KS) Journal of Commerce*, Apr. 13, 1877.

21. Alexis and Kucharzyk, *Texas Jack and the Peerless Morlacchi*.

22. Russell, *Lives and Legends of Buffalo Bill*, 226. The author gratefully acknowledges Paul Hedren's contribution to the background information.

23. Paul Hedren, *First Scalp for Custer: The Skirmish at Warbonnet Creek, Nebraska, July 17, 1876* (Lincoln: Nebraska State Historical Society, 1980; rev. ed., 2005), 27.

24. Cody, *Autobiography*, 344.

25. Hedren, *First Scalp*, 40.

26. Cody and Cooper, *Memories of Buffalo Bill*, 269.

27. *Kansas City (KS) Journal of Commerce*, Aug. 8, 1876, reprinted from the *Rochester (NY) Democrat & Chronicle*.

28. *Rochester (NY) Democrat & Chronicle*, Sept. 18, 1876; Russell, *Lives and Legends of Buffalo Bill*, 246.

29. *St. Paul (MN) Dispatch*, Sept. 13, 1876.

30. Henry Blackman Sell and Victor Weybright, *Buffalo Bill and the Wild West* (New York: Oxford University Press, 1955), 178–79.

31. Hickok was scouting for Colonel Augustus Armes of the Tenth Cavalry. Cody happened to be in the right place at the right time when Sheridan needed a scout. Nothing suggests Hickok was upset (Rosa, *They Called Him Wild Bill*, 113, 121).

32. The McCanles "gang" consisted of David McCanles, his son William, James Woods, and James Gordon. For a true account of the Hickok-McCanles fight, see Joseph G. Rosa's *They Called Him Wild Bill*, 34–49.

33. *Rochester (NY) Democrat & Chronicle*, Sept. 18, 1876.

34. Rosa, *They Called Him Wild Bill*, 287.

35. *New York Clipper*, Sept. 2, 30, 1876.

36. Paul Hedren, "The Contradictory Legacies of Buffalo Bill Cody's First Scalp for Custer," *Montana: The Magazine of Western History* 55, no. 1 (2005): 19.

37. Gordon Wickstrom, "Buffalo Bill the Actor," *Journal of the West* 34, no. 1 (1995): 66.

38. *Boston Evening Transcript*, Jan. 9, 1877.

39. Cody, *Autobiography*, 360.

40. Cody and Cooper, *Memories of Buffalo Bill*, 257, 258.

41. Cody, *Autobiography*, 349.

42. *Boston Evening Transcript*, Jan. 9, 12, 1877.

43. *Worcester (MA) Evening Gazette*, Jan. 17, 1877.

44. *Worcester (MA) Daily Spy*, Jan. 17, 1877.

45. *Cleveland (OH) Herald*, Feb. 20, 21, 1877.

46. *Oil City (PA) Derrick*, Mar. 7, 1877.

47. *Kansas City (KS) Times*, Apr. 10, 1877.

48. "Remember when Fred and Art Made Music?: Those Were the Days When the Opera House Was an Institution," Morton James Public Library, Nebraska City, NE, n.d., n.p.

49. *Nebraska City (NE) Daily News*, Apr. 25, 1877.

50. Russell, *Lives and Legends of Buffalo Bill*, 256.

51. Cody, *Autobiography*, 360.

52. *San Francisco Chronicle*, May 25, 1877.

53. *San Francisco Chronicle*, May 27, 1877.

54. *San Francisco Chronicle*, May 28, 1877.

55. Darlis Miller, *Captain Jack Crawford: Buckskin Poet, Scout, and Showman* (Albuquerque: University of New Mexico Press, 1993), 73.

56. Paul T. Nolan, "When the Curtains Rise, Scouts Fall Out," *Southern Speech Journal* 29, no. 3 (1964): 183.

57. *San Francisco Chronicle*, June 2, 1877. The reference is to the Russo-Turkish war of 1877–78.

58. Russell, *Lives and Legends of Buffalo Bill*, 320.

59. *San Francisco Chronicle*, June 9, 1877.

60. *Sacramento (CA) Daily Bee*, June 21, 23, 1877.

61. Geoffrey C. Ward, *The West* (Boston: Little, Brown, 1996), 292–96.

62. *Sacramento (CA) Daily Bee*, June 23, 1877.

63. Cody, *Autobiography*, vi–vii.

64. Paul Fees, "The Flamboyant Fraternity," *Gilcrease Magazine of American History and Art* 6, no. 1 (1984).

65. *Sacramento (CA) Daily Bee*, June 28, 1877.

66. *Gold Hill (NV) News*, June 28, 1877.

67. *Virginia City (NV) Territorial Enterprise*, June 30, 1877.

68. Clipping, n.d., William F. Cody collection, MS 6, BBHC.

69. *New York Clipper*, July 21, 1877; *Virginia City (NV) Territorial Enterprise*, July 4, 1877, quoting the *Reno (NV) Gazette*, July 2, 1877.

70. Miller, *Captain Jack Crawford*, 109.

71. Clipping, n.d., William F. Cody collection, MS 6, BBHC.

72. Russell, *Lives and Legends of Buffalo Bill*, 257–58.

73. William Frederick Cody, telegraph to Jack Crawford, Aug. 5, 1877, Western History Department, Denver Public Library Cody collection, WH 72, box 1, no. 27, hereafter DPL.

74. William Frederick Cody, letter to Jack Crawford, Aug. 7, 1877, WH 72, box 1, no. 28, DPL.

75. See also Cody's letter to Buckskin Sam Hall dated July 5, 1879, in which he accuses his former partners of badmouthing him when they failed on their own, cited in Sarah Blackstone, *The Business of Being Buffalo Bill: Selected Letters of William F. Cody, 1879–1917* (New York: Praeger, 1988), 2.

CHAPTER SIX

1. Russell, *Lives and Legends of Buffalo Bill*, 258–59.

2. *Davenport (IA) Democrat*, Jan. 15, 1878.

3. Will Bagley, *Blood of the Prophets: Brigham Young and the Massacre at Mountain Meadows* (Norman: University of Oklahoma Press, 2002), 87, 125–29, 142, 379.

4. Ibid., 144.

5. Ibid., xiv, 175, 313–17.

6. *Savannah (GA) Morning News*, Oct. 15, 1878.

7. *Brenham (TX) Daily Banner*, Dec. 12, 1879.

8. Hoyt, *Town Hall Tonight*, 55.

9. Hall, *Performing the American Frontier*, 63.

10. *Baltimore American & Commercial Advertiser*, Sept. 17, 1877.

11. Louis Pfaller, O.S.B., "The Galpin Journal: Dramatic Record of an Odyssey of Peace," *Montana: The Magazine of Western History* 18, no. 2 (1968): 19, 20.

12. Elizabeth Custer, *"Boots and Saddles"; or, Life in Dakota with General Custer*, in the Talewins Digital Library, http://www.talewins.com/ Treasures/novels/Boots/ (accessed June 5, 2004).

13. *Burlington (IA) Hawk-Eye*, Jan. 25, 1878.

14. *Lowell (MA) Daily Courier*, Nov. 19, 1877.

15. Russell, *Lives and Legends of Buffalo Bill*, 259–60; 1877 Ledgerbook, Peale Collection, no. 2, Colorado State Historical Society, Denver, CO, hereafter CSHS.

16. 1877 Ledgerbook, Peale Collection, no. 2, CSHS.

17. Russell, *Lives and Legends of Buffalo Bill*, 308; William F. Cody, *Buffalo Bill's Life Story: An Autobiography* (Farrar and Rinehart, 1920), 190.

18. *Baltimore (MD) American & Commercial Daily Advertiser*, Sept. 18, 1877.

19. L. G. Moses, *Wild West Shows and the Images of American Indians, 1883–1933* (Albuquerque: University of New Mexico Press, 1996), 6, 8, 18.

20. *Manchester (NH) Mirror & American*, Nov. 3, 1877.

21. Ibid.

22. *Waterville (ME) Mail*, Nov. 9, 1877.

23. *Worcester (MA) Daily Spy*, Nov. 21, 1877.

24. *Worcester (MA) Evening Gazette*, Nov. 20, 21, 1877.

25. *New York Clipper*, Nov. 17, 1877.

26. *Cincinnati (OH) Daily Gazette*, Feb. 19, 1878.

27. *Toledo (OH) Blade*, Dec. 26, 1877.

28. *Joliet (IL) Morning News*, Jan. 15, 1878; *Ottawa (IL) Free Trader*, Jan. 19, 1878.

29. Quoted in Francis Paul Prucha, ed., *Americanizing the American Indians: Writings by the "Friends of the Indians," 1880–1900* (Lincoln: University of Nebraska Press, 1978), 314.

30. Moses, *Wild West Shows*, 77.

31. *Chicago Tribune*, Jan. 9, 1878.

32. Cody, *Autobiography*, 361.

33. *New York Clipper*, Feb. 9, 1878.

34. *New York Clipper*, Mar. 21, 1873.

35. *Peoria (IL) Daily Transcript*, Jan. 30, 1878; Hart, "Buffalo Bill's Days on the Stage."

36. *Terre Haute (IN) Daily Express*, Feb. 1, 3, 1878.

37. *Louisville (KY) Courier-Journal*, Feb. 9, 1878.

38. *Worcester (MA) Daily Spy*, Jan. 17, 1877.

39. *Binghamton (NY) Republican & Times*, Mar. 22, 1878; *Fort Wayne (IN) Daily News*, Feb. 16, 1878.

40. *Wilkes-Barre (PA) Record of the Times*, Mar. 27, 1878.

41. Russell, *Lives and Legends of Buffalo Bill*, 506, 157.

42. "Sunbeams May Be Extracted from Cucumbers, but the Process Is Tedious" was an eighteenth-century political address by David Daggett, a New England lawyer.

43. *Brooklyn (NY) Daily Eagle*, Apr. 16, 1878.

44. Cody, *Autobiography*, 361, 363.

45. *Western Nebraskian*, Aug. 24, 1878; Yost, *Buffalo Bill*, 111.

46. *New York Clipper*, Aug. 24, 1878.

47. Clipping, n.d., William F. Cody collection, MS 6, BBHC; *Cheyenne (WY) Daily Leader*, Aug. 2, 1879; *Augusta (GA) Chronicle & Constitutionalist*, Oct. 9, 1878; *Charlotte (NC) Daily Observer*, Oct. 3, 1878.

48. Ford's Grand Opera House program, Sept. 12–14, 1878.

49. *Lancaster (PA) Daily Examiner & Express*, Apr. 8, 1878; *Wilmington (DE) Every Evening*, Apr. 9, 1878; *Newark (NJ) Daily Advertiser*, Apr. 13, 1878.

50. *Baltimore (MD) American & Commercial Advertiser*, Sept. 10, 1878.

51. Cody, *Autobiography*, 365; Russell, *Lives and Legends of Buffalo Bill*, 262; *New York Clipper*, Oct. 19, 1878.

52. *Richmond (VA) State*, Sept. 27, 28, 1878.

53. *Charlotte (NC) Daily Observer*, Oct. 4, 1878; *Spirit of the Times*, Oct. 12, 1878.

54. *New York Clipper*, Oct. 19, 1878.

55. Dr. H. A. Gant, "The Yellow Fever Epidemic of 1878," in the Yalobusha County MSGen Web Project, http://www.rootsweb.com/~msyalobu/yellofev.html (accessed May 8, 2004).

56. *Atlanta (GA) Daily Constitution*, Oct. 12, 1878.

57. *New Haven (CT) Evening Register*, Nov. 2, 1878; *Danbury (CT) News*, Oct. 30, 1878; *Boston Herald*, Oct. 2, 1927.

58. *Wilkes-Barre (PA) Daily Record & Times*, Jan. 25, 1879; *Titusville (PA) Morning Herald*, Jan. 31, 1879; *Pueblo (CO) Chieftain*, July 25, 1879.

59. *Cleveland (OH) Herald*, Oct. 24, 1879; *Dubuque (IA) Herald*, Sept. 6, 1879; *Hartford (CT) Courant*, Nov. 8, 1878.

60. *Providence (RI) Journal*, Dec. 12, 1878.

61. *Columbus (OH) Dispatch*, Feb. 27, 1879.

62. *Erie (PA) Morning Dispatch*, Jan. 3, 1879.

63. *Evansville (IN) Daily Courier*, Oct. 10, 1879.

64. *Watertown (NY) Daily Times*, Jan. 14, 16, 17, 1879.

65. *Wilkes-Barre (PA) Daily Record & Times*, Jan. 25, 1879; *New Haven (CT) Journal & Courier*, July 17, 1885.

66. *Cleveland (OH) Herald*, Feb. 7, 1879.

67. Cody, *Buffalo Bill's Life Story*, 190; Ward, *The West*, 359–62.

68. *New York Dramatic Mirror*, Mar. 8, 1879.

CHAPTER SEVEN

1. Clipping, n.d., William F. Cody collection, MS 6, BBHC.

2. *San Francisco Chronicle*, Aug. 13, 1916; Butsch, *Making of American Audiences*, 128.

3. *San Francisco Chronicle*, Mar. 30, 1879.

4. *San Francisco Daily Alta*, Mar. 30, 1879.

5. *Fort Wayne (IN) Daily News*, Oct. 17, 1879.

6. Ibid.

7. *New York Dramatic Mirror*, Apr. 12, 1879.

8. *Fort Wayne (IN) Daily News*, Oct. 17, 1879.

9. *San Francisco Chronicle*, Mar. 25, 1879.

10. Ibid.; *Sacramento (CA) Daily Bee*, Apr. 18, 1879.

11. Ibid.

12. *Carson City (NV) Morning Appeal*, Apr. 22, 1879.

13. William F. Cody, letter to Jack Crawford, Apr. 22, 1879, WH 72, box 1, no. 32, DPL.

14. *Salt Lake City (UT) Deseret News*, May 3, 1879.

15. Russell, *Lives and Legends of Buffalo Bill*, 271–73.

16. *Cheyenne (WY) Daily Leader*, July 31, 1879.

17. Cody, *Autobiography*, 365.

18. William F. Cody, letter to Jack Crawford, June 24 and July 4, 1879 (?),WH 72, box 1, nos. 33 and 42, DPL.

19. Blackstone, *The Business of Being Buffalo Bill*, 2.

20. *Cheyenne (WY) Daily Leader*, Aug. 2, 1879.

21. *Pueblo (CO) Chieftain*, July 27, 1879.

22. *Central City (CO) Daily Register Call*, July 31, 1879.

23. For more on the billboard, see http://www.reglenna.com/ buffalobill_press1.html (accessed Nov. 13, 2007).

24. Jack Rennert, *100 Posters of Buffalo Bill's Wild West* (New York: Darien House, 1976), 4, 5.

25. *Burlington (IA) Daily Hawk-Eye*, Sept. 9, 1879; *Western Nebraskian*, Nov. 15, 1879.

26. Butsch, *Making of American Audiences*, 61–63.

27. Blackstone, *The Business of Being Buffalo Bill*, 3–4.

28. Salsbury, "The Origin of the Wild West Show," 207–8.

29. Cody, *Autobiography*, 143, 225–27.

30. *Clinton (IA) Daily Herald*, Sept. 5, 1879.

31. *Columbus (OH) Daily Dispatch*, Mar. 3, 4, 1875.

32. Stephen Watt and Gary Richardson, eds., *American Drama: Colonial to Contemporary* (New York Harcourt Brace College Publishers, 1995), 150–51.

33. Wayne S. Turney, "Notes on Naturalism in the Theatre," in A Glimpse of Theater History, http://www.wayneturney.20m.com/naturalism.htm (accessed Aug. 6, 2006).

34. *Little Rock (AK) Daily Arkansas Gazette*, Dec. 2, 3, 1879; Fees, "Flamboyant Fraternity," 2; Butsch, *Making of American Audiences*, 123.

35. *Western Nebraskian*, Nov. 15, 1879.

36. Ibid.

37. *Burlington (IA) Daily Hawk-Eye*, Sept. 12, 1879.

38. Fees, "Flamboyant Fraternity," 2, 4, 8.

39. Richard Robertson, "Prentiss Ingraham," in *Lives of Mississippi Authors, 1817–1967*, ed. James B. Lloyd (Jackson: University Press of Mississippi, 1981), 253–54.

40. Kent Ladd Steckmesser, *The Western Hero in History and Legend* (Norman: University of Oklahoma Press 1965), 241–46.

41. William F. Cody, letter to Jack Crawford, Sept. 30, 1879, WH 72, box 1, no. 34, DPL.

42. William F. Cody, letter to Jack Crawford, Oct. 5, 1879, WH 72, box 1, no. 35, DPL.

43. Wilson with Martin, *Buffalo Bill's Wild West*, 209; Charles P. Fox, *Billers, Banners and Bombast* (Boulder: Pruett Publishing Co., 1985), 244.

44. *Columbus (OH) Ohio State Journal*, Nov. 12, 1879.

45. Bobby Bridger, *Buffalo Bill and Sitting Bull: Inventing the Wild West* (Austin: University of Texas Press, 2002), 7.

46. *Western Nebraskian*, Nov. 15, 1879.

47. Clipping, n.d., William F. Cody collection, MS 6, BBHC.

48. *Nashville (TN) Daily American*, Nov. 25, 1879.

49. *Little Rock (AK) Daily Arkansas Gazette*, Dec. 2, 3, 1879.

50. *Austin (TX) Daily Statesman*, Dec. 10, 1879, Jun. 15, 1881.

51. In a few months, Rampone would leave to become a professor of music at a Westchester County, New York, school. David Shiff filled his place. *New York Mirror*, Apr. 3, 1880; *Galveston (TX) News*, Dec. 18, 1879.

52. *San Antonio (TX) Daily Express*, Dec. 17, 1879.

53. Ward, *The West*, 63–65; Paul Fees, "The Hunter Hero in America," in *Sunrise in His Pocket: The Life, Legend, and Legacy of Davy Crockett*, ed. Paul Hutton (Austin: Bob Bullock Texas State History Museum, 2002).

54. *New York Mirror*, Feb. 21, 1880.

55. *New York Mirror*, Mar. 13, 1880; clipping, n.d., William F. Cody collection, MS 6, BBHC.

56. *New Haven (CT) Daily Courier*, clipping, n.d., William F. Cody collection, MS 6, William F. Cody collection.

57. Clipping, n.d., William F. Cody collection, MS 6, BBHC.

58. Clipping, n.d., William F. Cody collection, MS 6, BBHC.

59. *New York Mirror*, May 22, 29, 1880.

CHAPTER EIGHT

1. *Home Companion*, clipping, n.d., box 126, file FF19 Cody, CSHS.

2. Bret Harte, "Tennessee's Partner," http://www.classicreader.com/read.php/sid.6/bookid.813 (accessed Apr. 24, 2006).

3. *New York Mirror*, Aug. 14, 21, 1880; *New York Herald*, Aug. 24, 1880.

4. *Home Companion*, clipping, n.d., box 126, file FF19 Cody, CSHS.

5. Clipping, n.d., William F. Cody collection, MS 6, BBHC.

6. *New York Herald*, Aug. 24, 1880; *Brooklyn (NY) Daily Eagle*, clipping, n.d., William F. Cody collection, MS 6, BBHC.

7. "How He Hit Him," clipping, n.d., William F. Cody collection, MS 6, BBHC; Don Carlos Seitz, *Famous American Duels* (New York: Thomas Y. Crowell, 1929; repr., Freeport, NY: Books for Libraries, 1966), 30–31.

8. Mike Flanagan, *The Old West*, 324–26, 335.

9. *Milwaukee (WI) Sentinel*, clipping, n.d., William F. Cody collection, MS 6, BBHC.

10. Ibid.

11. *New York Mirror*, Oct. 16, 1880.

12. *Toledo (OH) Blade*, Oct. 19, 20, 1880.

13. Clipping, n.d., WH 72, box 1, DPL.

14. *New York Mirror*, Oct. 30, 1880.

15. *Easton (PA) Daily Express*, Jan. 14, 1881.

16. *Easton (PA) Daily Express*, Jan. 23, 1882.

17. *Brooklyn (NY) Daily Eagle*, Feb. 1, 1881.

18. *Louisville (KY) Courier-Journal*, Mar. 15, 1881.

19. *Dayton (OH) Daily Journal*, Mar. 17, 1881.

20. *Columbus (OH) Ohio State Journal*, Mar. 21, 1881.

21. *Pittsburgh (PA) Daily Leader*, clipping, n.d., William F. Cody collection, MS 6, BBHC.

22. *Elmira (NY) Daily Advertiser*, Apr. 2, 1881.

23. *New York Mirror,* May 7, 1881, June 18, 1881; *Nebraska City (NE) News,* Aug. 7, 1881; *La Crosse (WI) Tribune,* June 13, 1948.

24. *New York Mirror,* Sept. 10, 1881; Eric V. Sorg, "Buffalo Bill's Crony, Dr. Frank 'White Beaver' Powell, Brought the Art of Self-Promotion to New Heights," *Wild West* 7 (Oct. 1994): 8.

25. *New York Mirror,* Aug. 27, 1881.

26. *New York Mirror,* Oct. 1, 1881; *La Crosse (WI) Chronicle,* Sept. 23, 1881.

27. Cody, *Autobiography,* 360; *Des Moines (IA) State Register,* Oct. 2, 1881.

28. *Council Bluffs (IA) Nonpareil,* Oct. 4, 5, 1881; *Leavenworth (KS) Times,* Oct. 8, 1881.

29. Russell, *Lives and Legends of Buffalo Bill,* 77.

30. *St. Joseph (MO) Evening News,* Oct. 6, 1881.

31. Miller, *Captain Jack Crawford,* 108–9.

32. Cody, *Autobiography,* 362.

33. *Leavenworth (KS) Times,* Oct. 9, 1881.

34. William F. Cody, letter to Jack Crawford, Apr. 8, 1882, WH 72, box 1, no. 36; Wilson with Martin, *Buffalo Bill's Wild West,* 200.

35. *Leavenworth (KS) Times,* Oct. 2, 1881; *Atchison (KS) Daily Champion,* Oct. 11, 1881; *Louisville (KY) Courier-Journal,* Oct. 25, 1881.

36. *Springfield (IL) Illinois State Journal,* Nov. 2, 1881.

37. *Kokomo (IN) Dispatch,* Dec. 1, 1881; *Kokomo (IN) Saturday Tribune,* Dec. 3, 1881.

38. *Fort Wayne (IN) Daily News,* Nov. 29, 1881.

39. *New York Herald,* Jan. 13, 1874; *Fort Wayne (IN) Daily News,* Dec. 1, 1881.

40. *Columbus (OH) Ohio State Journal,* Dec. 13, 1881; *New York Mirror,* Dec. 17, 1881.

41. *Steubenville (OH) Daily Herald,* Dec. 16, 1881.

42. Salsbury, "The Origin of the Wild West Show," 206.

43. Wilson with Martin, *Buffalo Bill's Wild West,* 49; Salsbury, "The Origin of the Wild West Show," 206.

44. Yost, *Buffalo Bill,* 123; Russell, *Lives and Legends of Buffalo Bill,* 289.

45. *New York Mirror,* Mar. 11, 25, 1882.

46. Yost, *Buffalo Bill,* 115.

47. Cody and Cooper, *Memories of Buffalo Bill,* 280.

48. Stella A. Foote, *Letters from Buffalo Bill* (Billings, MT: Foote Publishing Co., 1954), 18.

CHAPTER NINE

1. Russell, *Lives and Legends of Buffalo Bill*, 285.

2. *Manchester (NH) Mirror & American*, Mar. 20, 1882.

3. Ibid.

4. Ibid.

5. Ibid.

6. William F. Cody, letter to Jack Crawford, Apr. 8, 1882, WH 72, box 1, no. 36, DPL. Cody remarks how, in spite of the Christian tradition of abstaining from entertainments during the week between Palm Sunday and Easter, he was doing a rollicking business.

7. *New York Mirror*, Apr. 28, 1882.

8. Ibid.

9. Raymond W. Thorp, ed. "The Letters of Doc Carver," *Outdoor Life-Outdoor Recreation* 65, no. 4 (1930): 19.

10. *New York Mirror*, May 6, 1882.

11. *New York Clipper*, June 28, 1873; *New York Mirror*, May 13, 1882.

12. *New York Mirror*, May 20, 1882.

13. *Denver (CO) Tribune*, June 1, 1882.

14. Wilson with Martin, *Buffalo Bill's Wild West*, 236.

15. Yost, *Buffalo Bill*, 209.

16. *Omaha (NE) Daily Bee*, July 7, 1882; Yost, *Buffalo Bill*, 116–19.

17. Yost, *Buffalo Bill*, 32, 104; John Bratt, *Trails of Yesterday* (Chicago: University Publishing Co., 1921; repr., Lincoln: University of Nebraska Press, 1980), 278; *New York Mirror*, July 22, 1882.

18. *New York Mirror*, Aug. 12, 1882.

19. Russell, *Lives and Legends of Buffalo Bill*, 315.

20. Hall, *Performing the American Frontier*, 66; *Burlington (IA) Daily Hawk-Eye*, Sept. 29, 1882.

21. *Janesville (WI) Daily Gazette*, Sept. 1, 1882.

22. *Milwaukee (WI) Daily Republican Sentinel*, Sept. 2, 3, 1882; *Chicago Times*, Sept. 5, 1882; *Clinton (IA) Age*, Sept. 15, 1882.

23. *Burlington (IA) Daily Hawk-Eye*, Sept. 29, 1882.

24. *Logansport (IN) Daily Journal*, Nov. 7, 1882; *Fort Wayne (IN) Weekly Sentinel*, Nov. 8, 15, 1882.

25. Levine, *Highbrow/Lowbrow*, 182.

26. *Cleveland (OH) Penny Press*, Nov. 21, 1882.

27. *Columbus (OH) Dispatch*, Nov. 18, 20, 1882; *Columbus (OH) Ohio State Journal*, Nov. 20, 1882; *Kokomo (IN) Dispatch*, Nov. 9, 1882.

28. *Lewiston (ME) Evening Journal*, Mar. 9, 1883.

29. *New York Mirror*, Feb. 24, Mar. 17, Mar. 24, Mar. 31, 1883.

30. *New York Mirror*, Aug. 26, 1882.

31. Salsbury, "The Origin of the Wild West Show," 206–7.

32. *Buffalo (NY) Courier*, Apr. 13, 1883.

33. *New York Mirror*, Apr. 14, 1883.

34. *Bradford (PA) Era*, Apr. 14, 1883.

35. Cody, *Story of the Wild West*, 693–94.

36. Wilson with Martin, *Buffalo Bill's Wild West*, 47.

37. *Waterbury (CT) American*, Feb. 5, 1883.

38. Yost, *Buffalo Bill*, 142.

39. *New York Mirror*, Aug. 11, 1883.

40. *Jacksonville (IL) Daily Journal*, Dec. 8, 1883.

41. Russell, *Lives and Legends of Buffalo Bill*, 295–96.

42. *Peoria (IN) Daily Transcript*, Dec. 3, 1883.

43. *Trenton (NJ) Daily True American*, Jan. 8, 1884.

44. *Trenton (NJ) Times*, Jan. 5, 1884; *Galion (OH) Inquirer*, Dec. 14, 1883, quoting the *Davenport (IA) Democrat*.

45. Fox, *Billers, Banners and Bombast*, 40, 151, 155.

46. *Fort Wayne (IN) Journal Gazette*, Feb. 17, 1884.

47. For more on the charges and countercharges, see Sandra K. Sagala, "Buffalo Bill Cody v. Doc Carver: The Battle over the Wild West," *Nebraska History* 85, no. 1 (2004).

48. Clipping headlined "No Lawyers at His Door," July 17, 1885, Carver's red scrapbook, BBHC.

49. Meserve, "The American West," 59.

50. William F. Cody, letter to Jack Crawford, Aug. 11, 1885, WH 72, box 1, no. 43, DPL.

51. *Quincy (IL) Daily Whig*, Jan. 29, 31, 1886.

52. *Lock Haven (PA) Daily Democrat*, Dec. 10, 1885, quoting the *Philadelphia Times*, n.d.

53. *Greensburg (PA) Evening Press*, Dec. 14, 1885.

54. *Steubenville (OH) Daily Herald*, Dec. 19, 1885.

55. Yost, *Buffalo Bill*, 157, 159.

56. *Clinton (IA) Daily Herald*, Jan. 26, 1886.

57. *Columbus (OH) Ohio State Journal*, Jan. 9, 14, 1886; *Atchison (KS) Globe*, Feb. 8, 1886.

58. *Burlington (IA) Daily Hawk-Eye*, Jan. 29, 1886.

59. Ibid.

60. *Monmouth (IL) Review*, Jan. 29, 1886.

61. Foote, *Letters from Buffalo Bill*, 22.

62. *Salt Lake City (UT) Herald*, Feb. 28, 1886.

63. *Keokuk (IA) Daily Constitution*, Jan. 26, 1886; *St. Joseph (MO) Daily Gazette*, Feb. 6, 1886.

64. *Boulder (CO) Weekly Herald*, Mar. 31, 1886.

65. Alfred Doten, *The Journals of Alfred Doten, 1849–1903*, ed. Walter Van Tilburg Clark, 3 vols. (Reno: University of Nevada Press, 1973).

CHAPTER TEN

1. Wetmore and Grey, *Buffalo Bill*, 223.

2. *Williamsport (PA) Gazette & Bulletin*, Nov. 26, 1873; *Bridgeport (CT) Daily Standard*, Jan. 7, 1874.

3. *Madison (WI) State Journal*, May 5, 1874.

4. Wetmore and Grey, *Buffalo Bill*, 136.

5. *Omaha (NE) Daily Bee*, July 28, 1873.

6. Cody and Cooper, *Memories of Buffalo Bill*, 251–52; Cody, *Autobiography*, 328.

7. W. F. Cody to John "Captain Jack" Crawford, Apr. 26, 1880, quoted in Joseph G. Rosa, "Hickok, Cody and the 'Slade Connection,'" *NOLA Quarterly* 29, no. 4 (2005): 12–13.

8. *Easton (PA) Free Press*, Oct. 20, 1875.

9. Don Russell, *The Wild West: A History of the Wild West Shows* (Fort Worth, TX: Amon Carter Museum of Western Art, 1961), 7.

10. Russell, *The Wild West*, 25.

11. William E. Deahl Jr., "Buffalo Bill's Wild West Show, 1885," *Annals of Wyoming* 47, no. 3 (1975): 142, quoting the *Chicago Tribune*, May 26, 1885.

12. Sell and Weybright, *Buffalo Bill and the Wild West*, 175.

13. "To Invade Europe," Carver's green/brown scrapbook, c. May 1899, BBHC.

14. *New York Mirror*, May 10, 1884; *St. Louis (MO) Globe-Democrat*, Sept. 22, 1890.

15. *St. Louis (MO) Globe-Democrat*, Apr. 26, 1884.

16. *New Haven (CT) Journal & Courier*, July 16, 1885.

17. Clipping, n.d., Carver's scrapbook, BBHC; see also Sagala, "Cody v. Carver."

18. From a eulogy written by Annie Oakley after Cody's death in 1917, published in the *Cody Enterprise*, n.d.

19. Russell, *Lives and Legends of Buffalo Bill*, 314.

20. Dick Kreck, "Listening to History," *Denver (CO) Post*, Apr. 14, 1996.

21. Rosa and May, *Buffalo Bill and His Wild West*, 157, 159.

22. Turner, "The Significance of the Frontier in American History," ch. 7.

23. Jack Nachbar, ed., *Focus on the Western* (Englewood Cliffs: Prentice-Hall, 1974), 22.

24. Brasmer, "The Wild West Exhibition and the Drama of Civilization," in *Western Popular Theatre*, ed. David Mayer and Kenneth Richards (London: Methuen, 1974), 146.

25. *New York Times*, Nov. 25, 1886, quoted in Brasmer, "The Wild West Exhibition and the Drama of Civilization," 145.

26. Cody, *Autobiography*, 362.

27. Sell and Weybright, *Buffalo Bill and the Wild West*, 168.

28. *Youngstown (OH) Vindicator*, Sept. 3, 1885, quoting the *Montreal Gazette*.

29. Rennert, *100 Posters of Buffalo Bill's Wild West*, 4, 5.

30. Slotkin, *Gunfighter Nation*, 68.

31. Blackstone, *The Business of Being Buffalo Bill*, 103.

32. Yost, *Buffalo Bill*, 343.

33. Cody, *Buffalo Bill's Life Story*, 183; Sell and Weybright, *Buffalo Bill and the Wild West*, 249; Mark Twain, letter to Mr. Cody, July 14, 1885, the Mark Twain Papers and Project, record no. 3259, source 252.1928.07.14, Bancroft Library, University of California, Berkeley.

34. Francis Parkman, *Oregon Trail: Sketches of Prairie and Rocky-Mountain Life* (Boston: Little, Brown, 1892).

35. Turner, "The Significance of the Frontier in American History," ch. 1.

36. Cody to his sister Julia, New Rochelle, NY, Feb. 8, 1916, cited in Foote, *Letters of Buffalo Bill*, 77.

37. Alan Gallop, *Buffalo Bill's British Wild West* (Phoenix Mill, UK: Sutton Publishing, 2001), 254.

APPENDIX ONE

1. *Cincinnati (OH) Daily Gazette*, Dec. 31, 1872; clipping, n.d., William F. Cody collection, MS 6, BBHC; *Boston Ray*, Mar. 5, 1873; *New York Clipper*, Apr. 12, 1873.

2. *The Scouts* program for Jan. 20, 1873, Franklin, PA, courtesy of Robert Pepper.

3. *New York Herald*, Aug. 30, 1873; *New York Clipper*, Sept. 6, 1873; Odell, *Annals of the New York Stage*, 1:155; *Indianapolis (IN) Journal*, Oct. 14, 1873.

4. *Springfield (IL) Illinois State Journal*, Apr. 14, 1874; *Quincy (IL) Whig*, Apr. 16, 1874; *Bridgeport (CT) Daily Standard*, Jan. 6, 1874; *Easton (PA) Daily Express*, Dec. 16, 1873; *Worcester (MA) Evening Gazette*, Feb. 18 1874; *Hamilton (ON) Spectator*, May 28, 1874.

5. *Boston Ray*, Mar. 5, 1873.

6. *Wilmington (DE) Every Evening*, Dec. 2, 4, 1874; *Utica (NY) Daily Observer*, Nov. 14, 1874; *Elmira (NY) Daily Advertiser*, Nov. 16, 18, 1874.

7. *Worcester (MA) Evening Gazette*, Jan. 22, 1875; *Erie (PA) Daily Dispatch*, Feb. 18, 1875; *Dayton (OH) Daily Journal*, Mar. 6, 1875.

8. *Easton (PA) Free Press*, Oct. 20, 1875; *Wilmington (NC) Daily Journal*, Oct. 26, 1875; *Columbus (GA) Sunday Enquirer*, Nov. 14, 1875; *Cincinnati (OH) Daily Gazette*, Jan. 25, 1876; *Worcester (MA) Evening Gazette*, Apr. 24, 1876.

9. *Rochester (NY) Democrat & Chronicle*, Oct. 3, 1876; *Elmira (NY) Daily Advertiser*, Oct. 19, 1876.

10. *St. Louis (MO) Daily Globe-Democrat*, Apr. 4, 1877; *Manchester (NH) Daily Mirror & American*, Jan. 3, 1877.

11. Program of the Buffalo Bill combination, 1876–77 season, file MS6.1.D.3/21, BBHC.

12. *Gold Hill (NV) News*, June 28, 1877; *San Francisco Chronicle*, May 15, 20, 27, 1877; *San Jose (CA) Daily Mercury*, June 16, 1877.

13. Odell, *Annals of the New York Stage*, 10:406.

14. Bowery Theater program for Sept. 8, 1877, William F. Cody collection, WH 72, box 1, DPL; *Erie (PA) Morning Dispatch*, Mar. 14, 1878;

Columbus (OH) Daily Dispatch, Feb. 22, 1878; *Springfield (IL) Illinois State Journal*, Feb. 1, 1878; *Peoria (IL) Daily Transcript*, Jan. 30, 1878; *Burlington (IA) Daily Hawk-Eye*, Jan. 25, 1878; *Philadelphia Times*, Oct. 5, 1877; *New York Clipper*, Sept. 29, 1877.

15. Program from Ford's Grand Opera House, Baltimore, MD, Sept. 14, 1878, program files, theater 1878–79, "May Cody," Enoch Pratt Free Library, Baltimore, MD; *San Francisco Chronicle*, Mar. 25, 1879; *Carson City (NV) Morning Appeal*, Apr. 22, 1879; *Georgetown (CO) Colorado Miner*, July 26, 1879.

16. *Carson City (NV) Morning Appeal*, Apr. 23, 1879; *New York Clipper*, Mar. 10, 1879.

17. *Fort Wayne (IN) Sentinel*, Oct. 16, 1879.

18. *Davenport (IA) Democrat*, Sept. 2, 1879; *Columbus (OH) Ohio State Journal*, Nov. 14, 1879; *Austin (TX) Democratic Statesman*, Dec. 11, 1879.

19. *Rochester (NY) Democrat & Chronicle*, Apr. 23, 1880; *Buffalo (NY) Daily Courier*, May 11, 1880.

20. *New York Herald*, Aug. 24, 1880; *Brooklyn (NY) Daily Graphic*, Jan. 31, 1880(?).

21. *Leavenworth (KS) Times*, Oct. 9, 1881; *Ottawa (IL) Free Trader*, Sept. 10, 1881; *St. Joseph (MO) Gazette*, Oct. 8, 1881; *Lacrosse (WI) Chronicle*, Sept. 22, 1881; *Keokuk (IA) Constitution*, Nov. 11, 1881; *Columbus (OH) Ohio State Journal*, Dec. 12, 1881.

22. *Janesville (WI) Daily Gazette*, Sept. 1, 1882; *Milwaukee (WI) Daily Republican Sentinel*, Sept. 2, 1882; *Clinton (IA) Daily Herald*, Sept. 13, 1882; *Des Moines (IA) State Register*, Sept. 26, 1882; *Burlington (IA) Daily Hawk-Eye*, Sept. 29, 1882; *Buffalo (NY) Courier*, Apr. 13, 1883; *New York Mirror*, Aug. 19, 1882.

23. *Trenton (NJ) Daily True American*, Jan. 5, 1884.

24. St. Joseph (MO) *Daily Gazette*, Feb. 3, 1886; *Salem (NJ) National Standard*, Nov. 18, 1885; *Allentown (PA) Chronicle & News*, Nov. 27, 1885; *Danville (PA) Sun*, Dec. 10, 1885; *Columbus (OH) Ohio State Journal*, Jan. 11, 1886; *Lincoln (NE) Daily Nebraska State Journal*, Feb. 11, 1886.

Bibliography

BOOKS, MONOGRAPHS, AND ARTICLES

Alexis, Peter, and Henry Kucharzyk. *Texas Jack and the Peerless Morlacchi.* Lowell, MA: Patrick J. Mogan Cultural Center, 1994.

Arlington, J. V. *Life on the Border.* 1876.

Athearn, Robert G. *The Mythic West in Twentieth-Century America.* Lawrence: University Press of Kansas, 1986.

Bagley, Will. *Blood of the Prophets: Brigham Young and the Massacre at Mountain Meadows.* Norman: University of Oklahoma Press, 2002.

Bank, Rosemarie K. "Rhetorical, Dramatic, Theatrical, and Social Contexts of Selected American Plays, 1871 to 1906." Ph.D. diss., University of Iowa, 1972.

———. "Frontier Melodrama." In *Theatre West: Image and Impact*, edited by Dunbar H. Ogden and B. V. Rodopi, 151–60. Atlanta: Rodopi, 1990.

Billington, Ray. A. "Best Prepared Pioneers in the West." *American Heritage* 7 (Oct. 1956): 20–25, 116–17.

Blackstone, Sarah H. "Buffalo Bill's Wild West: A Study of the History, Structure, Personnel, Imagery and Effect." Ph.D. diss., Northwestern University, 1983.

———. *The Business of Being Buffalo Bill: Selected Letters of William F. Cody, 1879–1917.* New York: Praeger, 1988.

Bordman, Gerald, ed., *Oxford Companion to American Theatre: A Chronicle of Comedy and Drama, 1869–1914.* New York: Oxford University Press, 1984.

Brasmer, William. "The Wild West Exhibition and the Drama of Civilization." In *Western Popular Theatre*, edited by David Mayer and Kenneth Richards, 133–56. London: Methuen, 1974.

Bratt, John. *Trails of Yesterday*. Chicago: University Publishing Co., 1921; repr., Lincoln: University of Nebraska Press, 1980.

Bridger, Bobby. *Buffalo Bill and Sitting Bull: Inventing the Wild West*. Austin: University of Texas Press, 2002.

Brown, Dee. *Wondrous Times on the Frontier*. Little Rock: August House Publisher, 1991.

—————. *The American West*. New York: Scribner's Sons, 1994.

Brown, John Russell, ed. *The Oxford Illustrated History of the Theatre*. Oxford: Oxford University Press, 1995.

Burke, John. *The Noblest Whiteskin*. New York: G. P. Putnam's Sons, 1973.

Burke, John M. ("Arizona John"). *Buffalo Bill from Prairie to Palace*. Chicago: Rand, McNally, 1893.

Butsch, Richard. *The Making of American Audiences: From Stage to Television, 1750–1990*. Cambridge, UK: Cambridge University Press, 2000.

Cawelti, John G. *The Six-Gun Mystique*. Bowling Green: Bowling Green State University Popular Press, 1984.

Cody, Louisa Frederici, and Courtney Ryley Cooper. *Memories of Buffalo Bill*. New York: D. Appleton, 1919.

Cody, William F. *The Life of Hon. William F. Cody, Known as Buffalo Bill, the Famous Hunter, Scout and Guide: An Autobiography*. Hartford, CT: Frank E. Bliss, 1879.

—————. *Story of the Wild West and Camp-fire Chats*. Philadelphia: Historical Publishing Co. 1888; repr., Freeport, NY: Books for Libraries Press, 1970.

—————. *The Adventures of Buffalo Bill*. New York: Harper and Brothers, 1904.

—————. *Buffalo Bill's Life Story: An Autobiography*. New York: Farrar and Rinehart, 1920.

—————. *Life and Adventures of "Buffalo Bill."* Golden, CO: Mrs. Johnny Baker, 1939.

Coleman, William S. E. "Buffalo Bill on Stage." *Players* 47, no. 2 (1972): 80–91.

Davies, Henry E. *Ten Days on the Plains*. Ed. Paul Hutton. Dallas: Southern Methodist University Press, 1985.

Davis, William C., and Joseph G. Rosa, eds. *The West*. New York: Smithmark, 1994.

Deahl, William E., Jr. "Buffalo Bill's Wild West Show, 1885." *Annals of Wyoming* 47, no. 3 (1975): 138–51.

Dickinson, Deborah Ford. *On With The Show! Theatrical Touring Companies in the 19th Century American West*. Bismarck: State Historical Society of North Dakota, sponsored by the North Dakota Humanities Council, 2004.

Doten, Alfred. *The Journals of Alfred Doten, 1849–1903*. Edited by Walter Van Tilburg Clark. 3 vols. Reno: University of Nevada Press, 1973.

Editors of Time-Life Books. *The Old West: The Gunfighters*. Alexandra, VA: Time-Life Books, 1974.

Fees, Paul. "The Flamboyant Fraternity." *Gilcrease Magazine of American History and Art* 6, no. 1 (1984): 1–8.

———. "The Hunter Hero in America." In *Sunrise in His Pocket: The Life, Legend, and Legacy of Davy Crockett*, edited by Paul Hutton. Austin: Bob Bullock Texas State History Museum, forthcoming.

Flanagan, Mike. *The Old West: Day by Day*. New York: Facts on File, 1995.

Folsom, James K., ed. *The Western: A Collection of Critical Essays*. Englewood Cliffs: Prentice-Hall, 1979.

Foote, Stella A. *Letters from Buffalo Bill*. Billings, MT: Foote Publishing Co., 1954.

Foster, Charles. *Twenty Days*. 1882.

Fox, Charles P. *Billers, Banners and Bombast*. Boulder: Pruett Publishing Co., 1985.

Gallegly, Joseph. *Footlights on the Border: The Galveston and Houston Stage before 1900*. The Hague: Mouton, 1962.

Gallop, Alan. *Buffalo Bill's British Wild West*. Phoenix Mill, UK: Sutton Publishing, 2001.

Goodman, Julia Cody. "Julia Cody Goodman's Memoirs of Buffalo Bill." *Kansas Historical Quarterly* 28, no. 4 (1962): 442–96.

Gray, John. "Fact versus Fiction in the Kansas Boyhood of Buffalo Bill." *Kansas History* 8, no. 1 (1985): 2–20.

Grossman, James R., ed. 1994. The Frontier in American Culture: An Exhibit at the Newberry Library, Aug. 26, 1994–Jan. 7, 1995. Essays by Richard White and Patricia Nelson Limerick. Chicago: Newberry Library; Berkeley: University of California Press.

Hall, Roger A. *Performing the American Frontier, 1870–1906*. Cambridge, UK: Cambridge University Press, 2001.

Hart, Phil. "Buffalo Bill's Days on the Stage Recalled by Fellow Actor." *Boston Herald*, Oct. 2, 1927.

Hedren, Paul. "The Contradictory Legacies of Buffalo Bill Cody's First Scalp for Custer." *Montana: The Magazine of Western History* 55, no. 1 (2005): 16–35.

———. *First Scalp for Custer: The Skirmish at Warbonnet Creek, Nebraska, July 17, 1876.* Lincoln: Nebraska State Historical Society, 1980; rev. 2005.

Henderson, Mary. *The City and the Theatre: New York Playhouses from Bowling Green to Times Square.* Clifton, NJ: James T. White, 1973.

Hewitt, Barnard. *Theatre U.S.A., 1665 to 1957.* New York: McGraw Hill, 1959.

Hine, Robert V. *The American West.* Boston: Little, Brown, 1984.

Hoyt, Harlowe R. *Town Hall Tonight: Intimate Memories of the Grassroots of the American Theatre.* Englewood Cliffs, NJ: Prentice-Hall, 1955.

Hughes, Glenn. *A History of the American Theatre, 1700–1950.* New York: C. Samuel French, 1951.

Hyde, Stuart Wallace. "The Representation of the West in American Drama from 1849 to 1917." Ph.D. diss., Stanford University, 1953.

Kasson, Joy. *Buffalo Bill's Wild West: Celebrity, Memory, and Popular History.* New York: Hill and Wang, 2000.

Ketchum, Richard M. "Faces from the Past." Pt. 20. *American Heritage* 17, no. 3 (1966): 64–65.

Leonard, Elizabeth J., and Julia Cody Goodman. *Buffalo Bill: King of the Old West.* Edited by James W. Hoffman. New York: Library Publishers, 1955.

Leonard, L. O. "Buffalo Bill's First Wild West Rehearsal." *The Union Pacific Magazine* 1, no. 8 (1922): 26–27.

Levine, Lawrence W. *Highbrow/Lowbrow: The Emergence of Cultural Hierarchy in America.* Cambridge, MA: Harvard University Press, 1988.

Lewis, Philip C. *Trouping: How the Show Came to Town.* New York: Harper and Row, 1973.

Limerick, Patricia Nelson. *The Legacy of Conquest.* New York: W. W. Norton, 1987.

Logan, Herschel C. *Buckskin and Satin.* Harrisburg, PA: Stackpole, 1954.

Masterson, W. B. "Bat." "Colonel Cody: Hunter, Scout, Indian Fighter." *Human Life* 6, no. 6 (1908): 135–46.

McPherson, James M. *Battle Cry of Freedom: The Civil War Era.* New York: Ballantine, 1988.

Meserve, Walter. "The American West of the 1870s and 1880s as Viewed from the Stage." *Journal of American Drama and Theater* 3, no. 1 (1991): 48–63.

Miller, Darlis. *Captain Jack Crawford: Buckskin Poet, Scout, and Showman.* Albuquerque: University of New Mexico Press, 1993.

Monaghan, James. "The Stage Career of Buffalo Bill." *Journal of the Illinois State Historical Society* 31, no. 4 (1938): 411–16.

Monaghan, Jay. *The Great Rascal: The Life and Adventures of Ned Buntline.* Boston: Little, Brown, 1951.

———. *Custer: The Life of General George Armstrong Custer.* Lincoln: University of Nebraska Press, 1959.

Moses, L. G. *Wild West Shows and the Images of American Indians, 1883–1933.* Albuquerque: University of New Mexico Press, 1996.

Nachbar, Jack, ed. *Focus on the Western.* Englewood Cliffs, NJ: Prentice-Hall, 1974.

Nieuwenhuyse, Craig Francis. "Six-Guns on the Stage: Buffalo Bill Cody's First Celebration of the Conquest of the American Frontier." Ph.D. diss., University of California, 1981.

Nolan, Paul T. "When the Curtains Rise, Scouts Fall Out." *Southern Speech Journal* 29, no. 3 (1964): 175–86.

Odell, George C. D. *Annals of the New York Stage.* 15 vols. New York: Columbia University Press, 1927–49.

Parkman, Francis. *Oregon Trail: Sketches of Prairie and Rocky-Mountain Life.* Boston: Little, Brown, 1892.

Peiss, Kathy. *Cheap Amusements.* Philadelphia: Temple University Press, 1986.

Pepper, Robert D. "Horace Greeley's Raffish Neighbor, or Ned Buntline, the Westchester County Truant." *The Westchester Historian* 71, no. 3 (1995): 67–68.

Pfaller, Louis, O. S. B. "The Galpin Journal: Dramatic Record of an Odyssey of Peace." *Montana: The Magazine of Western History* 18, no. 2 (1968): 2–23.

Prucha, Francis Paul, ed. *Americanizing the American Indians: Writings by the "Friends of the Indians," 1880–1900.* Lincoln: University of Nebraska Press, 1978.

———. *The Great Father: The United States and the American Indians.* Lincoln: University of Nebraska Press, 1984.

Rahill, Frank. *The World of Melodrama.* University Park: Penn State University Press, 1967.

Rattenbury, Richard. "From Showman to Shootist: A Stevens-Lord Presentation Pistol." *Man At Arms* 10, no. 6 (1988): 10–14.

Rennert, Jack. *100 Posters of Buffalo Bill's Wild West*. New York: Darien House, 1976.

Robbins, Hiram. "Wild Bill's Humors," *Arkansaw Traveler*, n.d.

———. *Wild Bill; or, Life on the Border, a Sensational Drama in 5 Acts*. Cincinnati: n.p., 1873.

Robertson, Richard. "Prentiss Ingraham." In *Lives of Mississippi Authors, 1817–1967*, edited by James B. Lloyd, 252–67. Jackson: University Press of Mississippi, 1981.

Rosa, Joseph G. *The Gunfighter: May or Myth*. Norman: University of Oklahoma Press, 1969.

———. *They Called Him Wild Bill: The Life and Adventures of James Butler Hickok*. Norman: University of Oklahoma Press, 1974.

———. *Age of the Gunfighter*. London: Salamander Books, 1993.

———. "Hickok, Cody and the 'Slade Connection.'" *NOLA Quarterly* 29, no. 4 (2005): 8–13.

Rosa, Joseph G., and Robin May. *Buffalo Bill and His Wild West*. Lawrence: University Press of Kansas, 1989.

Russell, Don. *The Lives and Legends of Buffalo Bill*. Norman: University of Oklahoma Press, 1960.

———. *The Wild West: A History of the Wild West Shows*. Fort Worth, TX: Amon Carter Museum of Western Art, 1961.

Sagala, Sandra K. "An Unlikely Trio: Buffalo Bill, Wild Bill, and Texas Jack—Actors." *True West* 40, no. 6 (1993): 23–27.

———. "Buffalo Bill Cody v. Doc Carver: The Battle over the Wild West." *Nebraska History* 85, no. 1 (2004): 2–15.

Salsbury, Nate. "The Origin of the Wild West Show." *The Colorado Magazine* 32, no. 3 (1955): 204–14.

Sanford, William R., and Carl R. Green. *Buffalo Bill Cody, Showman of the Wild West*. Springfield, NJ: Enslow Publishing, 1996.

Sarf, Wayne Michael. *God Bless You, Buffalo Bill: A Layman's Guide to History and the Western Film*. Rutherford, NJ: Fairleigh Dickinson University Press, 1983.

Schlereth, Thomas J. *Victorian America: Transformations in Everyday Life, 1876–1915*. New York: HarperCollins, 1991.

Seitz, Don Carlos. *Famous American Duels*. New York: Thomas Y. Crowell, 1929; repr., Freeport, NY: Books for Libraries Press, 1966.

Sell, Henry Blackman, and Victor Weybright. *Buffalo Bill and the Wild West*. New York: Oxford University Press, 1955.

Settle, Raymond W., and Mary Lund Settle. *Saddles and Spurs: The Pony Express Saga*. Harrisburg, PA: Stackpole, 1955.

Slotkin, Richard. *Regeneration through Violence: The Mythology of the American Frontier, 1600–1860*. Middletown, CT: Wesleyan University Press, 1973.

———. *The Fatal Environment: The Myth of the Frontier in the Age of Industrialization, 1800–1890*. New York: Atheneum, 1985; repr., Norman: University of Oklahoma Press, 1998.

———. *Gunfighter Nation: The Myth of the Frontier in Twentieth-Century America*. New York: HarperCollins, 1992.

Smith, Henry Nash. *Virgin Land, the American West as Symbol and Myth*. Cambridge, MA: Harvard University Press, 1950.

Smith, James L. *Melodrama*. London: Methuen, 1973.

Sorg, Eric V. "Buffalo Bill's Crony, Dr. Frank 'White Beaver' Powell, Brought the Art of Self-Promotion to New Heights." *Wild West* 7 (Oct. 1994): 88–94.

Steckmesser, Kent Ladd. *The Western Hero in History and Legend*. Norman: University of Oklahoma Press, 1965.

Thorp, Raymond W, ed. "The Letters of Doc Carver." *Outdoor Life-Outdoor Recreation* 65, no. 4 (1930): 18–21, 88.

Wallis, Michael. *The Real West: The 101 Ranch and the Creation of the American West*. New York: St. Martin's Press, 1999.

Walsh, Richard J. *The Making of Buffalo Bill: A Study in Heroics*. Indianapolis, IN: Bobbs-Merrill, 1928.

Ward, Geoffrey C. *The West*. Boston: Little, Brown, 1996.

Warren, Louis S. *Buffalo Bill's America: William Cody and the Wild West Show*. New York: Alfred A. Knopf, 2005.

Watt, Stephen, and Gary Richardson, eds. *American Drama: Colonial to Contemporary*. New York: Harcourt Brace College Publishers, 1995.

Wetmore, Helen Cody, and Zane Grey. *Buffalo Bill: Last of the Great Scouts*. New York: Grosset and Dunlap, 1918.

Wickstrom, Gordon. "Buffalo Bill the Actor." *Journal of the West* 34, no. 1 (1995): 62–69.

Wilmeth, Don B., and Christopher Bigsby, eds. *The Cambridge History of American Theatre, Vol. 2, 1870–1945*. Cambridge, UK: Cambridge University Press, 1999.

Wilson, Garff B. *Three Hundred Years of American Drama and Theatre*. Englewood Cliffs, NJ: Prentice-Hall, 1973.

Wilson, R. L., with Greg Martin. *Buffalo Bill's Wild West: An American Legend.* New York: Random House, 1998.

Yost, Nellie Snyder. *Buffalo Bill: His Family, Friends, Fame, Failures and Fortunes.* Chicago: Sage Books, 1979.

MICROFILM

Buffalo Bill and His Wild West Companions, including Wild Bill, Texas Jack, California Joe, Capt. Jack Crawford and Other Famous Scouts of the Western Plains. Chicago: M. A. Donohue, 190?. Western American Frontier History, 1550–1900, reel 79, no. 792.1.

Williams, Henry Llewellyn. *Buffalo Bill (The Hon. William F. Cody): Rifle and Revolver Shot, Pony Express Rider, Teamster, Buffalo Hunter, Guide and Scout.* London: George Routledge and Sons, 1887. Western American Frontier History, 1550–1900, reel 604, no. 6226.

Winget, D. H. *Anecdotes of Buffalo Bill Which Have Never before Appeared in Print by His Boyhood Friend and Pard.* Clinton, IA: n.p., 1912. Western American Frontier History, 1550–1900, reel 607, no. 6261.

ONLINE SOURCES

Custer, Elizabeth B. *"Boots and Saddles"; or, Life in Dakota with General Custer.* Talewins Digital Library. http://www.talewins.com/Treasures/novels/Boots.

"Dion Boucicault: Sensation and Melodrama." http://www.btinternet.com/~torichard/victorianplays/Boucicault1.htm.

Gant, Dr. H. A. "The Yellow Fever Epidemic of 1878." Yalobusha County MSGen Web Project. http://www.rootsweb.com/~msyalobu/yellofev.html.

"General Blunt's Account of His Civil War Experiences." *Kansas Historical Quarterlies* 1, no. 3 (1932): 211–65. http://www.kancoll.org/khq/1932/32_3_blunt.htm.

Harte, Bret. "Tennessee's Partner." http://www.classicreader.com/read.php/sid.6/bookid.813.

"19th Century American Theater." University of Washington Libraries. http://content.lib.washington.edu/19thcenturyactorsweb/essay.html.

Turner, Frederick Jackson. "The Significance of the Frontier in American History." American Studies hypertext collection, University of Virginia. http://xroads.virginia.edu/~Hyper/TURNER.

Turney, Wayne S. "Notes on Naturalism in the Theatre." A Glimpse of Theatre History. http://www.wayneturney.20m.com/naturalism.htm.

INDEX

Italicized page numbers indicate photographs.

Oakley, Annie, 197, 198, 204

Ogden, Josh E., 105, 108, 114, 158, 170, 178, 193

"Old Glory Blowout," 171, 198

Omohundro, John B. "Texas Jack," 20, 22, 23, 25, 28, 29, 41, 52, 53, 55, 59, 60, 63, 69, 80, 100, 110, 127, 136; activities outside theatre, 44, 57, 65, 67; as Cody's costar, 4, 13, 19, 21, 21, 32, 40, 43, 47, 50, 77, 78, 82, 184, 193; critiqued as actor, 21, 24, 31, 33, 34, 35, 37, 38, 51, 61, 82; death of, 82; early life of, 13, 56, 79, 169

Ouray (Ute), 152

Paiute, 102

Paul, Howard, 50

Pawnee, 15, 19, 20, 32, 113, 114, 116, 118, 128, 129, 184, 187

Pawnee Bill. *See* Lillie, Gordon "Pawnee Bill"

Ponca, 129

Powell, Dr. Frank "White Beaver," 157

Prairie Waif, A Story of the Far West, 147, *164*, 181, 182, 184, 196; plot of, 148; reviews of, 149, 153, 155–56, 157, 158, 161–62, 182, 183, 184

Quakers, 63

Rampone, J. G., 118, 141, 283n51

Randall, Fort, 172

Red Cloud Agency, 14, 82, 101

Red Right Hand; or Buffalo Bill's First Scalp for Custer, 89, 95, 147; plot of, 87; reviews of, 90, 92, 96

Remington, Frederick, 201

Rice, Dan, 133

Robbins, Hiram, 48, 49, 52, 54, 55, 58, 59, 71, 80, 90

Rocky Mountain and Prairie Exhibition, 178

Roosevelt, Theodore, 171, 198

Russell, Charles, 201

Safford, Lizzie, 47, 110

Salsbury, Nate, 46, 130, 163, 171, 176, 182, 195, 196, 197, 198, 202

Schoeffel, John B., 67

Schurz, Carl, 101, 116

Scouts of the Plains, 67, 73, 77, 81, 95, 184; plot of, 54; reviews of, 54, 55, 57, 61–62, 64, 65, 66, 67–68, 74, 94

Scouts of the Prairie, and Red Deviltry As It Is, 29, 40, 46, 54, 129; plot, 21–23; reviews, 22, 23, 24, 27–28, 31, 33–34, 35, 37, 38

Sellers, Harry, 157

Sheridan, Lt. Gen. Philip H., 2, 17, 19, 21, 40, 63, 82, 86, 96, 105, 140, 277n31

Shiff, David, 283n51

Simmonds, S. J., 80

Sioux, 14, 17, 19, 57, 64, 74, 81, 82, 83, 86, 105, 113, 157, 181, 197, 204

Sitting Bull (Sioux), 86, 172, 200

Skiff, Frank, 110

Smith, Frank, 181